THE HIGHWAY OF SPIRIT AND BONE

a novel

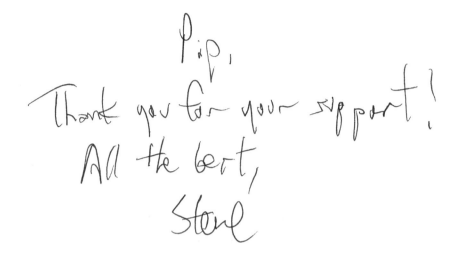

Pip,

Thank you for your support!

All the best,

Steve

THE HIGHWAY OF SPIRIT AND BONE

a novel

STEVEN OSTROWSKI

LEFORA PUBLISHING LLC

Author's photo by Susan Ostrowski.

Cover art by Eileen Snyder.

Published by Lefora Publishing LLC.

www.leforapublishing.com

Visit the author on digital media:

https://sites.google.com/view/stevenostrowski/home

https://www.facebook.com/steven.ostrowski.9

Printed in the United States of America.

In loving memory of my parents: Helen, for the unquenchable sense of wonder she felt deep in her bones; and Ben, for his gentleness and his artist's spirit.

All journeys have secret destinations of which the traveler is unaware.

—Martin Buber

You do not know what wars are going on

down there where the spirit meets the bone.

—Miller Williams

Table of Contents

Prologue

Marie and I decided that we didn't want to wake the kids at five a.m., so I said my goodbyes to them last night. I was only going to be gone nine or ten days, but I'd never been away from them for more than a week, and it felt to me, and maybe to them, like an immense period of absence. Genevieve blinked her eyes and told me to be sure to come back. "Oh, you know I'm coming back, Sweet Eyes. I always do and I always will." She asked if I'd send her postcards from all the states I'd be driving through. "I'll do my best," I told her. Then, wagging her finger, she told me to take extra good care of Grandma because, remember, she's old now. I assured her that her beloved grandma would be safe with me.

Teddy, hands in his pockets, was staring out the window when I walked into his bedroom. He didn't turn right away and when he finally did, I asked him if he was okay. He said, defensively, "I'm fine, dad." All I could do was nod, tell him to take good care of himself and his mom and sister, and to call me anytime he felt like it. I hugged him for longer than he wanted me to, but it was a hug I hoped he'd feel in his bones.

Now it's six a.m. and I'm standing beside the van with Marie, who's out in her silky mauve bathrobe and white slippers. Looking into her eyes, I want to find in their hazel depths sparks of longing, signs of deep, eternal affection. But what I see is distraction, perhaps impatience for me to get the show on the road. Maybe she's thinking about her own plans for the days to come.

"Hey," she says, "you didn't happen to get around to fixing that faucet, did you?"

"Damn," is my answer, with a drop of my heavy head.

"I'll get someone in."

"Sorry. No excuse." But immediately, I add, "You know I've been getting ready for this..."

"It's okay. It's okay, David."

When I say, "I love you, babe," her eyelids flutter a few times before she tells me she loves me, too.

As I back the van slowly down the driveway, Marie walks along the brick path to the sidewalk. In the empty street I idle, taking her in. I wave one more time and she waves back, but both of our expressions are somber, etched with a strange uncertainty. I sigh and shift into drive, and in the rearview mirror watch my wife watch me drive away.

Something's wrong, but I tell myself it's only this disruption in our lives, and that we'll be fine after I accomplish my unhappy mission and get back home where I belong.

Chapter One
Thursday, June 6, 2002

Intimacy Has Never Been This Close

On the van's radio, Imus presses some politician to fess up about the country's sorry state of preparedness for new acts of terror. The good senator does his best to deflect the question and eventually manages to reword it to his own liking. He then offers the host and his listeners a platitude-laden non-answer: we are confident that we are diligently preparing for what no one can ever be fully prepared for.

Here's to that.

Frankly, I'm not listening all that closely. I have a pressing question of my own to wrestle with: why the hell am I about to drive my 79-year old mother from Staten Island to Flagstaff to live out the rest of her days in the clutches of my aggressive, spoiled elder sister Debbie when I know damn well that Arizona is not where Ma wants to be. But Ma–being Ma has agreed to the move.

When an obnoxious male voice screaming about insane deals on electronics comes on, I flick off the radio. Through some series of synaptic associations, I find myself remembering the last conversation I ever had with my father. It took place in the mid-afternoon as I stood beside his bed in a blue-curtained, tube-dangling, machine-murmuring cubical of the IR at Staten Island Hospital. Da had been in and out of consciousness for a couple of days and in a matter of hours would die. Ma, Debbie and Jeanette had gone down to the cafeteria for coffee, but I was already over-caffeinated and relieved to be removed from the combustible chemical combination that was Debbie and Jeanette. I'd fallen into a melancholy, selfish reverie about how my own last days might unfold when suddenly my father's eyes blinked open and took immediate aim at my face. "Look it, David," he said weakly but gruffly, as if we'd been conversing the whole time, "listen up."

"Yeah, Da?" I leaned down.

"Of all of you, you're the one that let me down the least. You know that, right?"

I suppose I'd always known that I'd been the most "dutiful" child, at least from his perspective. I was gainfully employed as a tenured professor of anthropology, happily married (mostly), had two (basically) healthy children, was a semi-active member of St. Gregory parish in our rural western Jersey hamlet; this despite my long-evolving suspicion that Catholicism didn't have it all exactly right. Being dutiful isn't something I've ever taken pride in. In fact, I suspect my psyche still harbors a few ancient, unwaged, long-delayed youthful rebellions. Meanwhile I grow old…

"The one I thought I could trust most," Da went on, "goes and gets married and moves all the way the hell to Arizona. The other two…" He frowned and shook his head. The "other two" would be the thrice-divorced poet son and the ultra-conservative lesbian daughter. "They let me down almost every step of the way."

"They love you though, Da."

"That's not what I'm talking about, son."

"Look, don't get yourself upset. Maybe you should rest."

"I intend to. Listen, take care of your mother, okay?"

"Of course, though she's pretty capable to taking care of herself."

He frowned. "Can I trust you to do that for me? To make sure she's happy? Okay?"

I stared at his ungrayed blonde hair, his bulldog face, and my hands spread open and my head trembled, and I wanted to protest that it was insanely unfair of him to ask me to *make sure* his wife will be happy. But his eyelids had already slid down over his robin's-egg blue eyes. They would never open again.

* * *

"All set for the journey?" I say to my mother with forced cheer.

She looks as if she's trying to remember a rehearsed response. Pushing open the screen door of her garden apartment to let me in, she replies, "I better be, right?"

In the little foyer, under a cross made of a Palm Sunday frond that Ma has thumb-tacked to the archway, I lean down to kiss her cheek. She abruptly turns her head and I kiss her earlobe instead. I'm tempted to take her head in both my hands and hold it steady while I plant a long, firm kiss on her Hepburn-like high cheekbone. Whether she likes it or not.

"I have no coffee for you, David," Ma informs me. "Jeanette brought the last of my kitchen things down to the Salvation Army yesterday. I'm sorry, honey."

"It's okay," I assure her, even though for the five years since Da's death, whenever I've driven to Staten Island to visit and run errands for her, our having a cup of coffee together has been a ritual of reconnection. "I don't know how you managed to survive here the last few nights with everything gone."

Ma shrugs. "Jeanette's been taking me out for supper, and my friends have been inviting me over for lunches, and for my other meals I've been eating my *Wheaties* and bananas. I listen to my radio. It reminds me of when I was a girl. We ate and listened all the time. Where *is* Jeanette anyway? You picked her up, didn't you? She's still coming with us, isn't she?"

I nod toward the street, where my sister stands leaning against my '96, pearl blue Chrysler Town and Country van, muttering into her cell phone. Twenty feet away, some guy in a tight tank top and shorts lingers, letting his collie sniff the grass and attempting to catch the eye of the beautiful blonde babe with the cigar in her mouth. How is he supposed to know he has a better chance with the Queen of England?

Jeanette finishes her call, grimaces, and snaps the phone shut. She climbs up the front steps, lays her half-smoked stogie on the far edge of the top step, exactly the way Da always did, opens the door and nods to Ma. She squeezes by us and goes into the living room, where she pulls a rolled-up section of *The Wall Street Journal* out of the back pocket of her chinos, slams her cell phone down, and leans on the sill of the big bay window. Until recently, that sill had housed a gaggle of Ma's beloved plants—geraniums, begonias, wandering jews, pothos—all arranged around a gilt-framed, rosary bead-draped, 12 X 16 photograph of Da in his formal Army dress, circa 1944. The sill is now a warped wooden desert. Jeanette holds open the newspaper but glares down at her cell phone like she's ready to stomp on it.

"David," Ma says as we step inside, "don't let me forget my camera. I want to take lots of pictures. Everybody wants me to send them pictures of the country and of Debbie's place and all."

"Okay. Where is it?"

"It's...I put it...." She glances around the room. "Well, goodness gracious I had it a minute ago."

Jeanette lowers her paper and points with her eyes to the kitchen counter. "There."

"Oh, thank goodness." Ma retrieves the camera and hands it to me. "Hold it for me, okay David? If I know me, I'll leave without it."

The silver, compact, feathery light digital camera is a gift from Debbie and her husband Clint so Ma can document what Debbie calls Ma's "great westward adventure" to the upscale retirement complex she and Clint own and operate in Flagstaff. Debbie called me every day last week wanting to know *exactly* when we were leaving Staten Island and *exactly* when we would arrive in Flagstaff. I told her we'd be on the highway by nine on Thursday but that I couldn't possibly tell her *exactly* when we'd arrive; I supposed it would be sometime late Sunday or early Monday. She said we could be there by Sunday afternoon if we did a steady 70 and drove eight hours a day. "We'll be there when we get there," I told her. "Who knows, maybe she'll have a last minute change of heart." Debbie told me I was acting "just a bit like a selfish son of a bitch," said goodbye, and hung up.

I tell Ma we can go anytime she's ready.

"Let me make sure I'm not leaving anything."

She walks slowly through her three modest rooms, me trailing. In each room she glances around anxiously. But besides the refrigerator and Ma's relatively new Posture-Pedic bed, which Jeanette arranged to have sold to the incoming tenant, the apartment is empty.

"There's nothing here, Ma. You aren't leaving anything."

"That's what you say."

"Hel*lo-o*? *Li*-lly?" a high, thin voice quivers through the apartment. "Are you here, dear?"

"Oh, gosh," Ma says. "My friends. How could I forget? Thank goodness we didn't leave yet."

We greet them in the foyer. Ma's long-time best friend, tiny, white-haired, Scottish-brogued Edna McCauley, and right behind another elderly women who's wearing a dizzying, flower-patterned vinyl raincoat and wrap-around sunglasses, though it's only a little overcast outside. There's also a thin old man with coffee stains on his white, button-down shirt, a man Ma calls Minty, and a much younger, heavily made-up Hispanic woman holding a tiny pink infant whose tiny ears are pierced with gold studs.

The woman with the baby pretends to reach into her purse. "How much so you won't take Lilly away? My God, she's been more of a grandma to Lupe than my own mother."

I force a smile.

"I wish I could offer you coffee," Ma says to her friends, gesturing toward the empty kitchen.

"Don't be silly," the raincoat friend responds. "This isn't a normal morning."

"I know it," Ma says.

"By the way, Lilly," Edna says, "Father Jerzy said he was sorry he couldn't come say goodbye. He has a funeral mass today at 10. That poor Mr. Millstone. Or Milestone. You know the man."

Ma nods. "Young. Wasn't even seventy yet."

"He had a hard life," Edna says. "Lost a son in Viet Nam. His wife supposedly left him... oh, never mind all that."

Ma says, "Bridges under the water." Her head quivers, "Oh, you know what I mean."

The raincoat woman looks at me for half a second, then at Jeanette for a good long while. "What nice-looking kids you have, Lilly."

"Oh," Ma says, looking only at Jeanette, "she gets her looks from her father, not me. David gets his from me. Boy oh boy, I hope I have everything."

"The places life takes us, huh?" the raincoat woman says.

Ma glances away. "I know it. In a million years you could never guess when you're young where you'll end up when you're old."

"I always knew I'd end up here," the old man, Minty, says with a swell of pride. He adds, "What would your husband think, you going all the way out to Arizona to live?"

Ma's chin trembles. "Well, it's a big change. He didn't like things to change much. But sometimes they have to, right?"

Debbie's convinced that Ma is thrilled with the idea of moving out to

Arizona. She started pushing for it a week after Da died. Ma managed to avoid committing for five years. It finally happened this past Christmas. Ma, Debbie and Clint and their kids, Jeanette and her then-girlfriend Sheri, Marie and I and our kids, were all celebrating at our house. (Aaron had called on Christmas Eve, an hour before I was supposed to drive over to Newark Airport to pick him up, to say something had come up and he wouldn't be flying in.) All the adults were sitting at the dinner table eating dessert when Debbie said, "You know, Ma, I'm just thinking. If you don't move to Arizona soon, *my* kids are never going to have the kind of intimacy with their grandma that David and Marie's kids have always had. Is that really fair?" I watched Ma's face contort with guilt; Marie's face turned crimson, and Jeanette's jaw dropped. Me, I stabbed my pumpkin pie in the heart. There ensued a long debate about fairness, about Debbie's own choice to move to the other side of the country, about Ma's undying love of Staten Island and of her many friends there, etc. And still, by the time Debbie left my house a few days later, Ma had been talked into moving west.

While Jeanette and I load her luggage into the back of the van, Ma reminisces with her friends. ("What about the time we got to ride on that float in the Pulaski Day parade? Remember, all the way up 5th Avenue in the pouring rain? What fun!") When we're finished loading, Ma asks me to take a picture of her and the gang. They gather on the lawn in front of the big wooden sign that reads *Riverview Apartments; A Better Way of Life.* Everyone, including Ma, smiles gamely as I snap three more or less identical shots.

"I'll send you all a copy as soon as they're developed," Ma tells her friends.

"You know Lilly, you're probably better off where you're going," the raincoat woman says. "No crazy terrorist is going to want to drop a bomb on an old folks' home in Arizona. Over here, we could be blown to smithereens tomorrow."

I glance in the direction of Manhattan. Ma has what they call a "seasonal view" of the Big , which means that from late-November to mid-April you can see the skyline through a tangle of bare branches. If you want to see the skyline in the warm months, you have to go up to the roof. Which is where Ma and the other tenants of the building watched the towers fall on that sun-splashed morning last September.

"And you'll be sitting in a hot tub in your daughter's fancy-schmancy old folks' home, watching it on T.V.," adds Minty.

"I don't think anything like that will ever happen again," Ma opines. "We learn from our mistakes, don't we?"

"You're going to be living like the rich people now, aren't you, Lilly?" the young woman with the baby says.

Ma looks flustered. "My gosh, I wouldn't know how."

"No snow out there to worry about, eh, Lil?" Minty says. "Or is there?"

"Oh, there *is*. Debbie says we're up in the higher elevations. In fact, there's a ski resort right nearby, only a mile away."

"Snow in Ari*zona*?" The raincoat woman seems doubtful. "I thought it was always a hundred degrees out there. Isn't Arizona the state that's always on fire every summer?"

"No, there are mountains there, too. Fine with me. I love the snow, especially the big storms. Especially the blizzards."

"Oh, that's you all over, Lilly," Edna McCauley laughs. "Always looking for excitement." She shakes her head and says, "Bus rides to Atlantic City won't be the same without you. All the laughs we had, didn't we, dear?"

"And who's going to give me my mysteries?" Ma says, her voice going damp.

"Oh, I'll send them by the box load."

Ma looks away from Edna and notices, as I do, Jeanette's glance at her watch. "I guess we better be leaving, huh? We have a long way to go."

Each of her friends steps up and puts their arms around her, and for once Ma yields to their embraces—almost fully. Edna McCauley comes last and holds on longest. When she and Ma finally let go of each other, neither is able to speak. Their two white-gray heads bob, and they gaze bashfully into each other's eyes.

"Goodbye, dear," Edna says. "I'll miss you terribly."

Ma turns half away, sniffles and turns back. Finally, she climbs through the van's sliding side door into the middle row, settling herself into what my kids have dubbed the "pilot" seat, with its wide, cushy armrests, panoramic, tinted window and separate light, heat and air controls.

"We'll see you before long, Lilly."

"Be sure to write."

"Send back lots of pictures."

And from the woman with the cane: "Remember, you can always come home if you don't like it out there."

"Beg your pardon?" Ma's head lifts and her eyes brighten.

But old Mr. Minty says, "What? Come *home*? You don't make a move this big and then just change your mind about it. I'm afraid Lilly's not ours anymore."

* * *

And now Staten Island, Ma's home for all of her seventy-nine years, is at our backs. We've crested the Goethals Bridge and are descending into Jersey's wasteland of girdered towers and mammoth tankers and towering brick stacks billowing chemical smoke. I can only imagine what Ma is feeling.

We roll off the bridge in utter silence, though I heave a conspicuous sigh designed to signal to Ma and Jeanette that one of them should voice how sad we all feel. I would do it myself but I have to concentrate on the road.

"You know," Ma says, "stinky as it is, I'm going to miss the smell of Jersey blowing across the island."

I chuckle. "Must have been tough saying goodbye to your pals back there, huh Ma?"

"Oh...."

"It's got to be. Knowing you may not see them again. You must feel kind of ...."

"Okay," Jeanette says. "Let's end this before it starts, okay David?"

I glance at my sister, slouched in the passenger seat. At 39, she's still petite and youthful, with cobalt eyes and cropped white-blonde hair– these courtesy of Da's mother's Swiss genes. The rest of us are, like Ma, brown-haired and brown-eyed. Right now, Jeanette's mouth is a mere dash, eyes fixed upon the poisoned geometrics of Jersey's Cancer Ally, but inward, on thoughts infected with resentment. Her cigar protrudes from the pocket of her tee shirt– another legacy from Da, who was never without one except for the forty days of Lent, when he went cold turkey.

I maneuver us toward *West 287*. As we merge onto the highway a huge stars-and-stripes-backgrounded billboard reads *These Colors Won't Run*. You see it everywhere these days. Billboards, flags, homemade signs and posters: *God Bless the USA. Together We Can, Together We Will. Osama, You're a Dead Man.* A collective patriotic fever burns high: nobody messes with the USA and gets away with it. Fever, and a deathly, unspoken fear that somebody will mess with the USA and get away with it again. Any day now, any time.

A few hundred yards further down the highway another billboard looms. A dark-haired woman stands beside a breezy open window, arms folded across her bare breasts, wearing only the sheerest of panties. Across the bottom, the words: *intimacy has never been this close.*

* * *

"Get gas while we're still in Jersey," Jeanette says to me. "It's cheaper."

"I know. I live here, remember?"

"I want to pay," Ma says.

I tell her to save her money.

"Yeah, spend it in Debbie's paradise."

We pull up to a Mobil station/minimart just off the highway. Ma and Jeanette go inside to use the ladies room. The sky is overcast and the air feels both cool and humid. I feel like a machine crammed with color-coded wires and microchips, a contraption designed for intelligence but that is being thwarted by an overload of emotions. There is no valve for steam-letting. No vocabulary for the vagaries of sadness or the power of rage.

For distraction, I think about the "to do" list sitting on my desk at home. I've got to finish three articles, each focusing on a member of a family in Newark that I've been studying for the past two years: a single mother, her fifteen-year-old son, and her ten-year-old daughter. In July I teach my "Seminar in Advanced Domestic Ethnography" course. I've got two tricky remodeling projects to complete in the basement before September—not to mention the drip in the kitchen faucet that annoys the hell out of Marie and that I've been putting off fixing for reasons I can't seem to access. Marie turns 40 in late August, which has been troubling her; sometimes I find her lingering before one of the mirrors, frowning, and only recently she asked me if I were only meeting her for the first time now, would I find her attractive. I assured her I would, but she walked away after a skeptical "Hmmm." I've got a birthday gala to both plan and execute. And not least, I want to spend as much time with the kids as I can this summer, while there's time, while they're kids. While our lives, and the world, are still recognizable.

A clean-cut teenager hands me my credit card. "There you go, sir," he says all chipper and sincere. He's wearing a tee shirt with a picture of a thorn-crowned Jesus that reads *He Did It For You.* Maybe they shouldn't, since I myself am a believer/questioner, but such slogans tend to make me cringe. I'm guessing home-schooled evangelical.

"Nice *van*, by the way," the kid says. "That's one sweet engine in there. I like the slant six. Your oil's clean as water. You take real nice care of it, I can tell."

"Well, I try. Take care of things and they won't let you down. My dad…"

"That's true," he says. "I definitely agree with that."

Despite the tee-shirt, I think I like this kid. Seems genuinely…*good-hearted.* I don't sense that brainwashed, Pharisaic smugness you see in some so-called born-agains.

"Well, you seem to know your stuff," I tell him, and impulsively reach out and touch him on the shoulder. Thank God he smiles, doesn't seem to mind. In America these days you can be sued for less.

I glance away and spot them coming out of the store, Ma in her casual, matching pink cotton top and pants with bright pink and white sneakers, taking everything in, walking with the gait of an athletic fifty-year old, and Jeanette, eyes narrowed, striding, cigar puffs trailing behind her like the little engine that could kill.

"Have a safe trip, sir," the kid says to me. He helps Ma into the van. "God bless you all," he offers, and without a trace of self-consciousness.

I can't help but envy him.

* * *

I'm pointing out to Ma the big rectangular road sign that says, "*Welcome to Pennsylvania, the Keystone State*," when Jeanette's cell phone chimes. "Damn you," she mutters, straightens her legs, pulls the phone out of her pants' pocket and slowly lifts it to her mouth. "Yeah?"

"I still can't get over those things," Ma says. "That you can be on the phone in a moving car. Who would have thought?"

"I could live without them," I say, though mine rests as close as it possibly could in the breast pocket of my purple tee shirt.

"Oh, David, I should have taken a picture of the sign."

"The what? The sign? Why?"

"I don't know. Just to have it. To show where we were. Do all the states have them?"

"Yeah, sure. To let you know you've entered."

"From now on then. Remind me, okay?"

I really don't want to, but I offer: "We can turn around and go back. It's only one exit."

Ma doesn't answer right away. Which means, *yes, please do it, though I don't want to trouble you.* I get off at the next exit, take the highway overpass and then head back east into New Jersey.

Jeanette, listening to whoever has called her, makes an annoyed face.

"We've changed our minds," I tell her. "We're going home. The hell with Arizona."

But Jeanette's already turned her body toward her door and tucked her head into her shoulder. I can barely hear her voice. My guess is she's talking to Sarah, her girlfriend. Sarah's a psychologist– a "post-Jungian" is how she puts it. I don't know how her profession sits with Jeanette, but I know my sister is not likely to go exploring her inner daemons or dialoging with her anima or recognizing the stirrings in her soul of the collective unconscious. Jeanette believes in facts.

We reenter New Jersey, get off the highway at the first exit, take the underpass, get back on heading West. I hope this is not going to be a theme.

"Okay, Ma, get ready. Here comes the sign again." I slow down and Ma leans up between Jeanette and me, camera to her eye, and snaps away.

"Good, got it. Thank you, David."

I try, without success, to eavesdrop on Jeanette's conversation. Like Jeanette, Sarah seems to have a hard time making her face smile. And she doesn't say a whole lot, either. Have to wonder if two people as solemn and taciturn as they are can get very far as a couple. Then, too, Sarah seems to lean quite far left politically while Jeanette, being in this regard very much her father's daughter, is conservative to the bone. My sister is a financial consultant with a well-known investment firm in Manhattan. MBA from Princeton. (And judging from the advice, investment-wise, she's given to Marie and me over the years, she knows her stuff.) I just don't see this relationship lasting very long.

"Look, Sheri, stop it..."

Oh. Sheri. The girlfriend I wish Jeanette had stayed with. Though she's a cop (or was until recently), she's no brute. She's funny and funky and self-effacing, and pretty in a natural way: strawberry blonde hair, hazel eyes, smooth skin, on the tall side, nicely proportioned. She's also the kind of person who, when she asks you how things are going, how your work is proceeding, how your kids are doing in school, actually *listens* to your response.

Confession: I used to like to flirt with her at parties. With a few drinks in me, flirting with Sheri felt safe and harmless, though not without a certain low-wattage erotic charge.

"Hey, Girlie. You're looking fine as a knife."

"Yo, Studboy," – she'd say it sexy-like. We might both be in the kitchen, grabbing beers out of the fridge. Wiggling her head and her hips: "Where you been all this time, Mister Big Stuff?" And she'd drape her long arm over my shoulder and let her wrist go limp.

"Been biding my time. Doing what a man has to do."

Anyway, you get the point.

Here's the problem: Jeanette's girlfriends tend to fall more deeply in love with her than she does with them. I've seen it happen half a dozen times, and it's what happened recently with Sheri. Back in March, my sister gave Sheri her walking papers, which apparently Sheri never saw coming. Jeanette's description of Sheri's reaction went something like, "She's taking it like a big baby. She practically destroyed the kitchen." I would never have predicted Sheri to be a rager, even under bad circumstances. In all the time I'd known her, I'd never even heard her raise her voice. She and I did speak a few times on the phone afterwards, and it was obvious she was devastated, but quietly so, I thought. Neither she nor Jeanette would say much about the reasons for the breakup. Frankly, I don't think Jeanette knows why she ends relationships. Some kind of inner compunction: intimacy approaches; get out while you can!

Now Sheri's quit the police and gone back home to the Florida panhandle. Jeanette's begun a run with gloomy Sarah.

"Can't do it, Sher," Jeanette says into the phone, a little more loudly than she means to. She listens a while and says, "No way. Sorry, but I won't give you that information. I don't have time anyway. This isn't a vacation for me, okay? Hey, hey, I can't hear you, you're breaking up. Take care of yourself. I'll call when I get back." Then, "Yes, you can. You have no choice."

Long, awkward Pennsylvania highway silence.

"Was that your friend Sheri?" Ma finally asks.

"Mmm."

"How is she?"

"Don't ask."

"What did she want?"

"Don't ask."

We approach the decapitated carcass of a deer sprawled on the shoulder. A trio of fat crows waits in the wings for my van to pass so they can hop back to their feast.

"Can't blame the poor deer for wanting to get a head in life," I say. No response.

"Is everything all right with Sheri?" Ma queries on. She asks with a kind of lilt that implies she expects Jeanette to find a way to give an affirmative response.

"No," Jeanette says. "But please don't worry about it."

Ma makes a sound like a small breeze.

Roadkill splattered all along the highway. Smaller creatures mostly, though being Staten Island born and raised, I'm not particularly adept at distinguishing an opossum, say, from a mole.

"So, what's Sheri up to these days," I ask without looking in my sister's direction. "She working down there in Florida?"

Jeanette frowns. "No."

"What's she doing with herself?"

"Please, David."

"Jeeze, Jeanette. She's a friend of mine, too. And it's a pretty simple question. What, do you not want to be spoken to at all for next 2000 miles? Is that it?"

"She's obsessing, okay? She wants to meet me somewhere to talk. She says she'll drive anywhere in America so we can talk. The woman's insane. She makes me uncomfortable. I think she's losing it. All right? Like, dangerously so. Is that enough info?"

"Well, thanks. Now I know what she's doing. Obsessing. Same as everybody."

Jeanette frowns.

"Oh, good," Ma's voice rings from behind us.

"What's good, Ma?"

"It looks like the sky's trying to brighten."

I glance upward to see the same gray on gray on gray that I've seen all morning.

Jeanette says, "Looks like it's gonna pour."

* * *

No sun breaks through the sagging tent of clouds, but no rain falls either. An hour or so into Pennsylvania, I-87 West keeps its promise and brings us to I-81 South. While I feel a small sense of accomplishment at having made it to the next leg in the journey, I'm annoyed at having to keep fiddling with the air conditioner, which at one setting makes the air a tad too cool and at the next, not quite cool enough.

"Sorry about the air," I say.

"The air's fine," Ma says. "I remember when cars didn't have air conditioning."

"That must have been so uncomfortable on really hot days."

"Oh," she says, and waves her hand, "there are a lot of things we didn't have. Nobody minded. You don't miss what you never had. Plus, you really don't want your life to be too easy, do you? That's what I think. If it's easy, how can you appreciate anything? You know?"

We pass a mall the size of a small city. "Yeah, though the easier your life gets," I say, "the more time you have on your hands to make it difficult again. But in new ways."

Jeanette emits a kind of irritated animal sound.

So far, none of us has requested music. I don't know why *they* haven't, but my reason has to do with allowing the conditions for meaningful, honest conversation to remain optimal, though I can't seem to bring myself to initiate such a conversation. I hear myself thinking up conversation starters like, So, Ma, how do you *really* feel about this move? Manipulated? Ambivalent at best? Worried about adjusting? Concerned about making new friends? Fitting in?

But I keep all my questions to myself.

This time it's *my* little phone that sings against my chest.

"Hello?"

"Hi, David. It's me. How's it going so far? Where are you?"

"Marie. Hi, sweetheart."

"Everybody doing okay?" My wife's voice is full of bubbly, feminine energy.

"So far, so good. We're in the middle of Pennsylvania. Everything okay there? Kids okay?"

"They're fine. Off at school."

"So, what's up? You miss me so much you couldn't wait until tonight to hear my voice?"

"Actually, no. Well, yes, that, too. But I'm also calling because Brandon is out in the living room. He…"

"What? The guy across the street Brandon? What's he doing in our living room?"

"Well, I was talking with him this morning, outside. He came over after the school bus left, you know, to say hi."

"To say hi, huh? And you invited him in the house?"

"Yes, David, I did. He's here now because he wants to know if you have a hack saw he can borrow. I went down to get him one but your tool room is locked and I can't find the key. I'm sorry to bother you with this. You sound irritated."

Brandon, our neighbor, is a guy in his late thirties or so, a little younger than me, recently divorced. Good-looking, well built, dark hair and dark eyes. After the divorce he bought the four-bedroom farmhouse, and the twelve rolling acres that come with it, across the road from us. I don't know why he needs four bedrooms. He lives alone. I've only talked with him for any length of time twice–both times Marie was with me. The guy seems nice enough, although he's an attorney for a cable network geared for men– the "Peter Pan, let's never grow up" channel is what I call it. (Yes, I admit I've watched it. But after viewing some of the shows on that channel for ten minutes you feel dirty, and you either switch to PBS or take a long shower.) The other thing about Brandon is he's one of these guys whose gaze lingers on your wife's body too long. Maybe no guy is completely immune from doing such things, myself included I suppose, but Brandon almost seems like he's daring you to notice. Marie, to her credit, seems oblivious. Or if she does notice, she takes it for what it's worth. Just another thing about Marie that I admire. Except... No, never mind.

"The key's on the top of the boiler," I tell her. "I always lock that room when I go away. Bad combination, sharp tools and kids. There are two hacksaws in there."

"Yeah, good idea. Okay, hon. Thanks. We'll talk tonight, okay?"

"Hey, Marie?"

"Yeah?"

"Did you mention to Brandon what I'm doing? You know, that I'll be away for a few days?"

"Yes, we were just talking about it over coffee. Why?"

"Oh, you're having coffee with him?"

"I had a pot going when he knocked."

"Ah, good timing on his part."

"He's a good conversationalist. You should hear some of things he's done in his life."

"Oh? Well, maybe I will someday. I'm surprised he's not at work on a Thursday."

"Oh, he says he's able to do a lot of work from home."

"Lucky him. Home is where the heart is, after all. So, what were you conversing about?"

"Oh, this and that. Like I said, he's had all kinds of adventures. But also about making a living. Raising kids. All the demands. His divorce was rough on him. We were just now talking about, you know, trying to feel satisfied that you're doing something worthwhile with your life. He says he's not so sure he is satisfied. Which, I told him I could sort of relate to. I told him I didn't think that was ever an issue with you. Teaching and research, those are meaningful things to you."

"Pretty deep stuff you're covering. Intimate, almost. So, he's still there?"

"Yeah, he needs a hack saw."

"Key's on the boiler. Hey, look, I love you sweetheart."

"I love you too, hon. Call me tonight, okay? Say hi to Lilly and Jeanette. Bye." *Click.*

So why is the guy borrowing a hack saw *today*? Why didn't he borrow one yesterday, when I was home?

And he's a good conversationalist. Has had all kinds of adventures.

Oh, God. Calm down.

"Pew!" Ma says. "Smell those *cattle*?"

I sniff. Out beyond my already bug-speckled windshield, herds of brown and white beasts graze lazily or lie in the grass of the slopes that run for miles on either side of the interstate. They blink their big eyes like baby monsters. They seem patient, content with their lot. There seem to be an awful lot of cute little bovine toddlers, too, lingering close to their big mamas. Do cows only give birth in the spring? Imagine being limited to one mating season per year.

"I think that smell may be the manure for the fields," I say. "I don't think cows themselves smell like that."

"I hope we see some wild animals on this trip," Ma says. "Do you think we might?"

"Maybe," I say. "Especially as we get further west."

"Not likely," Jeanette says. "Not if we're on the interstate, which we'd better be if we want to get to Arizona by Sunday."

"Okay, but remember I promised Ma we'd get off once in a while and take a blue highway or two. Sunday, Monday. Doesn't matter."

"But don't if it's going to be any trouble," Ma says. "I know you both have to get home and back to your families and your jobs and such. It was so nice of you to drive me in the first place."

"Well," I say, "you don't like to fly and we certainly weren't going to stick you on a train or a bus."

"And Debbie would really like me to get there by Sunday."

"Look, Ma," I say. "We'll get off the interstate once in a while, just like I promised you. As a matter of fact, we're going to drive that Blue Ridge Parkway later today. Remember? It's marked as a scenic route in the road atlas I showed you. Supposed to be stunning."

"Oh, that's right. That ought to be terrific."

"It's going to add three hours to the trip," Jeanette says under her breath.

"That's too bad. How many more of these trips do you think she's going to be taking?"

Did I say that out loud? I check the rearview mirror. Ma's knitting is in her lap and her needles are in her hands. But at the moment she's staring out at the passing world.

* * *

By mid-afternoon we're in Virginia. Virginia feels significantly far enough away from home to cause me to think, *we really are doing this*. Because some part of me keeps thinking an epiphany is immanent: big mistake; turn around at the next bend; go home.

"Mind putting in my Sinatra tape?" Jeanette asks.

"Sinatra?" I say. "How about the Beatles? I haven't listened to the Beatles in a while and I was thinking this trip would be a good chance to catch up with them. I brought, like, six Beatles' tapes."

"Fine, play whatever you want."

"Well, never mind. Sinatra's fine. You asked first."

"No. Put in the Beatles."

"We'll listen to the Beatles later," I say. "You asked for Sinatra first."

"The Bea.... Oh, Christ. Pull over."

"What? What's the matter?"

"Just pull over please. Quick."

I lurch the van to the right, roll us up onto the pebbly shoulder and hit the break too hard. Our heads fly forward, then jerk back. "What's wrong, Jeanette? You okay, Ma?"

"Back there," Jeanette says matter-of-factly and tilts her head.

I glance through the rear windows and see, seventy-five yards back, a station wagon pulled over, hood up, and a woman and some kids milling around.

"What is it?" Ma says. "Did we hit something?"

"Somebody's broken down back there," I say and throw the van in reverse and start moving backward along the shoulder.

Why are we doing this, an observer might ask. Da simply could not pass a motorist in trouble without stopping to see if he could help, and, because he knew a lot about cars–his own father ran a service station for fifty-one years– he usually could. By the time we were ten, we could, too. Da never explained why he felt obliged to help motorists in need *every single time*, though I do remember one summer afternoon asking him why we had to stop to change some old man's flat tire when all I wanted was to get to whatever amusement park or picnic we were going to. He said, "Pay attention the next time they read the story of the Good Samaritan at Mass, okay David? Maybe you'll think about somebody besides yourself."

Da remained loyal to this requirement of his faith even after the time he was set-up and bashed over the head with a tire iron and left in a drainage ditch, bleeding profusely and badly concussed, some wannabe Bonnie and Clyde driving off with his wallet and our car.

"You stay in the van, Ma," I say as Jeanette and I get out.

"Be careful you two," Ma says. "Sometimes these things are a trick."

Jeanette, already ten no-nonsense steps ahead of me, goes straight to the wagon's hood. As I walk toward the car, the fumey gust and ground-shake of a passing eighteen wheeler exacerbates my sense of unease.

As I approach the car, a stone whizzes past my ear. "What the..." A ragtag, urchin-looking foursome of kids in dirty tee shirts and tattered pants stand around in the weeds, arms cocked. "Hey, stop that," I shout at them. More stones ping the dirt around my feet. One of them glances my knee.

"Hey, ma'am, would you tell your kids to stop throwing rocks at me, please. We're here to help you."

The woman is heavy-hipped, beer-bellied, droopy-bosomed. She's wearing a rather soiled-looking pink tank top (braless, I'm afraid) that reads *I'll buy it!* "They ain't gonna listen to *me*," she says. "Hey, you got a cigarette on ya?"

I glare at her, then at her kids, who stare back at me with chilling defiance.

Jeanette, standing beneath the hood, points at a thick crust of white/blue ash that covers both terminals of the battery. I roll my eyes, Da-like, at the sight of such criminal auto neglect.

Jeanette lights her cigar and says to me, "You carry jumper cables in that van of yours?" Which is a kind of Stepenski inside joke, since no Stepenski worth his dipstick would get *into* an automobile that wasn't fully equipped to handle all contingencies.

"Even got one of them there wire brushes," I say with a hillbilly twang.

In the van, Ma's craning her neck to see what's going on.

"Everything's fine," I tell her as I climb into the driver's seat. "We're going to try to jumpstart her, if she hasn't fried the battery. I just have to turn the van around so we can hook up the cables."

A few minutes later, after I've brushed away a decade's worth of crud, the big woman comes close and watches as I fit the cable clamps to her battery terminals. Comes a little too close, and her big saggy breasts brush the hair of my arm. That, and she smells of cigarettes and maybe sausages.

"Hey, you guys don't happen to have a dubie you can spare, do you? Man, I'm hurtin'."

No doubt about that. The thing is, what's the cure for her kind of hurting? I want to believe that even this woman carries a spark of divinity, is precious in the eyes of a merciful and loving God, is granted by that God, by virtue of her very existence, a certain dignity that is withheld from no one. And yet I want to get away from her and her dog snout-featured kids as fast as I can.

"*Fuck*!" one of those kids screams. He starts hopping around on one leg. "You asshole, Darryl."

"What the fuck's wrong with you now, Toby?" the big woman shouts.

"Darryl hit me in the shin with a fuckin' rock."

"Good. You deserve it."

"It's bleedin'" Toby says.

"Well, that's what it's supposed to do when a rock hits it, ain't it?"

Jeanette and I exchange glances. This is a line we may well invoke for comic relief later on. Jeanette walks around to the driver's side of the wagon and looks in. "Keys," she barks.

The woman digs into her pocket, tosses them to Jeanette, then says to me in a confidential tone, "Jesus, your wife's a piece of work, ain't she?"

"She's not my wife."

"She ain't?" The woman lowers her voice another notch. "You married?"

"Happily," I say.

And I'm certain Marie is not attracted to the likes of Brandon.

For a few painful, what-if-this-doesn't-work seconds, the engine only whines. I think, *are we going to have to give these people a lift somewhere?* But then, with a confused, messy rumble, the thing revs back to life. Merciful God indeed! Jeanette shuts the driver's door behind her and I quickly disengage the cables and slam down the hood. My sister climbs back into the van without so much as looking back at the woman or her kids.

The big woman squints at me. "You telling me you got nothin' in that van you could give me to help me out? A cold beer? A joint? Nothin?"

"You know something lady, I'm still waiting for you to say thank you. In case you haven't noticed, two strangers just helped you get your car running. I want a thank you for my sister and a thank you for myself."

The woman looks at me as if I'd asked her to pull out her eyeballs. When she starts to turn away, I step in front of her.

"I said I'm waiting for a *thank you*." Christ, who *am* I? What am I *doing*? The kids have stopped their stone-gathering and are staring at me. I get the feeling they've seen their mama in some ugly confrontations with men before.

Coming to my senses—a few of them, at least—I mutter "Never mind," and turn.

"Fine, crazy boy. Thank you. And tell miss pretty ass I said thank you, too."

"You're welcome."

"And fuck you, too," she adds. "Lucky thing for you Big Duckie ain't here. You'd be splattered all over this highway. Okay, get in the fucking car, you little shits." She gives the boy nearest her a hard smack on the back of the head.

I thrust the van back onto the highway, fifty feet in front of a noisy Mazda Miata that's going faster than I realize. The little car is on me in no time and its balding, bearded driver makes sure to give me a good long honk of disapproval as he jumps into the passing lane. He lifts his middle finger and jabs it in my direction, then swings back into the driving lane two feet in front of me. On his back fender is a bumper sticker with the word *Darwin* embodied in the outline of a fish.

Clever.

"How many people prayed to Darwin in the World Trade Center last year?" I mutter. I'm sorely tempted to ride up on his rear and find out which one of us is fittest to survive. But the minuscule part of me that retains any sense convinces the rest of me to ease off the accelerator and let him go.

"So," Ma says after an edgy silence, "everything okay now?"

"Yeah, Ma. Peachy."

"Good. Hey, let's try to enjoy the ride. Okay? Let's make this trip fun. Something we'll always remember."

"Do you know it never even oc*curr*ed to that fucking—sorry—that stupid woman to say thank you. Do you believe that?"

"She didn't even say *thank you*?" Ma says. Her scandalized tone appeases me.

From the passenger seat: "You know what your problem is, don't you, David?"

I glance at my sister. "You'd better enlighten me, Jeanette."

"Your problem is you expect too much from people. Really, you're just like that woman back there."

"Am I?"

"Yeah. She expects everybody to take care of her, and you expect people to appreciate every little thing you do for them. Except it doesn't work like that."

"If a frigging thank you is too much to expect then civilization as we know it is over."

"Is that supposed to be news?"

"Well, I hadn't quite given up. Guess I'm just not as advanced a cynic as you."

"Call it that if you like. But if you want to avoid getting frustrated every ten minutes, don't expect anything from anybody. The less you expect, the better off you are."

"Oh, Jeanette," Ma says, and sniffles, "that's so...pessimistic. We should pray for that family back there. They didn't look like they were doing so great. And think of the life those poor kids must have. I'll bet you they have no father, and to have to have a mother like that. Goodness, that can't be easy."

Chastened silence. The highway ahead of me, undulating but straight, looks endless.

* * *

We're on the last leg of Virginia's Blue Ridge Parkway, an extended, coiling, two lane mountain road that rides the tops and sides of a good stretch of a ridge of the steep and tree-covered Blue Ridge Mountains. The soundtrack to the afternoon has been provided by the Beatles. *She Loves You* is playing at the moment. *Yeah, yeah, yeah.* There is something about the harmonies of Lennon and McCartney that gets very close to touching whatever my soul is. If you doubt the existence of God, think of the sound their two voices, harmonizing, makes. This can't be an accident of evolution. Two hours ago, in a gesture of compromise, I actually popped Jeanette's Sinatra into the tape deck, but she insisted I take it out and put in the fab four.

"But I'm kind of in the mood for Sinatra now," I lied.

"Well, I'd like to listen to the Beatles," she insisted, though she doesn't really like the Beatles, or much else recorded after 1959, weird old soul that she is.

When we first got on this road, the vistas of lush mountainsides and green valleys enthralled us. Ma switched places with Jeanette and from the passenger seat snapped a dozen or so pictures, some at roadside, scenic-view pullovers and others while moving, Debbie having assured her that you can't take a bad picture with this incredible camera. But now we're tired. We've appreciated all the nature we can for one day. I'm achy in the lower back and my left butt cheek has gone numb. I'm looking forward to getting into a hotel room, touching base with the kids and Marie, then taking a long, hot, bone-soothing bath and going to bed. Thankfully Roanoke, our stopping point for the night, is not far off.

After consulting her laptop, on which she has stored all kinds of useful information for the trip, Jeanette reports from the back: "In Roanoke there's a Hampton Inn, a Motel Six, a Day's Inn, and a Red Roof Inn. I vote for the Hampton."

"Fine with me," I say. "All I need is a bathtub and a bed."

"I don't mind," Ma says. "But isn't the Hampton the more expensive one?"

"Exactly," Jeanette says. "We can afford it, Ma. The Depression's over. Your kids are all making plenty of money–except little boy lost in Vegas, that is."

Ma suddenly puts her hand over her mouth.

"What is it?" I say.

"How could I forget? I meant to remind myself this morning. Tomorrow's his birthday."

"Tomorrow?" I'm always ashamed that I don't remember my siblings' birthdays. "Well, why don't we call him tomorrow then?"

"Why bother?" Jeanette says. "Does he call you on your birthday, Ma?"

"Sure. Not just on my birthday. He calls me almost every single week."

"*Does* he?" I say. "*Aaron calls you every week?*"

"Or every other week, most of the time. He never goes too long without calling. I want to call him tomorrow."

"Ma, we can call him any time, anywhere, thanks to the magic of cell phones."

"Okay. Good."

Frankly, I don't want to talk to Aaron. I don't want to *think* about Aaron. I don't even want to think about why I don't want to call or think about Aaron. But I can't help seeing him, his unkempt, long, dark curls, his deep set, muddy eyes, his beefy but slouched body.

You might say he's the family's blackest sheep. Also, the older brother who, as a child, I idolized. The brother I trailed behind relentlessly, pestered for attention, found deeply, compellingly mysterious and hence tried desperately to figure out, to emulate. When Aaron got a beating from Da for answering back, say, or for not being home in time for curfew, he always walked out of the living room with his chin up and his eyes level and dry. My God, how I wished I could do that. But when I got it, my chin quivered and my eyes were pools of tears. Aaron got hit more than any of us; he seemed to have a genius for rubbing Da in exactly the wrong ways. He was stubborn and Da wanted obedience; he had ideas of his own and Da wanted us to adopt his ideas wholesale; Aaron was a poet (even before he was a *Poet*) and Da was all practicality; Aaron had to *believe* in a rule in order to follow it and a lot of Da's rules just didn't make sense to him. I, on the other hand, and Debbie (Da's "lieutenant") and to some extent Jeanette (as a child, Da's princess) seemed to know intuitively what he wanted us to say and do, and so most of the time we said and did them.

These days Aaron lives just north of Vegas, teaches as an adjunct at Jackpot Community College, or some such, writes and occasionally publishes poetry in obscure journals with names like *Steaming Locomotive* and *Frog's Recurrent Condition* and *Tentative Eternity*. He went away to college at 17 and stayed away for good. He's been married and divorced three times, a fact which, though Ma doesn't talk about it, has wounded her deeply. There aren't any children, thank God. His first marriage–to Trish–lasted a few years, until he told her in a three-sentence letter that he was leaving and that she could have the house and the car and everything else they owned. A few years later he married Stephanie. That lasted two weeks; Gail about a year.

Three years ago, Aaron called me and asked if I could lend him a few hundred dollars. Yes, yes. Of course. At least this was *contact*, a way I could be a small help to him. Maybe to appease guilt, maybe because love is thicker than common sense. I did and I didn't want my brother in my life. I sent him five hundred bucks. Ever since, when the twice-yearly royalty check for a textbook I wrote a while ago (with the sexy title, *Introduction to Domestic Ethnography,* and which, to my surprise, has been picked up for course use in a number of universities around the country) arrives in the mail, I send Aaron a little supplement to his adjunct's income. He always calls and thanks me, tells me he's keeping records, is going to pay back every cent someday. "I'll only take it if you come visit more often," I say to him. To which he replies, wearily, "Yeah, sure, David." And I say, "What? Can't bear to be too close to your kid brother?" And he says, "It's too complicated."

Which should be the Stepenski family motto.

Aaron does show up on the east coast once every three years or so, usually around the holidays, and stays at our place for three or four days max. Whenever he visits, Ma comes and stays with us, too. Not Jeanette. Jeanette and Aaron don't speak to one another. Who knows why? This, too, to Ma's great sorrow. Though we're all relieved when he heads back into the mystery of his life– relieved because something in the very grain of him drains you, haunts you– still there's heartbreak. Every time he leaves it feels to me like it's the last time I'm ever going see him.

Really, I don't want to think about Aaron.

* * *

Past six. The sky a cloudy soup with a swirl of dusky hues. We've left, at last, the scenic, 40 mile-per-hour parkway and are once again flying down I-81 at close to 80. Signs are telling us that Roanoke is near at hand. But then, wouldn't you know it, greeting us as the highway bends left around a foothill is a sudden sea of standing taillights.

"Damn," I say. "And we're probably four miles from the hotel."

"Who'd have thought there'd be a rush hour like this in Virginia," Ma says.

But this is something else: people are getting out of their cars and standing up on their toes and peering down the highway. I put the van in park and get out myself. The breeze carries the smell of heated gasoline and burned rubber.

In the lane beside mine, a man steps out of his pick-up. He's wearing a blue work shirt and a red NASCAR cap. His jeans are caked in mud. He calls to me, "You hear?"

"No. What is it?"

"Crazy." He comes around to the front of my van and stands a few feet from me, shaking his head. "Terrible, terrible. You know all them flags people been tying to the fences and rails on the overpasses? Well, one of 'em, big one apparently, come loose in the wind and blew down and covered over some guy's windshield. Drove straight into a concrete wall. Him and his wife and their little kid. All three killed. Ain't that something?"

All three killed. I peer down the road. "Just happen now?"

"Hour or so ago, I guess. It's all over the radio, CB. We're probably going to be sitting here a while. When there's fatalities...you know."

I look at my watch and sigh. "My luck."

The man, adjusting his cap, says, "Well now, I don't know about you, but I'm thinking, thank God that flag didn't come down over *my* windshield. You know what I mean? Though why it happened at all just blows my mind. Those poor folks. And all the other folks that care about them. Shame."

I stare at him: toothpick in his mouth, translucent blue eyes, a day's stubble on his chin, specks of grey in his black sideburns. "Point taken," I say.

"Still and all, it is a pain in the neck to have to wait around on the highway when you got someplace to be. I got my little guy waiting for me to take him to his t-ball game. Heck, I'd rather make the president wait than him. He don't understand late." Glancing at my license plate, he says, "Traveling, huh?"

"Yeah. Have to go out to Arizona."

"Beautiful country, I hear. Hot. Haven't been myself. Nice lookin' van, by the way. Got kids in there?"

"Not in the van," I say. "Two at home, though." It's funny, but I suddenly feel like I could cry at the thought of being a few miles from where some family's just been wiped out, and headed in the opposite direction of home and clan.

"Makes you see what's what, ain't it?" the man says, having read my mind. "I used to be a whole different guy before me and Ramona had little Benny. A *whole* different guy."

I give him a big old country boy nod. Lame. But he's right, of course. I guess he picks up on the fact that I'm choking on the enormity of it, of being a father, of being responsible for other people's lives. He raises his arm and slaps his hand down on my shoulder. "You'll be back home before long, no?"

"Yeah," I say. "Eight, nine days."

"Goes by fast enough. Appreciate 'em even more when you get back, know what I mean? And hopefully them you."

"Hopefully."

We stare in the direction of the tragedy until at last we see taillights begin to blink and people start getting back into their vehicles. Then, like some huge metallic snake, the traffic starts wriggling forward.

"Good luck on your travels, mister," the man says.

"Thanks. Hope you and your boy make it to the ball game."

"God willin'." He takes the toothpick out of his mouth and smiles.

"That's right," I say. Though I can't help but wonder why God wasn't willing to let the old stars and stripes stay fastened to that fence, or fall harmlessly into a ditch.

Not for me to know.

Back in the van, I say, "Some family got killed up here."

"Oh, no," Ma gasps. "Children?"

"One kid. And a husband and wife."

I watch her eyes peer up the highway, but before we reach the grim scene, now an aftermath of tow trucks and police cars and glittering shattered glass, she's closed them. Only her lips move.

* * *

We find the Hampton Inn right off the highway, just north of Roanoke proper. Standing beside the van, which radiates with the heat of a 500-mile sojourn, my body feels like it's still in motion, like it's moving backwards. Ma comes around from the rear and snaps a picture of me. I wonder if I'll be blurred at the edges.

"Boy, I'm hungry," she says. "The highway makes you hungry, doesn't it?"

I'd forgotten about food but I suddenly feel ravenous. "Sure does," I agree, then add, "That's one of the curious things about highways."

Ma and Jeanette share a room and I take one. It's clean and fairly spacious. There are two paintings on the walls, one of a country lane in snow, the other a still life of a bowl of fruit. (Boy, I'd like to have the concession for hotel room art.) From my third-floor window I have an unobstructed view of the parking lot, including, prominently, my van. Beyond the lot is the insomniac highway, and in the distance the mountains, which in the dying light of this gray day, really do look blue, as if they, too, feel like having a good, long, existential cry.

After a hot, sleep-inducing bath, I put on a fresh pair of shorts and an old Bob Dylan tee shirt (the design taken from the cover of the *Blonde on Blonde* album), take a deep breath and dial home on the cell phone. I'm anxious to touch base and yet calling the family right now feels like a weary obligation. The guilt machine kicks on.

Genevieve picks up. "Daddy!" she sings.

Oh, that word. That word out of that pure, loving, musical mouth. And just like that I want to sob, apologize for being so imperfect, drive home and swallow her up in my arms.

"Guess what, daddy?"

"What, honey?"

"I already started missing you. It started at supper when mommy said grace instead of you. She didn't say one thing funny, like, 'Thank you, Lord, for whoever thought of whipped cream.'"

When I was a child, God was an angry old man, a vindictive dispenser of punishments and guilt. To his credit, he's changed. Not quite the score-keeping cliché he once was. The God I recognize now (through the glass darkly, to be sure) has an infinite and sometimes bizarre sense of humor to go along with the other godly qualities like love, mercy and mystery (and it's the mystery aspect you have to invoke when a family is allowed to die in a car wreck caused by a free-floating American flag). I want my kids to share a belief in a God who's too big to figure out and yet so intimate and loving that you can tell him the most despicable thought, maybe even about *him*, and know he can take it, know he's not going to get all bent out of shape; know he loves you, yeah, yeah, yeah.

"Oh well," I say to my Spinning Jenny. "Mom's kind of a novice at funny graces. I'll bet she'll be hilarious at it by the time I get back."

"I hope so," she says with a tone of exasperation that makes me chuckle.

We chat a while about her day at school, her plans for tomorrow, the dream she had in which her school bus floated over the county and then morphed into grandma's living room, only her grandpa (Da, who died when she was four) was there, wearing a Burger King crown. Her little voice is like some irresistible music. I listen more to the music than the words, and so am surprised when she says abruptly, "Bye, daddy. Here's mommy."

"Hey, babe," Marie says.

"Nothing personal, but it's not your turn yet. Where's Teddy? Doesn't he want to talk to the old man?"

"I'm sure he would if he were here, but he's eating dinner at his girlfriend's."

"Girlfriend? He's twelve years old. Twelve-year old boys don't have girlfriends."

"Oh, you know what I mean. His friend Alison who happens to be a girl whom he spends a lot of time obsessing about. That better?"

"No."

"You sound tired."

"I am dead tired. Other than that, I'm fine. Pretty country we live in. I wish you were here with me to see it."

"I know. That would be fun."

"So, the day go well over there? You see any clients today?"

"No, I had the whole day free for household affairs. I don't see clients on Thursdays, remember?"

Marie has been my wife for thirteen years, my friend for fifteen, and I love her dearly. So, you'd think that I would know which days she works and which she doesn't. You'd think I'd know all about her various clients (she's an audiologist in private practice). "I forgot," I say. "Sorry. That's right, this morning you had that nice long chat over coffee with Brandon."

"Right. Hey, is Lilly there? Can I chat with her?"

"She's rooming with Jeanette. I'm in my room on the cell. I can walk over and put you on with her if you want. It's just next door."

"Well, no, never mind. She's probably exhausted. I'll talk with her tomorrow. I miss her already."

Like a headache, Brandon lingers in my head. Did he borrow the hacksaw and leave? Did he hang around? Did he return it and say thanks and go, or did he have another cup of coffee, or a drink, and a long conversation about life, all the while ogling my wife?

"David?"

"Yeah?"

"Are you okay?"

"Yeah."

"Want to talk about anything?"

"No, not now. I feel run down is all."

"Is everything going all right?"

"About as well as can be expected."

"You sure?"

"Yeah," I say. "If there was, I'd tell you. If not you, who?"

"Well, you know, it's funny you should say that. I was thinking, you've got your mother's ear for days on end right now. Maybe you could try and talk with her about things, ask her some of the questions you've always wanted to ask her. You know, some of the things about your father that bothered you. The hitting and all that. Maybe have a kind of, I don't know, *cleansing*. Though I suppose you don't want to upset her."

"Look, Marie…"

"It's just that you've always felt that parts of Lillian are a big mystery to you, right? I think you've got a real opportunity here."

"It's a good idea," I say. "I'm sure we'll talk, but I'm kind of tired right now."

"I understand. Try to relax, okay? Try to enjoy this. Connect with your mother and your sister."

"I'll give it my best shot. You take care of the kids. And yourself. And tell Brendan I'll be home real soon."

"What?"

"Never mind. Joke."

"Oh. I get it. Okay, I'll tell him."

I channel surf. The usual offerings: dramas and comedies. Sex too, of course. Here's tonight's line-up: *Sensual Siamese Sisters*; *Bed Time Tails*; *They Only Come Out at Night*; *Deeper Than Ever*; *Suzie Swivel*

Shipwrecked on Intimate Island; Naughty Nina Goes to Vegas.

Sex was not spoken of in the Stepenski household, unless you count Da's occasional remarks to the effect of: "Your private parts aren't for anybody else to see." It *was*, however, discussed at St. Albert's, the Catholic school we all attended first through eighth grade. At St. Albert's, as preached to us innocents by the good Felician sisters, sexual desire was essentially the way otherwise normal, otherwise decent people became, through their own weakness-of-flesh, major league, hell-bound sinners. "Would that we could live without our evil-inclined flesh," they, in essence, preached, "like angels of light."

I'm tempted by *Bed Time Tails*, but click "Power" and watch the words and colors on the screen implode to black. A small victory.

I grab from my duffle bag Flannery O'Connor's *The Habit of Being*, a book of her letters recommended to me by a guy in the English department named Tony Cappella. Tony teaches an elective called "Seen and Unseen: Catholic Writers and Their Visions of America." He once told me, "I like to watch these people wrestle with what they're up against. Which, being Catholic, is almost everything."

I manage four pages before my eyes grow so heavy they won't focus. Just as I'm reaching to turn off the light a single, aggressive knock, like a bird slamming into the door beak-first, startles me back to full consciousness.

"Who is it?"

"Me."

I get out of bed and pull on my shorts, open the door wide enough for Jeanette to come through, but she stays in the hallway. "Think we can make it to Nashville tomorrow?"

"Yeah. Pretty easily, I'd say. I was thinking we could get all the way to Memphis."

"I need to tell Sheri whether or not I can meet her. She thinks the best she can do in one day is Nashville."

"*Sheri*? I thought you told her..."

"She's called me three times tonight. She's losing it. She's saying some pretty crazy things. She'll do something stupid if I know her."

"Really? Sheri? I mean, I know she's hurting, but I wouldn't think..."

"You don't know her as well as you think you do, David. So, Nashville. Yes or no?"

"God forbid we have an actual conversation about our mutual friend."

Jeanette makes her I'm-trying-to-be-patient-with-you face, which for an instant makes me want to grab something sharp. "Yeah, fine. We'll meet her in Nashville. Make sure you…"

"Yeah, yeah. I know what to do."

I suck in air through gritted teeth. I don't want to have to try to sleep feeling angry at Jeanette. I want to say something like, okay, maybe we can all have a drink together and make her feel a little better. But I can't. Jeanette's gone.

Chapter Two
Friday, June 7, 2002

Scars

Jeanette drums her fingers on the side of her coffee cup. "What do they have to do, raise the chickens first?"

"I think they do," I say. "But it only costs a few bucks."

"You teach college or kindergarten, David?" Jeanette mumbles.

"Oh, a few *bucks*," Ma says. "I get it." She smiles. "You don't make jokes like that with your college students, do you?" She fears for my job security.

"All the time," I say. "But it's okay. I have tenure." I shoot a quick glance at Jeanette in anticipation of some snide remark about the scam of the tenure system. But she's into her *Wall Street Journal*, tracking investments. My eyes catch a headline: *Terror and the Declining Dollar*.

Somewhere late last night the words *turn back* were deposited into my head from the ether, and they were still there, branded into the big screen of my mind, at five fifty-three a.m. when I awoke from a nightmare, the details of which I couldn't retrieve except for the fact that a pistol pressed against my chest by a person of undeterminable gender figured in the anxiety. "Admit it," the person said. "Or die."

Lying in a king-sized hotel bed in the predawn gloom, I felt desperation coming on like a fever. I got up, took a long, almost scalding shower, then sat naked in the armchair in front of the big motel windows, drapes pulled apart, and gazed at the foggy mountain range to the west, trying to breathe/pray my way into something like calmness. After twenty minutes or so, I did achieve a semblance of it. The trick would be to hold on to it all day, many days.

Our waitress, seventeen or so, black, pretty, and wearing such a bemused expression that I want to ask her to share what she's thinking, carries a silver tray to our table and unloads the food. We go right at it, each of us in lively dialogue with our heaping breakfasts. Only after I register a degree of satisfaction of my hunger do I lift my head to say, "How's your omelet, Ma?"

"Delicious. You can tell the vegetables are fresh. I'll bet they grow them around here."

"Could be. How 'bout those pancakes, Jeanette?"

"They're pancakes."

"Well, that's what you get for ordering pancakes, huh?"

A man in his late fifties or early sixties and a woman in her thirties, both tall and dressed in conservative business attire, take seats in the booth beside ours.

"Addleson's a goddamned shithead," the man proclaims. His voice is polished, businessy, even as it speaks in crudities. "If he thinks we're going to cave in, he's got another thing coming. Goddamned stupid bastard."

"Tuckerson's just as bad," the woman says. "I swear he's going to get his balls cut off if I have any say in this. And I do."

My eyes zip from the woman to Ma. Ma looks back at me, then blushes and pokes her fork into her omelet.

"Look, we're going to screw that whole crowd right into their own assholes, for Christ's sake," the man says. "Mark my words."

"So, Ma," I say. "How did you sleep?"

"Oh, fine." She looks up, grateful for the distraction. "Like a baby. Did you call home last night? Everybody okay?"

"They're all fine. Oh, remind me to send postcards for Genevieve, will you? Oh, and she said to tell you she misses you already. Marie, too. She'd like to talk with you today."

"You know, David. It was so nice of you to offer to drive me out to Debbie's, but I could've taken a bus or a train. You and Jeanette didn't have to do all this for me. I should have flown. At my age it's time to stop being afraid of airplanes. Gosh, without you two...all you do for me..."

"We want to drive you, Ma. It's not just that you don't like to fly. It's a chance for you to see the country. And," I add with a sigh, "we..." I don't finish ...*love you*. Not that I *never* say it; I do. It's Ma who struggles with those words. Or it comes out through a blush and a cough and a down-turned head.

"I know one way we can fuck them *but good*," the man in the next booth says. "And we'll get the bank to fuck them, too. Listen..."

It just happens: I twist my body, lean over into their booth, and slap my hand on their table. "Excuse me. If you two don't mind, we'd rather not have to listen to that language while we're eating. Could just hold back for a few minutes? Would that be possible?"

The man stiffens; his eyeballs move from me to his companion, who looks straight back at him with steely blue eyes. "Maybe," he says to me, "you should mind your own business."

"As a matter of fact, that's what I'm doing."

"Oh, really?"

I gesture toward my mother and sister. "Yeah."

"Oh, fuck him," the woman says, looking away dismissively.

"Very articulate," I say.

"Let's go, Ray. There's a diner near their office."

Ray looks like he's ready to send a death laser out of his cool grey eyes. "Prick," he says.

"Appreciate it." I tip an imaginary hat as they grump out of the booth.

I watch them walk out, and then, like a little boy secretly checking to see if he's made his family proud, steal a glance at Ma and Jeanette. Neither of them so much as looks up from her plate.

"What a couple of assholes, huh?" I say.

"David!" Ma gasps.

From Jeanette, two dismissive shakes of the head.

"Humor," I mutter. "A little levity. No?"

Nope.

Jeanette looks up. "Who *are* you?"

Good question.

The sky is as gray as it was yesterday, though just now it feels stealthy and lower to earth. The air is so full of mist that you can see the particles spinning and zagging about. After a bathroom break and a five-minute wait beside the van while Jeanette puffs on her cigar and calculates something in a notepad, we're back on the road. Since we're only going as far as Nashville today, I feel no great pressure to push 80 like I did yesterday. My mission for today is simple: remain calm and, as much as possible, connect with Ma.

The earth rolls blue-green from the edge of the blacktop to the melancholy, mist-obscured mountains. A brown road sign informs us that we're approaching Hanging Rock, site of a Civil War battle.

"Yeah, lot of history in this part of the country," I say, ever-so-calmly. "Lot of civil war battles around here. This is blood-soaked ground, this is."

"I could never understand that," Ma says. She's behind me in the pilot seat, knitting a sweater for one of Debbie's kids.

"Understand what, Ma?"

"How people from the same country could kill each other like that. So many people killed, and all of them Americans. Some from the very same *family*. It doesn't make sense. Why couldn't they work something out? Compromise. All those people's lives lost. Such a waste."

I regard the stretch of spine of a green-coated mountain to my left, and the unbidden image of a barely bearded kid firing a bullet through his older brother's heart comes. The disturbing part is, it's me firing the gun, and big brother Aaron falling backward. I think, *this is not good. These are not the kind of thoughts I want in my brain.* So I hand Aaron the gun, and *I* take the bullet. This proves to be an unviable solution.

To Ma I say, "There were reasons, of course. Political, racial, economic. Stupid ones, but human beings are good at justifying stupidity, don't you think?"

She offers a small "hmm," which means that despite all the reasons in the world, the Civil War will never make sense to her. People in the same country, in the same family, just shouldn't fight with one another.

I hear the click of her camera.

"Didn't they have a plan B?" This was a comment I remember one of the students in my "Intro to Domestic Ethnography" course making, an older woman who'd been a financial planner for years and wanted out, needed a change. She'd made the remark in reference to one of the families I write about in my textbook, a Dominican family living in Jersey City: husband, wife, fourteen-year old girl and eight-year old boy. I studied them for a year and a half, by the end of which the couple was separated and the kids, especially the girl, were falling into a serious depravity of drugs and indiscriminate sex. They were a family of screamers, door-slammers, slappers and punchers. Except the little boy, Julio, who was a brooder and a

stoic. I witnessed violence in their home more than once. Always knew when it was coming: gradual changes in tone of voice; tightening facial muscles; fingers curling into fists. There was always the quickening of my own heartbeat, a quickening just like the one I felt as a child when Da was on the brink. I was there to observe this family, to chronicle their lives, to try to understand. But I couldn't change them, couldn't save them from themselves. "No Plan B," I remember saying to the woman. "They more or less always responded in the same, predictable ways." What I very much want to prove to myself, about *myself* at least, is that this is not inevitable, that we are capable of devising a "Plan B."

Jeanette's gazing out the passenger window. In the most sincere tone I can manage, I say, "Give us some insight into the Civil War. Could it have been averted? Was there any point at which it almost was?"

"Oh, please, David."

"I'm asking sincerely. You love Civil War history, Jeanette. What do you think?"

She frowns.

"Don't want to be spoken to? Would you be content to sit there for this whole trip and not be spoken to at all?"

"I don't see myself feeling content on this trip under any circumstances."

"What do you think is going to happen when you see Sheri tonight?"

"Sheri?" Ma says. "Your friend, Sheri? The police officer?"

I'm tempted to say, "Her ex-*girl*friend Sheri, Ma." Not that Ma doesn't know her daughter is gay. She isn't stupid. As for why Jeanette hasn't made a formal declaration, I don't know. Maybe she feels a declaration isn't necessary. Or maybe she's afraid if she says something, Da's ghost will appear and attempt to beat some sense into her.

"I'm meeting her in Nashville tonight," she says to Ma. "We're going to have dinner."

"Apparently Sheri's having a hard time getting over Jeanette." Why I volunteer this information, I don't know. But I do regret it.

Silence. Angry silence to the right of me, trembling silence from the back seat. Finally Ma says, "Boy, you're in some mood today."

"To*day*?" I say. "This has been her mood since we left."

"I meant *you*, David. You seem so....hostile."

Hostile? I stammer, "But she's the one who's seething. I'm just frustrated. I'm trying to accomplish something here."

Jeanette mock-recoils. "*Accomplish* something? Do me a favor, don't accomplish anything that involves me, okay?"

"Wait a minute," Ma says. "You mean Sheri's coming all the way from Florida to have dinner with you? Isn't that crazy?"

"It's the definition of crazy," Jeanette grumps.

Driving with one hand, I press two fingers into my temples and make small circles. I, too, feel crazy watching myself fail this way.

* * *

We're on I-40 now, a little past Knoxville at the eastern end of Tennessee. This road, God willing, will carry us all the way to Flagstaff.

It's been a morning of silence punctuated by Ma's occasional Ma-esque comments: "They call that a river? I call that a stream"; "I guess there aren't any Dunkin' Donuts out here, huh? What a shame"; and "That was the nicest smelling bathroom of the trip so far."

I chuckle to myself, remembering a few of her other nuggets through the years. "Well, if it ain't broke, don't break it, right?" "Oh, I'd love a nice hot cup of herberbial tea." Once, when we were pretty young, Ma overheard Aaron telling me that Jimi Hendrix had died. "Didn't he used to live around the corner on Harrison Avenue?"

Oh, Ma, Ma, Ma.

By early afternoon we're hungry. A sign showing a knife and fork indicates food at the next exit, so we leave the highway. But at the ramp's end, we find nothing but a rural road, a long range of lush, tree-covered hills, and a cool, drifting fog filling in the dales.

"Turn around and get back on the highway," Jeanette says. "There's nothing here."

"Wait a minute," I say. "There's probably a place within a mile. There *was* a sign."

"Oh yeah? Which way?"

"I don't know. We'll go a mile one way and if we don't find something, we'll turn around and go a mile the other way. It'll take two minutes. If we don't find anything, we'll get back on the highway."

"Wow," Ma says as we cruise along an undulating, white-fenced country lane. "This is pretty, isn't it?"

"It is." The lush greens of the overhanging trees, many of them willows, the rising and falling road, the occasional opening out of the woods into pastures where sheep or cattle graze in the thickening white mist makes for a landscape from a dream. Seduced by the *calm* of it, I drive on for well more than five miles.

Ma snaps pictures of a grazing goat, a full-bodied stream cutting down a steep grass-and-stone hill, a misty meadow. "How could anyone look at something like this and not believe in God? Where do they think it all came from?"

"Too beautiful for randomness and chaos," I say.

"What?" Ma says.

Jeanette says, "We're gonna have to shoot our lunch if you keep going in this direction, David."

"Okay, okay. I'll turn around the next chance I get."

The next chance I get is in the small, dirt parking lot of *Luke's Deluxe Lunch Shack*. It seems to be little more than a big plywood box, as if someone had repurposed a large tool shed, left it unpainted, allowed it to lean slightly, then invited people in to munch out.

"Well?" I say. "Do we dare?"

"They say these little, out-of-the-way places have the best food," Ma opines.

"I don't care," Jeanette says. "Let's just eat fast and get moving."

We go in through a screen door patched with duct tape. Inside, the walls are bare except for one small American flag– it too is fastened at its four corners by four torn strips of silver duct tape (and the upper left hand corner strip is curling loose, I notice.) A stand-up fan near the front door listlessly blows lukewarm air toward the ceiling. There's a small counter with three stools in front of it, and two plastic tables with plastic chairs around each. No customers in the place, and possibly no employees either.

"I don't think so," I say. That's when a man in a white apron pushes through the swinging doors behind the counter from what looks like a very cramped kitchen. "Oh, hi," I smile. "Serving lunch?"

The man nods. He's at least six-five, with narrow eyes and thin black hair. There's a large, unsightly, eggplant-colored birthmark above his left eye. We take seats at one of the tables and he hands us three laminated menus and goes back into the kitchen. The prices on the menus are written in pen on tiny squares of masking tape (too hard to write on duct tape, I guess), and the small mound made by the various additional pieces of tape added over time has become substantial enough to feel like brail to the fingertips. The anthropologist in me wants to peel away the layers to see the price of, say, a ham and Swiss sandwich in 1961, the year of my birth. In fact, my thumbnail flirts with the edge of the top layer of tape, upon which is written $1.50– pretty reasonable for ham and Swiss in 2002.

"I'm going to have the chicken noodle soup," Ma says to Jeanette and me. "Bet it's delicious."

The tall man reappears, already writing in his little notebook. "Anything else, ma'am?"

"A cup of coffee. Is it good and hot?"

"Yes, ma'am."

"I'll have a ham and Swiss sandwich," I say. "Is it really only a buck-fifty?"

The man cocks an eye, peers down at my menu. "Supposed to be a dollar eighty-five. Sometimes people pull off the prices. Got nothing better to do with their time, I guess."

I scratch my nose. "I'll take that, on whole wheat. Lettuce and tomato. Mustard. And I'll have coffee, too."

The tall man looks at Jeanette, then looks again. "And for you, ma'am?" His voice suddenly sounds like sugar mixed into gravel.

"Cheeseburger and fries," she monotones. "And a Coke."

"Pepsi all right, ma'am?"

Not looking up at him, Jeanette shakes her head. "I hate the taste of Pepsi. How about Mountain Dew?"

"Oh. Mountain Dew? Sorry, ma'am. Would a Sprite be okay?"

She makes a face. "Do you have Ginger Ale?"

His face begins to break out in spotty blotches. "Used to carry Ginger

Ale. Not many people ordered it, so we cancelled it. Awfully sorry."

Jeanette finally looks up at the man. "How about bottled water? Do have that? Evian or something?"

Now he's positively crestfallen. His droopy shoulders double-droop. "Got water from the tap, ma'am. It's clean, cold well water. Best water in the county. And it's free. No charge."

"Fine. Can you put ice in it?"

"Yes, ma'am. 'Course I can. Be happy to. Make it nice and cold for you."

We all breathe a sigh of relief at the resolution of the drink crisis. Our host says to Jeanette, "Anything else I can get for you? Anything at all?"

"No thanks."

When he's gone, we share a smile. Even Jeanette. At the sight of her smile, slight and fleeting though it is, I get a glimpse of the beauty that captivates so many.

After a deep breath I say, "So, Ma. How are you feeling? You doing okay so far?" I reach across the table and touch her arm, briefly.

"I'm fine," she says. "I feel good."

"You must be a little apprehensive about all the changes coming up. I know I'd be."

"A little," she concedes.

"It's a really difficult thing you're doing, making this move. I think that has to be acknowledged. A lot of people your age wouldn't do it. Couldn't do it. Make a move this big..."

"What are you trying to do," Jeanette says, "make her feel worse than she already feels about this whole fiasco?"

"Look," I say, "This is probably going to amaze you, Jeanette, but one of the most basic human needs– for *most* of us, anyway– is to *talk* about what we're feeling and..."

"It's not a fiasco," Ma says. "Don't say that. How would Debbie feel if she heard that?"

"Debbie's feeling pretty good right now," Jeanette says. "It took a little longer than usual, but she got what she wanted. Just like always."

"I want to know how *you* feel, Ma," I say.

"Don't you see..." But Jeanette's cell phone rings and she turns her back to me to answer it.

Ma says, "You know, you don't have to worry about me, David. I'm going to be fine. You worry too much. I thought this trip was going to be fun, but you're…" Her chin crinkles as she says it, and she turns away and pretends to look for something in her purse.

"Did I *say* I would meet you in Nashville?" Jeanette says under her breath. "Then trust me, okay? You've got to pull yourself together, Sheri. I'll see you between six and seven at the Sheraton. I gotta go."

The front door opens and a little blonde girl skips into the shack. Behind her is a tall man who looks remarkably similar to the guy in the kitchen. Twins? Except the man with the little girl is wearing a cap with a Tennessee Titans logo on it, so I can't tell if he's got the birthmark.

The cook comes out of the kitchen and stares at the pair, who take seats at the other plastic table.

The seated man says to the girl, "Tell him the delivery's coming at four. Tell him I'll be back in time to unload with him."

The little girl drawls, "Daddy says he'll come back at four to help you unload."

"Tell him okay," the cook says.

"Tell him to get us a couple of Pepsis."

"Can we?" the girl says to the man I assume is her uncle.

The man fills two glasses and leaves them on the counter for the girl to come and get. "Tell him I'm ordering Mountain Dew from now on," he says and takes a shy glance at Jeanette, though Jeanette's doodling what looks like skulls and crossbones on a napkin and doesn't notice.

"Daddy and I used to like to drive along country roads like this," Ma says. "Oh, I never wanted it to end. But he'd get tired after a while. He always wanted to go home before I was ready. I could've stayed out and driven all day."

"It was nice you and Da got to do a little traveling after we all left the house, huh, Ma?"

"Oh, I loved it."

"Da really mellowed as he got older, didn't he?"

"He had so much responsibility when you were all young. Some years two jobs, one year *three*, his own parents in bad health. You have to remember that when you think about him. I think he was as good a man as you'll ever find. He'd give you the shirt off his back if you needed it." She says this and looks at Jeanette, but Jeanette's into her doodling. Looking closer, I see that she's not doodling anymore, she's calculating figures.

"You miss him, I'll bet. He was your partner."

Ma's head trembles and she looks away. In her old lady/little girl eyes I find moisture. "Every single day I do."

"What do you miss most about him?"

"Oh, I don't know. Lots of things." I sense that she might be willing to try putting some of these feelings to words.

"Tell me just one of them. If you want to."

"You push and push and push," Jeanette says.

Stay calm. Remain calm.

"Oh, Jeanette," Ma says, "he's been that way since he was little. Always the questions! 'Ma, how does the sound get made inside the fire engine?' 'Ma, how come different people have different colored skin?' 'Why did God give us two eyes and two ears but only one mouth?' I used to tell all the neighborhood girls what you asked me. Oh, how we laughed! 'Does God have to eat lunch?' Isn't that a question? Sister Joan, when you were in second grade, used to tell me her religion class couldn't get through two paragraphs without your hand going up: why did God do that? How can God do this? Oh David, you drove people crazy with your questions. Including your father. I remember one time he got so exasperated he said to you, 'If God wanted us to know everything about himself, he'd tell us.' And you said something like, 'You mean He *doesn't* want us to know about him?' And Bernie said, 'No. He wants us to wonder about him.' I always remember that, because I didn't know how in the world he was going to answer you, and I thought that was a pretty good answer, really. *I* wouldn't have thought of it. If you'd have asked me, I would have just said, 'Go ask your father.'"

"He wants us to wonder about him," I repeat. "I *do* like that. What do you think of that, Jeanette? Theologically-speaking?"

"I wonder about *you*," she says.

"I'm flattered."

"Okay, enough," Ma says. "You two are worse than little kids sometimes."

The tall man places our dishes in front of us. Before he goes he says to Jeanette, "I made sure there was plenty of ice in your glass, ma'am. Should be good n' cold."

Jeanette looks at him, mutters "Thanks." I feel a pang of sadness for this man, and another bolt of rage toward my sister. But I hold my tongue– or rather, use it to eat. The sandwich is good. The coffee's hot. I remember my mission.

"Go tell him we're leaving now," the seated maybe twin says to the girl and stands up.

Dutifully, the little girl runs to the counter and calls through the swinging doors into the kitchen. "Uncle Mitch (she pronounces it Me-itch), we're leavin.' Anything you want me to tell daddy?"

"No."

When they go out, Ma leans over the table and says, "Isn't that sad?"

I gesture at Jeanette and myself.

"Oh, don't say that, David. You can't compare. You two do a lot of things together."

"They mostly revolve around you, Ma," I point out. And it occurs to me that with Ma living in Arizona, Jeanette and I may not find ourselves in each other's company much in the years to come. It was Ma inviting us to her place for one of her frequent "parties" (consisting, usually, of my family, Jeanette and a "friend," one or two of Ma's neighbors, and Edna McCauley.) Or it was Jeanette and I on the phone, coordinating which one of us would take Ma to the doctor's, or food shopping, or to an appliance store to get an air conditioner, etc. The thought of losing contact with Jeanette troubles me. A lot. I mean, although I often can't stand her, I do love her.

"I think we have a special family," Ma says. "Edna always tells me that. 'You should be so proud, Lilly,' she says. She's right. Look at you all. You a college professor. And you, a successful businesswoman. And Debbie an owner of a fancy retirement home. Even Aaron's a college teacher. And a published author, too. If someone told me when I first got married that my kids were going to do this well, oh, I'd have said that's too much to expect." Suddenly her eyes widen and her hand flies up to her mouth. "Goodness gracious, we were going to call Aaron and wish him a happy birthday, remember? Today."

"Oh, yeah," I say. But my thoughts are about our "special family." Yes, there have been modest successes, and coming from her girlhood in the depression, Ma has a right to be happy about them, proud even.

But the idea of calling Aaron dampens my already moist spirits. "He's, what," I say, "43 today? Okay, well, we'll call and we'll all wish him a happy birthday."

"Don't include me in that call," Jeanette says.

"Oh, come on," Ma says. "Just a quick happy birthday. He's your brother, for goodness sake."

"Technically. Everybody finished eating? Can we go?"

The women reach for their purses, I for my wallet.

The tall man comes out of the kitchen. He's slicked back his hair and changed his tee shirt from a green one to a red one. We all stand up and Jeanette takes a quick step forward and hands the man her Visa card.

His prominent Adam's apple rises and falls. "I'm sorry, ma'am, but we don't take that."

"American Express?"

"No, ma'am. We're a cash only outfit, I'm afraid. I'm working on a plan to get in a credit card machine..."

She hands him a twenty.

"I'll get your change directly, ma'am."

"Keep it."

"Oh, no ma'am, that's a nine dollar tip."

"It's okay," she says, turning for the door.

"Why, thank you, ma'am. You're very kind. You have a good day now. Come back any ...."

She's out the door.

"You have a good day," I say to the man.

"The food was delish," Ma adds brightly.

Outside, a great, God-like silence hangs over the little gravel parking lot. The air feels cooler than it did half an hour ago, and the hollows between the hills have become eerie lakes of fog. The surrounding woods are slipping into a milky oblivion, too.

"Gosh, look at this," Ma says. One of the things I've always admired about Ma is her undying and boundless capacity for awe; her wonderfully pure sense of wonder.

The tall man comes out of the shack and calls to us, "You all know there's no re-entrance onto the highway down here, don't you?"

"No," I say. "So, how do we get back on 40?"

"Just ride this road here fourteen miles. Might get a little foggy in the hollows. Next entrance'll come up on your left. In Tullsville. They got a diner there but people say the food ain't much."

"Tullsville. Thanks."

"And ma'am, I'm going in to order a carton of Mountain Dew. Next time you come through, we'll have it ready for you."

"Say thank you," Ma whispers to Jeanette.

"Thanks."

"My pleasure." The tall man smiles and blushes and stays out and watches us climb into the van and drive out onto the road. A surreal stick figure fading in mist, he offers a bashful, futile wave to his never-to-be lover, who's rolling a plastic-wrapped cigar around in her small fingers and looking the other way.

The road bends, then dips into a white soup. Unable to see more than twenty feet ahead of me, I ease up on the pedal.

"Do you think you should drive in this, David?" Ma says.

"It's not that bad," Jeanette interrupts, and glances at her watch. "He can handle it."

"It's okay at the moment, Ma." Though I do feel the need to move up on the seat and arch over the steering wheel. I see nothing outside on either side of me but gauzy, hanging smoke. "If it gets any worse, we'll pull over and wait it out."

"In my father's town in Poland," Ma says, "near the mountains, they used to get terrible fog. Some days, it never lifted. The whole day passed and you couldn't see your hand in front of your face."

"Did he tell you that?"

"No," Jeanette says. "She read his mind."

"Hey, Jeanette, stop. Please. Just, stop."

"My mother told me. My father didn't...he never..."

"Never what, Ma?"

No reply.

A cramp spreads across my shoulder blades like a crack fissuring through a beam of wood. "Damn."

"We were taught that swearing is a sin," Ma says from the back. "And we taught you that, too."

"Venial," I say.

"Using a bad word is a sin. And a sin is a sin."

So I risk this: "Do you think you were taught that using too many words to say *anything* was a kind of sin?"

"What on earth do you mean by that?"

Long inbreathe. "Well. Take us, for example. We've never been a family that...that *talked* a lot. I mean we talked plenty about the everyday things, I guess. Sports. How to fix things. How to get a job done the right way. But we sure didn't *emote* much. You will admit that displays of affection, verbal or physical, were kind of rare in the Stepenski household."

"Oh," Ma says. "I don't know about that. I think we were just like everybody else."

"I'm just conjecturing that maybe the reluctance to express emotion came, some of it anyway, from your parents, from that Eastern European culture of, of, you know, keep your nose to the grindstone, don't talk about what's on your mind, your feelings, your troubles..."

"Here we go again," Jeanette says. "Can we stop this discussion before it starts this time? Can we *please*?"

"You'd be the one to benefit most from *not* stopping it, Jeanette."

"Give me a break. You think everybody's 'issues' are the same as yours. *You* may need to talk about yourself on and on, David. *You* may need all this touchy-feely babble crap. Maybe you should get yourself a therapist and pay him a lot of money to let you talk for forty-five minutes non-stop about your problems. Go to Sarah. She'll give you the family discount."

I'm tempted to say, 'I don't think I'd want my sister's lover as my therapist,' but that would hurt Ma. "I've done my therapy," I respond. "You should *really* do yours."

"I thought you only went to counseling?" Ma says.

That *was* the word I used when I reluctantly mentioned it to her and Da (at the time, fifteen or so years ago, I considered myself brave for mentioning it to them it at all); they could, I thought, tolerate the idea of me getting a little "counseling" after a painful break-up with a woman I believed I was madly in love with, but they wouldn't understand why a normal guy like me would need to engage in anything so scandalous as seeing a shrink for "therapy." Therapy was for really disturbed people.

"Counseling, therapy. Whatever. It helped me get through some of the stuff I was dealing with." To my dismay, my voice cracks as I add, "But it's no substitute for honest conversation with the people you love."

Jeanette (to her credit, I suppose) simply turns and looks out the window at the thick curtains of white outside. Ma, I sense, is sitting there behind me, head trembling, struggling to think of words of comfort. But then, who in her life ever comforted her with words?

I cough and say, "Anyway, another seven miles and we'll be on the highway. Maybe it'll be a little less foggy on the highway."

"The fog seems to be getting denser," Ma says.

No, that's Jeanette I want to say. But I don't. Small win.

A phone bleeps, jarring us. My sister and I both dig into our pockets. It's mine. "I'm going to change the ring on this so we know which is which," I announce. "Hello. David Stepenski speaking."

"Dad?"

"Teddy? Hey, buddy. Good to hear your voice. Missed you last night." I feel like I haven't spoken with him in weeks, though it's only been a couple of days. His voice sounds deeper than I remember it.

"Mom made me call you. Just because I got home a little late last night."

"How late?"

I can barely hear the word, "Midnight."

"*Midnight*? Are you kidding? That's way too late for a twelve-year old, bud."

"I'm going to be thirteen in September, Dad. Everybody else can stay out as late as they want."

"I doubt that, Ted. Unless their parents are downright negli... Never mind. In our house, you come home when you're told to. Look, you're a smart kid. You know why we do what we do."

"No, I don't. Besides I was just at my girlfriend's. We were watching a movie."

The road curves this way and that through the feathery oblivion. I'm down to eleven miles an hour now, and our speed drops even more as I deep-breathe my reaction to his word, "girlfriend." Of course, I'm all too aware that if you say the right thing to a sensitive twelve-year old in the wrong way, you'll achieve the wrong result. Mostly, you'll engender silence and psychic distance. I know something about that.

"Listen, Ted. Our rule is you're home at nine-thirty. Whether I'm there or not. You must have worried your mother sick."

"She's always talking to that guy across the street lately."

"*What*? Teddy, she is not *always* talking to him. And I know you worried her."

He offers a mopey, "Sorry."

"Well, thank you for saying that."

"You're welcome. Okay, see you." He adds, perhaps perfunctorily, "Tell Grandma Lilly I said hi. And Aunt Jeanette."

"I will," I say. "Hey, wait a minute Ted." There's a millisecond of processing in my brain: do it or not?

"Yeah, dad?"

I do it. "Listen, you're not going out tonight." I know damn well that at another time, under less stressful circumstances, I might say, "Last warning."

On the other end of the line, silence smolders.

"You there, Teddy?"

"Yeah."

"Look. I love you, buddy. I love you like crazy. (I wonder, when Ma hears me say this to my son, what she thinks.) But there are consequences to our actions."

Teddy says, "Yeah, okay. Here's mom."

I hear the phone drop onto the kitchen counter, footsteps stomping away.

"Hi, honey. Wow, what did you say to him?"

"That he's not going out tonight. It's not that big a deal. He'll survive."

"Well, except that it's Friday, and all his gang of friends like to go out together on Fridays."

I'd forgotten it was Friday. I can still remember that early adolescent thrill, that first taste of semi-freedom: going out on a weekend night with friends, no adults involved. But, damn it, I want to be firm. The whole world feels so flimsy and tentative and compromising. And maybe Teddy's right: maybe his friends *are* allowed to come home whenever, do whatever. Which makes me feel even more compelled to draw a line, as if I represent some dwindling core of sane parents who may be civilization's last hope. "Well," I say, "he made a bad decision and now he's got a consequence."

"Fair enough," Marie says. "And I agree with you." She speaks with that lovely light touch of hers, the breeze that rights the tipping ship. I haven't heard her sound this way in a while. Would that I could learn such deftness of tone. "You know what we'll do. We'll rent a movie and get a pizza. Make it a family fun night. Of course, I'm no substitute for Michelle, so it'll still be a punishment. Is that okay?"

With an ache I realize how badly I want to be part of that movie and pizza deal. The unassailable *rightness* of all of us together in the same cozy room; the way one or another of the kids will just plop into my lap unbidden. Is there a better feeling? Oh, I want to wrestle them to the floor, squeeze them against my chest, not let go. "Yeah, that's fine. And, hey, you know what, you can invite Brandon. Teddy seems to think you're spending a lot of time…"

Out of nowhere a car in the opposite lane flies through the fog, becoming visible only as it zooms by, inches from me, and disappears back into the smoke. Even Jeanette emotes a "Whoa."

"Oh, gosh, David," Ma says.

"Look, I'll call you back later. It's really foggy out here."

"Well, why don't you pull over?" Marie says.

"I should. Okay, talk to you later."

As soon as I end the call, I slow down and begin angling the van to the right toward what I hope will be a decent-sized shoulder, or a shoulder at all, for that matter.

"What are you doing?" Jeanette says.

"Stopping. This is nuts. I can't see a thing. You'd think they'd have cat's eyes on the side of the road for situations like this. Hey, roll down your window and guide me over, will you?"

Jeanette makes a face but rolls down the window, leans out and peers down. "Okay. Keep coming right."

"What's that?" Ma says.

"What's what?"

"I thought I saw an animal. Maybe not. My eyes play tricks sometimes."

"Keep coming," Jeanette says. "We just went over a white line, I think. Go slow."

We're crunching now, still angling right. I want to get as far from the road as possible. There's nothing to guarantee that the driver of some eighteen-wheeler, having just had lunch at old Luke's Lunch Shack, won't decide to pull over right at this spot and wind up shoving us into a tree. *Mother, daughter and son killed in freak back road fog crash.*

I feel my right front tire rubbing against something, a good-sized rock maybe, and stop the van.

"Let me see if I can get some bearings here," I say. "Maybe there's a field or a lot or something where we can be sure we're far enough off the road."

"Be careful, David," Ma says. "God forbid we're still in the road."

I step out into the cloud and, arm out in front of me, Tiresias-like, take a few tentative steps forward to see what my front tire's up against. It's a small boulder, the size of a warped beach ball. No damage to the tire and not a problem as far as pulling back out goes. I take a few steps and my hand touches the prickly ends of a clump of pine-needles. I close my eyes, inhale streams of moisture and pine; the scent bathes my lungs and I entertain a fleeting, unfocused but happy sensation of Christmas' past. I walk ten or so steps farther and find more pine branches, a thick wall of them. I conjecture that there's an extended line of pine trees here and, satisfied that I can drive no further in, turn and walk back toward the van.

Except it isn't there. Or else I'm not where I think I am. I feel around, certain that I'm only a few feet at most from it; after all, I only walked fifteen paces or so, and was careful to retrace my steps. I walk around some more, arms out like a blind man, expecting to feel metal or glass.

Nothing but air. I could, of course, simply call out to Jeanette and Ma. But that would be to admit that I'm lost. Not ready to do that, fool that I know I am.

This brings back to me one of those cringe memories I try to avoid dwelling on whenever it imposes itself into my mind, but which nevertheless comes, and which I nevertheless dwell on, like a math problem you're sure you're on the brink of solving, but never do.

I must have been seven (Jeanette would have been five or six, Aaron nine, Deb eleven). Da took us to Clove Lakes Park, which was maybe a hundred acres of lakes and hills and woods in the middle of Staten Island. "Today is survival day," Da declared. He was in a bad mood, I remember, though there was nothing unusual about that: maybe he'd worked overtime on his second job the night before; maybe he was doing something he believed necessary but not enjoyable (which probably summarizes much of his life, maybe most lives). His instructions were essentially this: "I'm going to take each one of you to a certain part of the park, and your job is to find your way back here, to this spot in front of the Parkee station." He explained that this was one of the best ways he knew to help us become confident that we could take care of ourselves in a tough situation. The key point was, everyone had to make it back on their own. If we should happen to see one another, whoever was the older one had to wait until the younger one was out of sight before continuing on. (In our family, the older sib was always held responsible for the younger. If a situation involved two, three, or all of us and anything went wrong, the oldest one paid the harshest price.) In this situation you had to get back alone. *Alone*. I don't know if it occurred to any of us to think that attempting to "survive" *together* might be preferable.

Da led us into the woods, taking a circuitous route and then, after a half mile or so, said, "Aaron, wait here ten minutes and then head back." And so on with the rest of us. The reason we had to wait ten minutes in the area he dropped us off was so that he could get back to the meeting place before we did and be there when we arrived.

I actually enjoyed this challenge, as well as a lot of the other ones Da devised over the years. I didn't question the point, the usefulness of any of his exercises. I saw them as grand and exciting adventures, marred only by the fact that generally neither Da nor anyone else shared my enthusiasm, with the possible exception of Jeanette, who in those days, as Da's favorite, was actually quite happy, even sprite-like, much of the time.

On that morning I was disappointed that Aaron wasn't excited to be there. The two of us spent hours in the woods playing together. He would decide what game we played and who we would be (him the Lone Ranger, me, Tonto; him Batman, me Robin, etc.). The sidekick role was fine with me, as long as we were together. But that morning, Aaron seemed to view the task as Da's design to get him in trouble.

After being dropped off, I spent ten minutes choosing a walking stick, watching squirrels and birds scamper and flit, pretending to be Davy Crockett in hostile Indian country. Finally, I headed in the direction of the meeting spot. I was so confident that I'd find my way back that I intentionally meandered off course. Coming down a steep trail, I spotted a pair of legs stretched out from the base of a tree and recognized my brother's sneakers. Da's instructions forbade me to go to him, but it was Aaron down there, and I wanted to be with him.

When he spotted me coming he barely looked up.

"What are you doing?" I said. "How come you're not on your way back?"

"I'm not doing anything. Get out of here before he finds out you saw me."

"I know it, I'm gonna go now. Don't wait too long, okay? Hey, want to play wiffle ball when we get home?"

"Nah."

"Aaron? How come you're so...you know...sad and all?"

I see it very clearly even now: he's peeling a piece of bark off a small stick, then looking up at me, eyes brimming. My eyes brimmed, too.

"Go away, David."

"What's wrong? You can tell me, Arron."

"He hates me, okay?" Aaron shouted. "I'm the only one he hates."

I shook my head, *no, no, no, it isn't true.* You can't say that. He's our father. He *can't* hate us. *Any* of us, even you. *He believes in God.*

"He wishes I was dead."

"That's not true, Aaron. Don't say that."

"Then why do I get beat the most? Why do I get the hardest chores? How come he never laughs or jokes around with me like he does with Jeanette?"

I don't know, I don't know. Just stop. Shut up.

"It's because he hates my guts, that's why."

"No, Aaron," I shouted back through my own tears. "Shut up, okay?"

"You know it's true, David."

I shouted louder, "*Shut up. He can't.*"

But when he said, "And I hate him, even more," something in me broke. In one motion I whipped my walking stick at Aaron's face. The sharp tip of it ripped open the skin above his left eye and blood gushed out.

I dropped the stick and gaped at the bleeding, torn open flesh. My brother's blood was a deep satiny red. He pressed his tee shirt to the gash and in no time the shirt was a glistening, heavier and darker red.

"Get away from me," he cried. "Get out of here."

I ran, trembling, gasping, *Oh God, Oh God.* I know the girls were already at the Parkee Station when I approached, because Da always made it a little easier for them. They were sitting on a bench and I think Da was showing them how his watch worked. As I got close, he looked at me for a second, stood up and said sternly, "What's the matter?"

I bellowed out the first thing I could think of: "I saw, I saw a bear."

He laughed. "No, you didn't. It was probably a big dog." When I came to the bench, he ruffled my hair, which he almost never did. I remember thinking, *he loves me and he loves Aaron, too. He loves us all, like God does. No matter what.*

When, after what felt like an hour, Aaron finally came walking down the trail, pressing the sopping tee-shirt to his brow, but still holding his head up straight, he wasn't crying. Da spotted him while he was a ways off, saw the bloody cloth, and took off at a run. As he ran, he pulled off his own tee shirt. He flung Aaron's shirt to the ground and pressed his own against the cut. They stayed up there for a few minutes, the girls and I watching in silence. When they finally came down, we all hurried into the car and drove straight to the hospital. Aaron received fifteen stitches and a permanent scar above his left eye. On the way home, he told Da he'd slipped on some leaves and fallen on the sharp edge of a rock.

I really don't want to think about Aaron.

Okay. The van is near. Very near. I know this because it has to be very near. I try to call up one of those intuitive powers new-agers are always claiming humans possess. Sixth sense. I begin to walk, carefully, in the direction I think my greater MIND wants me to go in. Twelve paces, it tells me. I count them out: three, four, five; at step eight my face slams into a needly tree branch. I touch my right cheek and feel a bead of blood. "Damn."

Oh, just call out to them, for crying out loud.

But no-can-do. Not the Stepenski way. I will find them or die trying. (Which feels too much like a real possibility, and a chill shivers up through my bones.)

I decide I'll walk no more than ten yards in any direction, always turning just a few degrees to the right at the end of any ten steps. I do it: ten yards, half-turn to the right. Ten yards, half-turn to the right. I end up brushing into pine branches again.

So why hasn't Jeanette called out to me? Because Da would say, let him be? He's got to learn.

I stand there, hands on hips, turning around slowly, squinting, trying to make a search light of my eyes. Just as I complete a revolution, I hear a soft padding sound. It's not Jeanette, not human. An animal. I'm thinking, *fuck, it's a big old bear.* Coming this way, by the sound of it. I don't know anything about bears. We have three goldfish at home. I know that with dogs you're supposed to remain calm, that if they sense your fear, they may panic and attack. *Domestic Ethnographer Killed In Fog Bear Attack.* I send up a quick prayer to the God of mercy. The footsteps come very close, then stop.

Suddenly, just visible and no more than an arm's length away from me is the tawny head and upper torso of a horse. The head only comes up to my shoulders, and I wonder if he's standing in a gully. My heart pounds at the sheer animality of this creature. We stand still and stare into each other's eyes. His moist, contracting nostrils feed the fog with small puffs of smoke. I know that a person comfortable with horses, Marie for example, whose family owned several when she was growing up in the Berkshires, would rub it just above the nostrils on its long snout, or pat the side of its head behind its magnificent dark-roast-coffee eyes, and make comforting clucking sounds. Me, I stand statue-still. I try to appeal to the horse's intuition that I'm a calm, friendly, fellow creature. And I'm not so nervous that I fail to realize that this is a creature of stunning beauty, and that I just might be a veritable horse whisperer in-the-rough. As I gaze into its coppery eyes, and it into mine, the pounding of my heart subsides. It dawns on me that this is probably a foal. Its dark mane is short and fuzzy and growing upward, Mohawk-style. I lift my arm and slowly, gently message its face below the eyes. "Hey there, fella. Where's your mama? Huh?"

The horse takes a step closer to me.

"You're a good boy," I say, "or are you a girl? Doesn't matter, does it?" I pat it on its warm, muscular shoulder. Then, to my new friend, I confess, "I don't know about you, but I'm lost."

A tire-squealing vehicle, blasting wailing and tortured guitar licks within, suddenly blazes invisibly along the road. What the hell? The foal throws back its head and whinnies, then trots away into the white. I'm sorrier than I can say to see it go.

Very quickly the thrumming silence returns, more vast than before. In the foal's absence, I feel a new degree of aloneness. Things are just strange enough for me to wonder, seriously, whether or not it *really* was just here.

I jump backward at my cell phone's sudden tinny bleat. My hands fumble into my pocket.

"Hello."

"Did you get lost?"

I process the remark, try to conjure a quick rejoinder: *Not as lost as you are, sister*; *Who among us isn't? No, I hear that standing out in the fog is good for your complexion.* But I already feel like a first-class lame-o, so all I say is, "Hit the horn a few times, okay?"

The honking comes immediately from approximately twenty yards away. I make my way back to the van.

"Did you have to go to the bathroom or something?" Ma says when I climb back into the driver's seat. "I thought maybe you had diarrhea or something? Sometimes it comes at the worst times, doesn't it?"

"It wasn't anything like that. I was just checking out the lay of the land."

"What happened? Did you cut your cheek?"

I touch the place where the small blob of blood has begun to jell. "Scratch. Boy, you can really get disoriented in fog like this. Sense of direction just sort of goes haywire."

"Especially if you're disoriented to begin with," Jeanette says.

"Right. Obviously you, being the correctly-oriented one in the family, should have been the one to go out there."

"True. We'll know better next time."

Ma says, "I feel that way sometimes."

"What way, Ma?"

"Disoriented. You know? Like… Oh, never mind."

"No, tell me," I say, turning around to face her. "That could be a symptom of something."

"Oh, I don't think it's anything but getting old," she says. She's knitting, and as she talks she keeps her eyes on the work her fingers are doing. "It's just...well, like waking up in the middle of the night. Sometimes it takes a minute to remember where I am. Or even sometimes in the day.... Anyway, that's all I meant."

"That happens to everyone," Jeanette says. "You're not alone, Ma."

"I know it," Ma says. "We all forget things."

That's when I remember again that we are supposed to call Aaron today. But I don't mention it. Things are foggy enough as it is.

* * *

We wait it out mostly in silence. At one point, Ma says, "I should get a picture of this fog." And she points her camera out the window and takes one.

It's two-thirty-two when we're finally able to pull back out onto the road. Ma's come up to the passenger seat; Jeanette's gone in the back to nap. The fog has broken up enough so that when the road rises, the sky overhead shines blue and scrubbed. The dips and hollows still hold a soup of mist.

"What a trip so far, huh?" Ma says. "Boy, what else can happen?"

"Not much, let's hope."

"Oh, I like the excitement."

"Think we can get to Nashville by six?" Jeanette mutters.

"I think so. Probably two, three hours from here. You meeting Sheri at a particular hotel?"

"Yeah. I already made reservations for us, by the way. Near the Grand Ole Opry."

"Is Sheri staying there, too?" Ma asks.

"Who knows? She can take care of her own arrangements."

Ma says, "How come she left the cops? It wasn't just because you two stopped being friends, was it?"

I get a fleeting picture of my sister and Sheri making love. I see Sheri much more clearly than I do Jeanette. Sheri's full of passion, moving her body around Jeanette's like a snake around a pole. Or like Sheri's a flock of starlings and Jeanette's a stolid old oak. I catch myself with a full-bodied shudder and run away from the image.

"Let's just say," Jeanette answers, "that some of the boys on the force gave her a hard time and she finally had enough."

That, unfortunately, is not hard to imagine. Since 9/11, we've gained a new, or a renewed, respect for the job cops and firemen do, but that doesn't mean some of them aren't ignorant, arrogant sons of bitches. Nasty people (mostly men) with unresolved grievances who carry guns wherever they go. Sheri's a good person, and the idea that some of the "boys" gave her a hard time pisses me off. Macho sons of bitches.

"That's hard work for a woman," Ma says. "Don't you think so?"

"I'm a guy," I respond, "and *I* can't imagine doing it. I sure don't want a gun anywhere near me."

"But doesn't it seem like there's less of a difference between men and women nowadays? It must be confusing for kids, don't you think? Sometimes I think we're making it too hard for kids to grow up."

The faces of Teddy and Genevieve flash into my mind. What if today is the day some terror-driven lunatic blows up an American power plant, or a mall or school in rural New Jersey?

"Though," Ma continues, "some of the things *we* always had to do you men can do for a change. I don't think men know much about women, to tell you the truth."

Do I know Marie? I don't know. "You turning into a feminist in your old age, Ma?" I raise my pointer finger. "For the record, I've changed many a diaper, cooked many a meal, washed many a dish. Still do. Marie's no fool. We divvy up the domestic chores pretty fairly, I think. Not that I'm promoting complete homogenization of the sexes. I like femininity in a woman."

I check the rearview. Jeanette's eyes are shut tight.

Tullsville consists of the one main street, which we're riding down, and a few side streets of scattered, sleepy, neglected, early-to-mid-century houses, and not a soul in sight. The kind of place that makes you feel melancholy, sad that anybody has to live here. Or maybe it resembles some inner, psychic town that we all live in sometimes.

The entrance to I-40, a sign tells us, is one mile up the road. Just before the ramp we see the Tullsville Diner, a charming old railroad car. There are six or seven pickup trucks in the parking lot.

"That guy at the shack was really sweet on you, Jeanette." I don't know if I'm trying to taunt her or compliment her. Maybe I just want to *reach* her.

"Oh, lots of men are," Ma says. "Why wouldn't they be? She's always driven the men crazy. I don't know why she doesn't find herself a good one and settle down."

"*Ma*," Jeanette says. "I'm not invisible. Let's change the subject."

"You know what Edna said to me once? A lot of men are intimidated by attractive women. She thought maybe that was the problem. I told her, well Jeanette can't help how attractive she is. You know what she said?"

"Cut," Jeanette says. "End of conversation."

"Okay, okay," Ma says. "Just let me finish. She said, 'Oh, yes she can.'"

* * *

It's almost six when we walk into the bustling lobby of the Best Western Nashville North, a few miles from downtown, the modest skyline of which you can see in the hazy distance. The hotel is located on a boulevard of the usual hotels and motels, although a few are distinguished, as their marquees boast, by the fact that "Elvis Slept Here" or that you can "Stay Where Dolly Stayed." On the lobby walls hang assorted glass-encased guitars, dobroes, banjos and cowboy hats once played or worn by country music semi-luminaries.

I feel uneasy about the prospect of seeing Sheri under these circumstances. I associate her with parties, good conversation, the bearable lightness of being, even a kind of casual intimacy. But apparently, she's a different animal when she's at the end of her rope.

If Jeanette's anxious about the meeting, it doesn't show; she stands on the end of the check-in line with an expression of mild impatience, staring straight ahead, tapping her foot. Ahead of her on the line is a group of fifteen or so youngish Japanese men and women, all full of chatter and merriment, most of them wearing cowboy hats and tight blue jeans with big silver-buckled belts. In front of them, a huge man in a brown leather jacket seems to be scolding the young, auburn-haired woman he's with about something she should have said to somebody when she had the chance. And in front of them, a mother with a toddler-loaded stroller-for-three is searching through her purse while her husband talks to the clerk behind the desk. Since the parents aren't looking, the toddler in the front seat decides it's a good time to smear his banana into the face and hair of the toddler in the middle seat. Through the doors people come and go in a steady stream. My eye finds a still point in all this movement: an elderly gentleman in a white suit sitting in a wing-backed chair amid a set of six other, unoccupied chairs. His snow white, shoulder-length hair is well-groomed, his legs are crossed daintily, revealing argyle socks and a snazzy pair of tawny alligator shoes. He's reading *USA Today*, the headline of which proclaims that India and Pakistan may be on the brink of nuclear war. Will this be the trigger for all hell to break loose? But the gentleman strikes me as utterly imperturbable, and my heart swells with envy.

When Jeanette's finished checking us in, I tell her, "If you want, I'll bring your bag up to your room so you can wait down here for Sheri."

She bites her lower lip, then hands me the bag. She even says, "Thanks."

After quick showers, Ma and I meet in the lobby to head out for a bite to eat and a short sight-see while there's daylight. We find Jeanette outside, leaning against the wall near the front door, smoking.

"She still isn't here?" Ma says.

White gray smoke floats out with Jeanette's words: "She'll be here soon. She managed to get lost."

"Haven't we all," I say. "Have a good dinner, Jeanette. Give Sheri my love. I'd really like to see her before we leave tomorrow. Ask her to have breakfast with us, okay?"

"I don't intend to prolong this."

I ask Ma to wait while I take Jeanette aside. "Look, she's driven from Florida to Tennessee to have a friggin' *conversation* with you. That's mind boggling. I mean, she's got to be absolutely desperate. You know what I mean. So…just be careful what you say."

Jeanette looks up into pale evening sky. "She basically threatened to kill herself if I didn't agree to meet her. She can be dramatic sometimes, but sometimes she makes good on her threats. I'll try to talk some sense into her but then, sorry, it's bye-bye."

As Ma and I step down into the parking lot, I turn and catch my sister's lonely eye. I recall, thirty years or so ago, finding her lavender journal on her bedroom floor. I can see it clearly, the garish color, the cheap lock. What I remember most was what was written in emphatic black magic marker on the cover: *Keep Out! Stay Away!* And then, in smaller, tighter script, the saddest parenthetical phrase I've ever read: *(You Don't Want To Know)*.

Sadder still: she was right.

* * *

"Oh, my gosh," Ma says as she lifts a fork full of seafood enchilada.

"Aaron," I say, before she can. I check my watch. "It's only nine-thirty. Eight-thirty in Vegas. We can still call him. Let's wait until we finish dinner. I hate when people talk on phones in restaurants."

"Okay." But disturbance rides like a kick of dust across Ma's features.

"Or we can call him now," I say. I find his number on my cell phone, punch it in, hope for an answering machine.

Three rings, then, softly, "Hello."

I hand the phone to Ma. She's reluctant to take it, but collects herself and does.

"Aaron? It's me, your mother. Beg your pardon?. Uh, Nashville, Tennessee. Oh, terrific. We're having a grand time. Well, we'll see soon enough, won't we? I know, swimming pools, a sauna. It should be lovely. How are you, dear? Are you sure? What?" Her voice suddenly flatlines. "What? But...why so far away?"

Ma listens, finally says, "Gosh, I don't know. I would love to, but.... Can you ask David? He's right here." She thrusts the phone at me.

"Hey, brother," I say, like I'm happy as a pig in mud and expect him to be, too.

"Hi, David. How are things in the ethnography business?" He sounds okay. Get him when he's gloomy and it feels like every word is costing him an ounce of blood.

"People are watching a lot of T.V.," I say, trying to be clever. "Waiting for the other shoe to drop."

"Give it time."

"How are you? How's Po-Biz? You famous yet?"

"Look, I was telling Ma that I'm heading up to Alaska. I'm leaving...what's today, Friday?"

"Yeah, it's Friday night."

"I'm leaving Monday, maybe Tuesday."

"Nice of you to tell us. Alaska, huh? That's a haul."

"Going to drive up along the spine of the Rockies. So look, I was saying to Ma, any chance you guys could come up here for a day or two so I can see you before I go? I'd come down to Flagstaff, but I have a lot to do before we take off. Besides, I sold my car. I'm borrowing one at the moment."

"You know Jeanette's with us, right?"

"Ah, that's right. I forgot that." Long silence. "You know what, I'll bet Debbie's expecting you guys, like, yesterday. She's not going to put up with any delays. Especially if they're caused by me. Never mind."

"Ma's got the rest of her life to be with Debbie."

"No, let's forget it. It's just more time in the car for you guys, which I'm sure you don't need. Especially her. I'll be coming east one of these Christmases anyway."

I *am* relieved—but I'm also pissed. "Look," I say, "we'll see what we can do. I'll put in a call to Deb, talk with Jeanette and Ma, figure out logistics. We might make it over there for a day or two."

"No, David, listen..."

"Hey, here's Ma." And I hot potato the phone back to her.

"Aaron?" she says. "I forgot. Happy birthday, honey. Did you get the card I sent you? Listen I....I hope we can come see you. What? Don't be ridiculous. I *want* to see you before you go."

They talk a little while longer, say their goodbyes. As soon as she hangs up, she says to me, "We're going to see Aaron. It's not that far out of the way. Like you told him, if we're a day later to Debbie's, what difference does it make? I'm going to be there the rest of my life anyway, right?"

"If you really want to see him, we'll go. We'll go straight from here. Jeanette's not going to be happy about it, but...."

I am suddenly aware that the fortyish couple at the table next to ours have not spoken a word to one another, so intent on our conversation are they. When I turn and glare at them, their faces blanch.

"*David*!" Ma whispers. "What are you doing?"

"Let them mind their own business."

"My goodness, I've never seen you like this before. You've been so...what's the word for it? My goodness, you're not like this at home."

"That's because at home I'm...." A dish drops in the kitchen and like Peter hearing the cock crow, I recall my morning vow to *stay calm*. I feel like I can't control a single damn impulse. I shake my head three times. "I'm sorry," I say, "sorry, sorry."

"It's all right. You're a little tense, that's all." Ma seems hesitant, but she manages to say, "David, why don't they talk to each other?"

I glance at our neighbors, who slowly lift their forks to their mouths and gaze at their plates. "I have no idea. Really, I don't."

"Are you telling me the truth?"

"Yes. I don't know what caused them to stop speaking. It must have been something that hurt, but I don't know what it was."

"So many years. Why can't they just forgive?"

Ma's hands, set out on either side of her plate, tremble. I reach across the table to put my hands on hers, but she pulls them quickly back into her lap.

"They're *brother and sister*, for goodness sake," she says. "I don't understand it. They were okay until around eighth grade, then all of a sudden they wouldn't talk to each other. Not a word!"

I shove a pile of rice and beans around my plate with my fork.

"*I* did something wrong," Ma says, her head suddenly tipping downward. "When I first noticed it, I thought it would blow over. I should have said something to them before it went on too long. I should have had a meeting with them, like you and Marie do with your kids when there's a problem. But in those days, people didn't do that kind of thing."

"Ma," I say, "I don't know what triggered their problem, but it is hard to undo all the unhealthy habits in a family all through its history. And then there are the norms of particular cultures. And…"

"Oh, I hate it when you talk like that. All intellectual. I don't even know what you mean, but it makes our family sound so terrible. And I feel like you're putting down the Polish and maybe the Swiss, too, with all that talk about cultures. We were just like everyone else when we were a young family. You make us sound so…I don't know what. *Abnormal*. But let me tell you we had a lot of…," now her head begins to tremble along with her hands, "…you know …."

"A lot of what, Ma?"

"A lot of love, dammit." She turns away, as if the speaking of the word may unleash some force she won't be able to control.

"I know love was there, Ma. I never doubted that you or Da loved us."

"Goodness gracious, I should *hope* not. My gosh. Why do you even need to say that?"

I frown and Ma blushes; her eyes move around the table as if they're watching a ball roll.

The eavesdroppers are nibbling at their salads. Maybe an earful of our problems is making their own lives look a little brighter.

"*You* get along with your siblings, David. *You* talk to them all fine."

"How can you say that? You see how Jeanette and I keep butting heads. And I resent Debbie and I'm mystified by Aaron and frankly tend to want to avoid him."

"Oh, no, it isn't that bad. This trip is just a little tense for all of us, that's all. Back at home, you and Jeanette do things together all the time. And you and Debbie…well, she's right about her kids never really getting to know their grandma. And it *is* exciting for me to live somewhere new. Sort of. Don't resent her for this, David."

"I accept it," I say and blink at the sting in my eyes.

Suddenly Ma leans forward and says, "David, *do* something, please. Bring Aaron and Jeanette closer together before he goes off to Alaska. Who knows how long he'll be away this time. It would make me so happy to see them talk to each other again. Can you try to have a meeting with them, like you do with your kids? Please, David. Just try."

"But, *Ma*, they're adults. They make their own choices. What the hell can I do at a meeting?"

Her eyes plunge back to the tabletop. She frowns. "You're right, it isn't fair to ask you to try to fix this up."

My teeth grind into my gums. I glance at the couple at the next table. They're kissing.

* * *

When we step into the hotel lobby at a little before ten, only a few people mill about. I notice right away that sitting in the wing-backed chair is the same elderly gentleman in the white suit, although he's replaced his newspaper with a novel. I try to be inconspicuous as I stroll closer and peek at the title. *As I Lay Dying*. Haven't read it, though I liked *The Sound and The Fury* as an undergrad, mostly because the professor I had was passionate about Faulkner. She made you feel that if you understood Faulkner, you were in on some mysterious knowledge of life that remained unknown to all non-Faulknerians.

I feel a strong urge to sit near the old guy and try to strike up a conversation. Pick his brain for wisdom, because he just looks so damn wise and I feel so damn lacking. But Ma is tired and so I escort her to her room. Opening the door, we see that Jeanette's not there. "I guess they're still out eating, huh?" Ma says. "Gosh, I hope they're doing okay."

"You know, they may have stayed and eaten here in the hotel. I'll take a walk down to the restaurant and peek in, see if I can find them."

"Would you? Thank you, David. I'm a little worried. Sheri's a very nice person but there's something about her that makes me nervous. And if she would come all this way just for a dinner with Jeanette, that seems, you know, crazy."

"It is crazy."

Ma opens her handbag and peers in. "I wish Jeanette would find some nice man to marry, the way you found Marie and Debbie found Clint and I found daddy."

"Ma," I say, weariness making me brave, "you know Jeanette's not going to find a man."

Her head jerks away as if it's following the flight of a bird; her jaw begins to quiver. "I know it." Still looking in the direction of the bird, she says, "Do you think our religion ever makes mistakes about what it teaches?"

"She—mother church, I mean—sure has been doing a lot of apologizing lately."

Ma gazes into my eyes, waiting for more.

"There's that line in John's gospel that says: *God is love.* It seems impossible to get to the bottom of a statement like that. Love is such a mystery, you know? Maybe the church tries too hard to take the mystery out of God. Turn God into a mathematical equation, when in truth God is more like a poem."

"Well, that isn't how we were brought up to think of God. The way they taught us, He wasn't *that* mysterious. He wanted us to be good and to follow his rules."

"Well, you'll never go wrong trying to be good. But maybe some of the rules are more human than godly."

Ma's head tilts. It's too much and it's too late, and I give her a kiss on the forehead and suggest she get some sleep.

Before heading down to the restaurant, I go back into my own room, pace, glance out at the twinkling Nashville skyline. I'm thinking about Aaron. Da's wake. At some point toward the end of the first night, my brother, whom I hadn't seen in two years, caught me between conversations with cousins and asked if I'd like to go downstairs to the lounge with him. We'd all been on our feet for the better part of three hours in the sickly perfumed air, greeting friends and relatives and receiving condolences.

We settled into one of the sofas in the small, cedar-walled, lamplit room. "So who's idea was the cigar in his hand?"

"His. Remember?"

Aaron hadn't.

"Well..." I shrugged. "He made it known to us any number of times. 'Bury me with a cigar or don't bury me at all.'"

"There should have been a belt in the other hand."

"He mellowed," I said. "He changed. Give him that."

"Too late to do me any good."

I raised, lowered, then bent my head to look at him sideways.

Aaron's big-boned fingers forked into his tangle of curls. "At least now there's nothing I can do," he said. "It's always eaten at me that we had this lousy relationship and I didn't know how to fix it. It was broken beyond repair by the time I was ten, but, well, you know, David, Stepenskis are supposed to be able to fix anything, right?"

"I think that applies exclusively to mechanical things."

"I've always had this fucking buzz in my head: *Do something. Confront him. Make him apologize. Make him fucking confess. Something. Fix it.* Now he's dead and I'm thinking the obsession's finally gonna start fading. I think it's already started. Sorry if I sound insensitive. I know everybody's grieving. Just thought I'd let you know where I was, head-wise."

"So, there's no grief in you?"

He rested his elbows on his knees. "I've been grieving that man all my life. I was obsessed with him. Obsessed with trying to please him, to rile him, to become him, to become the opposite of him, and then not give a damn about him."

Debbie shepherded Ma into the lounge toward the other sofa. Jeanette moped in behind them, her hands drilled into the pockets of her chinos. In those days she wore her blonde hair long, a just barely parted curtain behind which she hid her stunning face. She was about to drop into the pink Queen Anne chair in the corner when she spotted Aaron and did an about-face.

I can still see the big, sad, muddy lakes of Aaron's eyes following her out and lingering at the doorway.

I flip on the T.V. and, standing in front of it, watch Letterman wax ironic about an indicted congressman. Of course, if Letterman couldn't be ironic he'd be mute. Irony is too much with us these days: ironic commercials and ads, ironic T.V. shows, ironic websites. Many of the younger faculty at Rutgers, men and women alike, speak, conversationally as well as in their classes, as if life is an inside joke that they get and the rest of the world doesn't. As far as I can see, though, inside of the inside of this running joke is pure nullity. Irony for the sake of irony for the sake of irony, *ad infinitum*, all the way to the gates of hell. Irony in the service of a larger idea, yes. As an arrow for piercing to the heart of a matter, yes. But irony for its own sake? Nope.

In the bathroom, I brush my teeth and comb my hair. I change clothes. I'll look for Jeanette and Sheri at the bar, but if I don't find them, I won't be all that disappointed. Might even sit down and have a stiff drink.

Chapter Three
Saturday, June 8, 2002

It Ain't Me, Babe

I head down a hallway lined with autographed pictures of country music stars, most of whom I've never heard of, and come to the restaurant's entrance. *Damon's*: a low-lit, roomy sports bar/restaurant with candles flickering in red-ribbed plastic holders on the tables, a dozen or so big T.V. screens mounted high on the walls, and twangy, good time music playing at a healthy but not obnoxious volume. The Friday night crowd is young, professional, casual. I tell the blonde, busty, tight-jeaned hostess at the podium that I'm just checking to see if my friends are inside. She says, in that everything-is-beautiful way that young, attractive hostesses sometimes speak, "Sure thing, sir. Hope you find them!" The "sir" part stings.

Inside, I amble around, scan tables and booths. A woman or two glances up, a certain linger in the eyes, a certain question. Why do I even notice this when my answer is, *thank you, truly, but it ain't me, babe*. Is it because I like getting the attention of a woman, even if I have no intention of acting on it? Something to do with wanting Ma to hug me?

Okay, stop the psychoanalysis, David. You're looking for your sister. But into my mind flashes Marie, then Brandon, then, *no*. Resume the search.

Beneath a giant T.V. screen I scan a series of booths in a far corner of the big room. In the most remote one, I spot them, sitting across from one another at the dark-stained wooden table, their faces tinged red by candle glow, a couple of heavy steins of dark ale at their elbows. Sheri's talking; Jeanette looks dazed.

I want Marie here. Want to confess to her that I've fucked up royally today, failed to keep my cool half a dozen times, failed again to be the man I want to be. I want her sweet absolution, which might lead, on a good night, to a purging, purifying, red hot roll in the hay.

But I'm not home and now that I know Jeanette and Sheri are alive (if not well), the question is, should I stay or should I go. A big part of me wants to go back to the room, collapse on the bed and pursue the dream of lovemaking with my wife. On the other hand, this is likely the last time I'll ever see Sheri.

On the *other* other hand…

I'm still waffling when Sheri turns and our eyes meet. She scrambles out of the booth and dashes over to me.

"David. Oh, David." She presses her body against mine and I feel something hard push into my thigh. A *gun*? Is it a fucking *gun*? "It's so good to see you, David."

"Good to see you, too, Sher," I say, and make an effort not to stare at her waist. "How are you doing?"

"Oh, God." She takes a step back, though she keeps a hand wrapped around my wrist. The watermelon-colored tank top and snug cut-offs and green and red bandana tied around her head with a sprout of auburn hair falling down over one side make for a sexy look, but there's no denying that around the eyes her all-American prettiness has been marred by the effects of extended misery.

"It must be tough," I offer lamely. "You guys were pretty tight."

"I love her so much." She smiles bravely. "Come have a beer with us."

"I can't stay, Sher. I have to call Marie before it gets any later. I just wanted to say goodbye. I mean, and hello."

"Have a beer with us. Please. I've come an awful long way. Don't turn me down. I'm at my worst when people turn me down. You don't even know…"

Do I discern a threat? "One beer. I admit I was a little surprised when Jeanette told me you were willing to drive all the way out here for...well…"

"Don't be surprised. Aren't there people in your life you would do anything for?"

"You know there are."

As we take our seats, I nod to my sister, who says, "Didn't know you got invited to the party."

"I'm the comic relief."

"I was just telling Jeanette," Sheri says, "that my cousin wants me to be the godmother of her baby. She's due in September. Isn't that cool? Know what I did after she asked me? I went out and bought a bible. I may not be a big believer like you guys (Jeanette and I simultaneously wince), but at least I'm willing to read the material. That counts for something, doesn't it? Maybe it'll get through to me."

"Worth a looksee," I say.

"Anyway," Sheri says, "I want her to come down to Florida for the baptism in November, but she won't do it."

Sheri doesn't take her eyes off my sister. Except that when Jeanette frowns and looks away, she squeezes her eyes closed, reaches across the table, gathers some of the skin on Jeanette's forearm, and gives it a fierce, prolonged pinch. Jeanette yelps and pulls her arm back.

Wait. Did that just happen? And is my sister now going to bash her stein over Sheri's head?

Jeanette lowers her head like a chastised puppy and examines the raw blemish on her forearm.

"Why doesn't she love me anymore, David?"

I blink.

A waitress with glistening black hair and big, owl eyes appears at the table and asks if I'd like a drink. The sweetness of her voice is jarring.

"I'll have a mug of whatever these guys are having."

"Coming right up," she smiles. "Another round, ladies?"

Jeanette nods without looking up. Sheri says, "Yup."

When silence descends over the table the ambient noise of the bar becomes pronounced. Somewhere nearby a male voice bellows, "...so the Polack says to the Ginny..."

It's three guys in their thirties: well-groomed, polo shirts, Dockers. Central casting.

"Don't even think about it," Jeanette mumbles.

"...and the Polack jumps up and says, 'Excuse me, but that's not the monkey I was referring to.'"

As they burst into laughter, I feel the impulse to punch the joke teller's big, horsy, upper middle-class teeth.

The waitress lays our beers in front of us with a generous smile that tempers my anger. I reach to get my wallet but Sheri's already stretching her body straight to pull out some bills from the front pocket of her shorts. Her bright tee shirt rises over the top of her jeans to expose a sleek black pistol tucked behind her belt buckle. She sees I've noticed and, after she hands the waitress a twenty, says, "Don't worry, it's registered."

"You carry it all the time?"

"Not all the time."

"I never noticed it on you before. Mind if I borrow it real quick?"

"Or I can do it for you. I kind of feel like using it anyway."

"But make sure you do the one who told the joke last, okay?"

"I'm not stupid, David. Desperate, maybe, but not stupid."

We sit, make a little small talk. Jeanette stares into the wishing well of her stein, her right hand covering the spot where the pinch must still sting.

"Do you find me attractive, David?"

I muscle something like a smile onto my face, lift my mug to my lips and take a long sip. "Sure. You're an attractive woman, Sher." Another long sip—I want to finish my beer and go. "And a good person, too."

"Not attractive or good enough for some, though."

Helpless shrug. I drink up. "Hey, I gotta get some sleep."

Sheri stands before I do. "Tell me what to do," she says, smoky eyes pleading, as we walk away from the table together.

"Break ups are hard, Sher. But you'll start feeling better in a little while. Everybody goes through this at some point in their lives. I certainly did. You get over it."

"Time doesn't pass anymore."

"It will," I say. "It has no choice. You'll feel better." This kind of pep talk can go on and on as the clichés line up on your tongue, so I stop talking and give Sheri a goodbye hug.

"I can't stand *needing* her this much," she says into my ear. Her hand grips my wrist.

"Look, you'll find someone else. Someone less problematic than Jeanette."

"Don't you understand, David? I need *her*. Nobody else counts. Nobody else *exists*."

"You won't always have that point of view."

Sheri's tone hardens. "There's a Jeanette you don't know, David."

"I'm sure there is."

"Things have happened to her. I *know* her better than anybody."

"I don't doubt it. I, I don't feel like I know her at all." I step back, say,

"Look, call me any time, okay, Sher? If you ever need to talk."

She nods and releases my wrist, which goes swinging down to my side. "Take care of that beautiful family of yours."

Sigh.

"David." Her eyes are a smear of tears and mascara. "You're like a brother to me. You're an extension of her to me."

I feel diminished by the comment.

"I love you, David."

"I love you, too, Sher."

Sheri smiles, sadly; it isn't my love she craves.

* * *

When the elevator arrives at my floor and the door slides open, there stands the old man in the white suite.

"Evening," I say as I step out.

"Evening."

"Um…"

He waits while my mouth malfunctions, then says, "Pardon me," and steps into the elevator. But he presses the button that keeps the door open, looks at me frankly and says, "Everything okay, sir?"

I'm tempted to go back into the elevator with him, ask him if I can buy him a drink, shoot the breeze a while.

"Just finding things out that aren't so pleasant."

"Sooner or later," he says, "you find out all the things you never wanted to know." He lets the button go. "That's the sign to start again."

* * *

"David, it's almost one o'clock in the morning. Why didn't you call earlier? I'm fast asleep." The last thing I want is to turn defensive and start a fight. "I'm sorry, hon." I'm lying in bed in my skivvies. T.V.'s on CNN, sound off. They're showing footage of another bombing in Israel, a dazed young woman on a stretcher, a gang of men waving bystanders out of the way as they run her toward an ambulance. "I should have called earlier. The day got away from me."

"Has it been a good day, though?"

"It's been a hell of a day. But I'm not up to reliving it right now. Nothing tragic. It's just hard." A commercial for women's shampoo comes on; a woman, ecstatic in the shower. "God, I wish you were in this room with me."

"Oh, yeah? Why is that?"

"It wouldn't be for stimulating conversation. Not at the moment."

Coyly, "What on earth would we do then?"

"Hmm." I find the remote and dispense with the T.V.

"Hmm?"

"You want specifics?"

"David…"

"Help me out here, Marie. Please. It won't take that much of your energy. And I miss you."

Long sigh. "Well, I'm wide awake now anyway."

"Okay, thank you," I say, trying to find the appropriate tone of voice for this. "First thing I'd do is bring you close to me and kiss you a while. Little nibs all over your face and neck. Then I'd unbutton your blouse, but really slowly, and get that first little thrill of seeing your bra exposed, the pink one, the sheer one where the rise in your nipples shows through."

"Mmm."

"Then I'd cavalierly toss your blouse to the floor. And then I'd... Well, wait. Your turn."

"Oh, David, I don't know. I feel so silly."

"Just try, Marie. Please. This is all I've got right now."

"Okay. Well, I guess I'd unbutton *your* shirt, and toss it away. And then, well, then I'd take little licks of your chest. Maybe even suck on those cute little nipples of yours."

"I love your tongue, Marie. You have the sexiest tongue. I love the way it glistens. I love watching it do its thing. Especially when you make your way down...."

"Slow down, big boy."

"Speaking of big...."

"Really? Just from that? Oh, David, this seems so…"

"Really. And it's desperate to be inside you."

"Mmm."

"Take it into...."

"Oh, God, honey…"

Three violent raps on the door. "Holy shit, Marie. Someone's here. I mean at the door."

"But who could it be so late?"

"Beats me."

More knocks.

"Coming" I call. "Can I call you back?"

"That *was* kind of interesting. I've never done that before. Have you? Never mind. Don't answer that."

"I haven't," I say. "They didn't have phone sex when I was a young stud." Although it occurs to me that possibly I *have* done it, with, of all people, Sheri. A straight guy and a gay woman goofing around. "Can I call you right back?"

Two more raps. "One sec," I call.

"No, it's too late, David. You better see who that is."

"Really?"

"It's too weird. I tried, though."

"Hey, so what's up with Brendon, or Brandon? Whichever. Is he coming back over tomorrow for coffee? Borrow a screwdriver or two?"

"Stop. Go answer the door. If it's Sheri, give her my love. We can talk tomorrow."

Erection now a sagging memory, pissed off again, I pull on my pants and go to the door. "Who is it?"

"Maintenance."

Maintenance? I peek through the peep hole, see an older black man's gaunt face; he's wearing a blue shirt with the hotel logo stitched on the breast pocket. I open the door a few inches.

"You called about the T.V?" He's tall and lanky, with grey temples and short, graying hair. Has the aging athletic look of a former wide receiver.

"No I didn't. The TV's fine."

"You sure?"

"I never called for any maintenance."

He looks confused and reaches into the breast pocket of his work shirt. "This is 233, ain't it?"

"No. 223."

"Oh, my goodness. My my. I'm sorry, sir." His bullet-shaped head swivels apologetically. "My brain..." he says, and touches the side of his head.

"I hear you. I know about that. Don't sweat it."

"Hope I didn't wake you up or nothing."

"No. I was up."

His eyes peer around me into the room. "T.V.'s alright then?"

"It's fine. You have a good night, okay?"

"Thank ya. You do the same. Sorry about the mistake. My brain…"

"Mine, too, believe me. It's not a problem. Have a good night now."

Ten seconds after he leaves, I hear footsteps in the hallway. Angry footsteps. I open the door.

"So, how's she doing?" I ask softly as Jeanette stops in front of her door and pulls her key out of her wallet.

"She scares me. But, never mind. Don't ask."

"Too late?"

"You can say that again."

* * *

The phone bleats on the night stand. I answer with a wary hello.

"Hi, daddy. Mommy said if you heard my voice first thing in the morning it would cheer you up."

"Genevieve." The red clock numbers say seven-o-seven. "It *is* good to hear your voice, sweetheart."

"But why did she say that, daddy? Are you feeling sad?"

"A little."

"Because you have to take Grandma to live so far away, right?"

"That's a big part of it."

"That makes me feel sad, too. Mommy says she's sad about it, too. We're *all* sad."

"Well, at least we're all sad together. That makes it a little easier, don't you think?"

"Sort of. Mommy said she'll talk to you later. My friend Sammy's here, but he's making a coloring book, and I don't like it. It's all airplanes crashing into buildings and stuff like that."

Fuck you, Osama.

"Teddy said he doesn't feel like talking to you." Pause. "Is Teddy mad at you, daddy?"

"No, no" I say. I stand up from the bed and turn, and as I do, I catch a glimpse of my naked, silhouetted self in the full-length mirror on the closet door. I look pathetic. Or maybe "sad" is the more accurate word. "Actually," I say, "I think Teddy *is* angry at me. I guess we'll both have to live with it for now. But we'll fix things up. We always fix things up."

"You're good at fixing things up, daddy. You're the best fixer-upper in the world."

The door booms with a hard wrap and "Let's go, David. I want to get the hell out of here."

"I love you love you love you love you love you," I chant to my little daughter.

She giggles and loves loves loves loves loves me right back. It's reassuring to know that *something*'s right with the world.

I meet them in the foyer of Damon's. Ma, I'm pleased to see, looks perky and refreshed, dressed in an optimistic pink-flowered blouse and white slacks, and ready for action. Jeanette's eyes are as gloomy as a storm sky over a prairie. I'm sure I look like hell on a bagel myself, bleary and disheveled in my wrinkled yellow tee shirt and khaki shorts.

Damon's is going full tilt: waitresses hustling steamy pots of coffee here and there, patrons swarming the buffet tables, patriotic country music in the background, all the T.V's showing highlights of last night's baseball games.

"Y'all go on and get started at the buffet any time," our waitress says. Her hair is the color of stainless steel and almost as stiff and her face is thin, but she's got a tank full of wiry energy. "Grits are real tasty this mornin'." Then, conspiratorially, "Biscuits are drier than the Sir Harry Desert." She looks from Jeanette to me, then turns to Ma and says, "I can *see* these two need some coffee fast. I'll be back in a Nashville minute."

"Bring some for me, too," Ma calls to her back. She leans across the table. "I just love their accents, don't you? It really makes you feel like you're in a different place."

Jeanette rubs her palms into her eyes. "You are in a different place, Ma."

"Oh, I know that, wisenheimer. But nowadays a lot of places look the same, don't they? But at least they sound different. Listen, this is my treat, so get my money's worth, okay?" And off she goes to explore the offerings.

"So," I say to Jeanette as we try to rouse ourselves to the task of food gathering, "where did Sheri wind up staying last night?"

"No idea."

"You didn't ask her where she was staying?"

"I made a point *not* to ask."

One tuft of Jeanette's hair sticks up like a small animal's tail, and I reach over to pat it down. She swats my arm away.

"Whoa," I say. "Just helping groom you."

"Thanks, but no thanks."

I notice that a pink remnant of injury lingers on her forearm.

"You don't think Sheri drove after she left you last night, do you? You guys were fairly loaded by then."

"Who knows? Probably got a cheap motel room close by. She can't afford this place."

"Well then why the hell did you let her pay for a round of beers?"

She shrugs. "She'd insist. Not worth the fight. Hey, I sent her a thousand bucks a couple of weeks ago, though that's got to be close to drained by now. I just hope to hell she's heading southeast at eighty miles an hour right now."

It doesn't surprise me a bit to know that Jeanette would break up with a woman and continue to support her financially. "She carries a cell phone, right?"

Jeanette nods, then drops her head a notch like a boxer about to throw a jab. "Look, I can't fix her problems anymore. She's got way too many of them. I tried. I give up."

She's her father's daughter. Da viewed life in terms of problems to be solved. He spent his years digging into the guts of everything from inefficient car engines and balky household appliances to convoluted tax and financial aid forms. Everything was either broken or in need of re-imagining. I can still hear him speaking to the four of us in the dining room at some hastily-called family meeting, having caught one of us trying to fit a square peg into a round hole. "Look, you guys," he's saying through swirling cigar fumes, "there's a right way and a wrong way to do everything, see? The right way's the only way. Otherwise everything breaks down. If you live that way, sooner or later you're gonna get in trouble and you ain't gonna know how to get out of it. You understand me?"

Yes, yes, Da. I see. I *understand.*

Jeanette sure got the message. She was the most Da-influenced of all of us. Look at her politics. Her mechanical and technical competency. The cigars. The outlier, of course, is her sexual orientation. If God hadn't seen fit to throw that particular monkey wrench into the plan, Jeanette would no doubt be the compliant wife to an all-American, card-carrying NRA husband. But God seems to have an affinity for the monkey wrench.

"Believe me, David," she goes on, "you don't even know the beginning of that girl's problems. You always saw her at her best. You don't know the other side."

"Tell me something I don't know about her. Besides the fact that she apparently feels free to assault you physically when the spirit moves her."

Jeanette's eyes fall, but she recovers quickly and smirks. "You don't want to know." She gets up from the table and walks toward the chow line.

Here's what I do know about Sheri's life: her parents split up when she was six, and not too long after that her father, a cop, dropped out of her life for good. ("Maybe that was for the best; at least he wasn't there to beat us up anymore," I remember her telling me. She'd blushed, as if maybe she said something too sensitive, given my father's own proclivities.) I also know that her mother has got some sort of pretty serious skin cancer but still sits out in the Florida sun every day, smoking Camel after Camel and drinking whiskey sours. I know she's got two brothers, both in Florida: one is a state trooper and the other runs a warehouse. That much I know; fact is, when we were together, Sheri and I tended to either discuss metaphysics or engage in our ritual flirtations.

I don't have much of an appetite, but the right thing to do is fuel up my body for another day on the odyssey.

"...Staten Island," I hear Ma saying to a good-looking older black man who's dishing himself some scrambled eggs as she tongs a biscuit onto her plate. I join them on the line.

"Nice place, is it?" the man asks her. He's got small, coppery eyes and salty hair. Izod shirt and smart-looking tan pants. Retired high school teacher, I'm guessing. History. Maybe Earth Science. The gentle, sensitive teacher all the students liked, the one who baffled the white kids with racist parents.

"Oh, yeah," Ma says emphatically. "I love it. The nicest people. Lots to do. We have parks and a nice zoo and beaches. Good schools for the kids. Three different colleges. And New York City right there, a ferryboat ride away."

"You folks have been through a lot up there lately though, huh?"

"Oh, my." Ma's hand covers her mouth and her eyes fly to heaven, and she tells the man, as they move on to the pancake and waffle trays, about some of the grown children of friends she knew who were killed in the attacks. A bond trader. A fire fighter. "Staten Island lost a lot of people that day," she says. She starts to choke up and turns and gestures toward me. "Oh, by the way, this is my son, David. He's a college professor."

We smile and nod to one another. Staten Island, I think, is losing its greatest apologist.

"Well, you all have a good trip out west," the man says as we come to the end of the kiosk. "Nice to meet you, Lillian. Now, David, you take good care of your lovely mother. She's a treasure, as I'm sure you know."

He keeps his eyes on me until I answer, "I do know that, and I will."

"Nice man," Ma says as we head back to our table. "Although, when you think about it, most people are. Don't you think?"

"Most people are pretty much like we are," I say unreflectively. When I do reflect, I realize that can't possibly be true.

I wait until we've each had a dose of coffee (which is, Ma proclaims "good 'n hot") before I broach the subject of visiting Aaron.

Jeanette jabs her fork into a piece of French toast. "We can't do it. Call him and cancel."

"I'm not canceling," Ma declares. "I want to see him." Her own fork trembles in her hand. "He's going to Alaska in a few days, and I'm going to see him before he goes. God knows when I'll see him again after that."

Jeanette is taken aback by Ma's assertiveness. "Okay, fine. I'll get a hotel in Flagstaff and wait till you get back."

"But, honey, he's your brother."

"That's not my fault."

"No, it's mine," Ma says curtly.

Jeanette lays her fork on the table. "Ma, I take responsibility for my relationships. I don't happen to have a relationship with Aaron, and I don't want one. You two go see him. I've got plenty of work I can do. That's why I brought the laptop."

"No, come and talk with him, Jeanette," Ma says. "Just come and say hello and ask him about his life. Just be nice to each other for a day or two. My goodness, is that so hard?"

"It's impossible."

Ma's all a-tremble now, fumbling for words. Jeanette's face remains expressionless, though her skin has blotched at the neck. I think about the relative simplicity of my livelihood: taking a lot of notes and turning them into papers and articles and books about other people's messy lives, pretending, largely, in scholarly, jargon-laden language, to have uncovered the reasons for their troubles. What the hell would I make of us?

"Ma," I say, "you're still going to get to see Aaron. Maybe that has to be enough."

"I just wish I understood why the four of you can't all get along better." She lifts her cup to her lips. "You don't get along too well with Debbie either, Jeanette."

"Debbie the princess? I love Debbie the princess."

"Sarcasm," Ma says.

Resting her head in her hand, Jeanette says, "Listen, it's a fantasy. How many people out there get along with everybody in their family? One in ten? One in fifty?" She turns to me. "You're the *domestic ethnographer*. How many families..." But she notices something over my shoulder and blanches. "Oh, good God."

Near the entrance, the ragged figure of Sheri searches the place for her lost cause.

"What's the matter now?" Ma asks

"Let me go talk to her," I say.

"Suit yourself. I'm not going to." Jeanette rests her fork full of scrambled egg on her plate. "You can let her know that, too. We talked for six hours last night. Enough is enough. I'm going to the ladies room." When a group stands up near the front, she steals away, in a crouch, toward the far bathroom.

"I'll be back soon, Ma," I say. "Have some more coffee."

When I reach her, it takes Sheri a second to acknowledge me. "Where's Jeanette?"

I feel a pang of insult. "Not here at the moment. Let's go outside and talk." I take her arm, but she resists.

"I have to see Jeanette." She scans the room, but doesn't seem to take it in. Her eyes are glassy and bloodshot.

"You don't look good, Sher. You don't want to talk to her now. Come on."

"I have to see her. What if she leaves?"

"She can't leave without me."

She pans the room again. When she spots Ma alone in the corner, she flushes a little. Reluctantly, she turns away.

I hold the heavy glass front doors for her and squint. For the first time in three days the sun is shining. You can smell heat building. We sit down together on a wooden bench in the ample shade of a great live oak adorned with hanging Spanish moss; the odor of warming soil reminds me of something from my childhood that I wish I could linger on.

"Have you been drinking, Sher?"

"Not since one or two this morning, with Jeanette. I've been trying to sleep, but I can't. Jesus Christ, I haven't slept in two months, David."

The bruised-colored bags under her eyes testify to that. As do the baby crow's feet that etch out from the corners of her eyes.

"I shouldn't have come out here," she says. "Oh, God. Oh, Jesus fucking Christ." She presses her hands to the top of her head as if it might blow off. "I don't know what to do. I don't know what to do."

I say again: "You'll get over her. Takes time."

"Spare me the Wal-Mart self-help book crap. Please."

These are the harshest words she's ever spoken to me and I feel their stab. I stand up and pace along the flagstone path, then stop to watch, in the distance, the worry beads of traffic sliding along I-40.

"I'm going crazy. I'm going crazy." Her voice sounds adolescent in its naked pain. "I'm worse than lost. There's a claw in my gut that never goes away. It claws and claws and claws at me." Her fingers curl, animal-like. "It's clawing me to death."

"Don't let it." My own fingers in-fold to fists. "Damn it, don't let it, Sher. She's not...nobody's worth that."

Her eyes jump around my face but won't focus. "Oh, Jesus Christ, David," she cries. "You don't hear me, do you? She *is* worth that. She's worth everything. I...I'd do anything to have her. Just to be in the same room with her. You, you're so lucky. I'd give my life to be you. To be with her whenever you want. To be so close to her for days at a time."

I start to offer yet another lame cliché but instead I say, softly, through gritted teeth, "It must make you want to rage. It must make you want to rip something to fucking shreds."

For the first time, Sheri looks into my eyes. Heat and silence fill my ears to the throbbing point.

"I...I can't..." She throws her head from side to side, stands up, stutter-steps in three directions, and finally starts to walk out toward the sea of cars glinting in the sprawling lot.

"Where you going, Sher?"

"I don't know. To sit in the car. I don't know. I can't talk right now. I can't think."

She steps from the shade into the sunlight, makes her way, slowly, circuitously, to her car. For a long time she simply stands in front of the dented green Civic, looking here and there, pressing her hands against her head, bending forward, standing up again. Finally, she gets into the car. I wait to see whether or not it pulls away. I very much want it to, but it doesn't.

Ma and Jeanette pick at the remains of their breakfasts. Ma's eyes, when she sees me, grow wide and full of fret; Jeanette's don't rise from her plate.

I drop into my seat, push my plate of cold eggs and pancakes aside. "She's a wreck."

"Doesn't she have any other friends?" Ma says. "Why is she so upset with Jeanette?"

"Ma," Jeanette says. "Would you mind if I talk to David in private? Maybe you can go up and start packing."

"I'm already packed. And I don't see why you two have to keep keeping things from me."

"Because you have enough on your mind already. You don't need this crap."

Frowning, Ma pushes out from the table and stands up. "I'll go pay at the register," she says. She glances over the table. "Neither of you even ate that much."

"I don't know," Jeanette says as she watches Ma walk away, "what the hell possessed me to agree to meet her." To drive home the point, she hits the side of her head with her open palm. "You thought you could help her," I say. "Honest mistake."

"At some point you start doing more harm than good."

I realize I've turned my wedding ring around my finger so many times that the skin is chafing.

"The absolute worst part of her personality is the part that's running the show right now. God help her." Jeanette looks frankly into my eyes. "She knows where Aaron lives, David. And Debbie."

"And your point is...?"

"She's got nothing to go home to. She's at rock bottom. She can go wherever we go."

"But would she do that? Follow us...follow *you* around the fucking country?"

"Unless she's got some reason not to."

"But what would she accomplish?"

"Didn't you stalk Sarah Remillard for three months after she broke up with you in tenth grade?"

"I didn't *stalk* her," I say. "I *haunted* her. There's a difference. Anyway, how does Sheri know where everybody lives?"

Jeanette pushes her seat back from the table. "We used to live together, remember? She always wanted to know everything she could about every single one of us. It was like she was writing our family friggin' biography.

She has this thing about our family. Don't ask me. But over time she got all kinds of information. Who knew she'd ever want to use it?"

"She probably knows more about us than I do."

Jeanette stands up. "That's a fact."

* * *

By 10:30 we've checked out of the hotel and are sitting in the van in the parking lot, letting the air conditioner cool the inside. Las Vegas is next, though, damn it, I don't want to go to Las Vegas. I don't want to see Aaron right now. I'm not in the right condition for it. It's like agreeing to run a marathon when you haven't even been jogging.

I shift the van into drive, then, allowing myself to remember something I've been trying not to think about, shift back to park. "Wait here one minute, okay? I'll be right back."

"Where are you going now?" Ma says.

"He'll be right back," Jeanette answers for me.

I jog through three sections of the parking lot until I come to where Sheri's Civic is still parked. Heat and humidity have moistened my hair and sheened my skin. I peer in through the rolled-up passenger window at a front seat cluttered with Styrofoam coffee cups and granola bar wrappers and a stiff new Rand McNally Road Atlas. Sheri, though, isn't there. I glance into the back and find her curled in the fetal position across the seat, face pressed into the upholstery. Beads of sweat gleam on her cheeks and arms and legs, but, by God, she looks completely knocked out.

It's got to be over 90 degrees in there. I put my hand on the passenger side door handle and it opens. Stale heat globs over me as I climb in and roll down the driver and passenger windows. When I turn and lean over to roll down the windows in the back, trying not to wake Sheri, I spot, tucked under the driver's seat, her sleek, palm-sized black revolver.

I stare at the gun. *It's okay. She's a cop.* Then I think, *If she kills herself with it, I'll never sleep again.* Then, *this is not my problem.* Then I lean all the way over and begin to lift the thing, crane-like, between my forefinger and thumb. It's heavier than it looks, and cold to the touch, despite the fact that it's been baking in the car. I bring it carefully over the top of the seat and, holding it the way you'd hold a dead mouse, I close the door as softly as I can. I slip the little killer into the deep front pocket of my khaki shorts and pray it doesn't go off before I get rid of it.

Jeanette's outside the van, sucking on a cigar. "So, she gonna live or what?"

"Take a walk with me, will you?"

"Oh, Jesus. Now what?" She flicks away a wad of ash.

Treading between cars and SUVs and minivans until we're out of Ma's view, I tell her what I've just done, and nod at the bulge in my pocket.

"You *what*? What the hell are you thinking, David? That's larceny."

"Larceny? Holy smokes, I never even.... But she's so unstable. The condition she's in and gun don't go together."

"You gotta put it back. Or I will."

"Aren't you concerned she'll use it? I mean, you'll be rid of her all right."

An even more frightening thought occurs to me: Sheri could just as easily decide to use the damn thing on Jeanette before she turns it on herself. The classic jilted lover murder-suicide.

My sister sucks on her cigar, her delicate, creamy cheeks collapsing around the crude-looking log, and releases a gray cloud into the Tennessee blue. "She's had that thing as long as I've known her, and a lot longer than that. She has a license for it. She's trained to use it. And as far as I understand the law, we aren't legally allowed to relieve her of it. You want to put it back or you want me to?"

"Oh, damn it, I'll do it. I just hope we don't regret it."

"I'll come with you."

"You will?"

"If you don't want me to, I won't."

"No, come on."

We walk back toward the Civic. "I opened all her windows; if she's still asleep I can put it back without going in. But I really don't know about this. This just can't end well."

"Look, David, it ain't exactly difficult to get a gun in this country if you want one. And even if she couldn't get a gun and did want to kill herself, there are other ways to do it."

"What if she wanted to kill somebody else before she killed herself?"

Jeanette frowns. "Then let's hope that that somebody else has her house in order. Let's get this over with and get out of Dodge."

Ten feet from the car Jeanette stops and leans against a gold Lexus. I walk slowly forward. My tee shirt at the back and shoulders is so wet it sticks to my skin, and sweat beads run down my face like bugs. Where the hell did the breeze go?

Sheri hasn't budged. My hand twitters as I pull the gun carefully out of my pocket and glance around to make sure there are no witnesses to this act of reverse larceny. I reach in through the open back window and lower the gun to the floor, lay it there, and push it forward a few inches so that it's right back where I found it.

Chest rising and falling like a sea, Sheri sleeps on.

* * *

"Jeanette," Ma says as I ride in the late morning flow of interstate traffic, "I want you to come with us to Las Vegas. I don't feel right about leaving you somewhere else. I, I *insist* you come with us."

Ma sounds vulnerable; a little girl playing at authority.

"If you really won't see Aaron, okay then, stay in the room or something. But I want you to come with us."

"Fine."

"Well, that's..., thank you," Ma says. "That makes me feel a little better at least."

"What are *you* looking at?" Jeanette says to me. "Pay attention to the road."

The road indeed. This continent-long unfurled banner of tar and painted white lines. And that blue-with-red- and-white metal shield, recurring like a motif in a dream: *Interstate 40, West.* Oh, Lordy Lord, we're still moving west; still such a long way to go. And the recurring bashed, squished, decapitated animals. The oases of commerce that spring up around every exit, their bright gas, food, souvenir signs reaching up into the air like neon palm trees. And the proud flags on the overpasses, and the angry spray-painted signs aimed at the ever-lurking, unseen enemy. And the occasional bedraggled, sunken-eyed hitchhiker who may or may not, we used to be told in religion class, be an angel in disguise, even Jesus himself, there to test our ability to love the unlovable; the hitchhiker who, on the other hand, may or may not, once he's gained entrance to your moving abode, pull out of his ratty trousers a long-bladed knife and force you off the highway and down a lonely country road, and then, somewhere in a chirping, darkening wood, listening to the devil's voice in his head, slit your throat and rape your sister and maybe even your mother and then slit their throats, too. And because this is America, there's a good chance the tale will become a made-for-T.V. movie: *The Interstate Murders. Death on I-40. Samaritan Slaughter.*

So, change the subject. The variety of skies one travels under, for example. The unmarred afternoon blue dome; the gloomy slate; the slow-gathering green/black mass that smells of tree-snapping wind; the sky that floats whipped cream clouds and makes you a child again, wondering if you might catch a glimpse of God floating by. *The Skies of I-40.* Potential coffee table book? I've seen dumber.

We cover green and hilly Western Tennessee in a little over three hours. For most of that time, Ma and Jeanette doze. Which is nice; I relish the quiet, the semblance of peace. In fact, I feel more awake than I'd have thought I would, given everything. Though I'm concerned for Sheri, I'm relieved to be driving away from her.

And who should come slinking into my mind but Aaron. When we were little kids he and I used to play in the fields, each with our own gang of friends, which sometimes joined to become one gang of older and younger kids playing baseball or football together and at other times remained two separate groups playing separate games of army or explorers or Batman. We played until we heard Ma's voice: *Daaaaavid, Aaaaaron,* calling us home for supper and the doing of our tedious homework. God, how I hated doing homework. I felt so put upon. I would drag it out, mope and procrastinate my way through every pointless subject. Aaron never complained, just did the work. Of the two of us boys, he was by far the better student (both Debbie and Jeanette were straight-A types). Then came his sophomore year of high school, when he started down the long hill he seems to this day to be descending. The fall was precipitous. His grades plummeted in the course of one marking period. Teachers called home telling my parents that Aaron was not himself, asking if there might not be a medical issue. I don't know what happened; if it was the influence of the kids he hung around with in those days, or if it was something inside of him, or something else altogether. Ma seemed utterly baffled and worried sick. Da was always angry at Aaron back then, and the anger often resulted in beatings. The girls seemed to be pushing him out of their minds altogether. I was baffled and worried and angry at him. I was beginning to learn to pretend that he didn't exist.

And as usual, the gloomy, hovering cloud I associate with Aaron starts moving over me, *into* me.

But Ma stirs and says, "Where are we?"

"Almost out of Tennessee."

"We're still in Tennessee?" Jeanette grogs, and pulls herself up in the seat. "Give me a break."

At mid-afternoon we drive through Memphis and approach the mighty Mississippi.

"Daddy always wanted to see this," Ma says.

I say, "He must have seen it once or twice, no? In the Army? Wasn't he stationed in Kansas for a while?"

"I don't mean *your* father," she says. "I mean mine. When he came over from Poland, he settled on Staten Island right away and stayed there all his life. He never left it once, right up to the day he died. Seventy years. He never even took the ferry into Manhattan."

"*Really*? Why didn't I know that about him?"

"I don't know why," Ma says defensively.

"Was he afraid of it, do you think?"

"He worked at the tire plant ten, twelve hours a day, six days a week. When he was home, he loved to listen to the radio. We had two Polish stations we could get."

What about spending time with his daughter?

"He loved to read. He loved Mark Twain the most. We had his books in translation. My father used to say how much he'd love to see the Mississippi River, where Huck used to float on his raft. He loved Huck."

"Why did he read it in Polish?"

"Oh, you know why, David," Ma says.

"No, I don't."

"He never..." Though I can't see her behind me, I feel waves of discomfort emanating from her body. "...he never learned to speak English. Or how to read it. But you knew that."

"No, Ma, I didn't. He died when I was three, but I thought I remembered talking with him. In English. Did I dream that?"

"Oh, he could say a few phrases: 'How are you?'; 'You want a glass of soda?' He mostly smiled at you kids. He got such a kick out of you all."

"How did I not know he never spoke English? I feel like I've just been told that I was adopted."

"Well, there's that, too," Jeanette says.

"Haha."

"Seriously, David. *I* knew it. Lots of immigrants didn't speak English. They had a whole Polish community down there in New Brighton. He didn't have to speak English."

After a protracted calming breath, I say, "I get the impression Ma wishes he'd have learned. Is that right, Ma?"

"He never.... Lots of other people did it. Mothers and fathers. They learned. He was stubborn about it. But it kept him kind of...isolated. He never came to our school to meet the teachers. He never...."

We're on the bridge, crossing the quintessential American river. If Ma was a crier, she'd sure as hell cry right now. They'd be tears that have been sitting in a pool at the bottom of her heart for decades. I can only imagine how good it would be for her to finally drain that pool. But she's not, and she says, "Oh, he was a good man."

"Even good men have flaws," I say. "Goes with being human."

"Well, of course," Ma says. Something in her tone tells me she's taking some solace from my truism. I think maybe she's giving herself permission to acknowledge and forgive her father.

"Get out your camera, Ma," Jeanette says, "we're entering a new state."

Arkansas starts out flat and nondescript. Road work-related single lane traffic goes on for a lot of dusty, hot, sleep-inducing cropland miles. I can't tell what they're growing here. I wish they'd put up signs, so travelers could learn something as they creep across a region. At one point twenty miles or so into the state we get some entertainment: a small white puttering crop duster flies low over the highway, then circles tightly and flies back over again, dips and begins to spray its chemical cloud over the fledgling crops.

"Wow," Ma says, "they really fly low, don't they? I could almost see the pilot. He looked like Henry Modeliewski from Brighton Avenue."

I laugh. "What? Who's that?"

"A friend of daddy's and mine from the old neighborhood. You know him. He used to come over and have a beer with daddy in the yard Sunday afternoons in the summer. Nice man. His brother played professional baseball for a few years. He was on the Philadelphia A's."

I can vaguely picture Da and his friend sitting in plastic chairs in the yard, smoking cigars and drinking whatever beer was cheap then, Rheingold or Schmidts or something. "He still alive?"

"No, he died years ago."

"So, it's probably not him flying the plane then."

"Wise guy," Ma says.

We drive right through some of the drift of the chemical cloud. "Don't breathe," I say. "Who knows what the hell's in that stuff."

"They say that's how the terrorists may try to get us next time," Ma says.

"The way we're using those chemicals is terrifying enough."

"Hey, listen, if they didn't spray," Jeanette says, "those crops would be dinner for bugs instead of people. That what you want?"

"No. I want a Plan B."

We decide we'll eat in the car as we drive. I've got it in my mind that we can make Vegas by Monday afternoon, stay until Tuesday morning, and have Ma in Flagstaff by Tuesday evening. I've got Jeanette and me heading home on Wednesday afternoon, and, by breaking all kinds of records and speed limits, I've got myself diving into the arms of my wife and kids sometime next Saturday evening.

Just east of Little Rock, we get off the highway and cruise along a boulevard that is exactly like a boulevard nine out of ten Americans live within a few miles of. McDonald's. Burger King. Wendy's. Conoco. Pizza Hut. Taco Bell. Garrett's Guns and Ammo (with a giant poster of a bull's eye with Osama Bin Laden's picture in the middle. We don't see this kind of shop in the New York metro area; guns and ammo transactions are handled privately and discreetly, usually on dark street corners). Domino's Pizza. Burger King. Waffle House. McDonald's (I can still see the golden arches of the first one in the rearview mirror). Fantasy Adult Video. Arby's. St. Francis Christian Books and Gifts. And look what's coming: why it's a McDonald's!

"Unfortunately," I say, "there are only three McDonald's to choose from, and we're running out of boulevard. What's it going to be then, eh?"

"Junk food is junk food," Jeanette comments. "You're choice, Ma."

"McDonald's is fine with me."

"Okay," I say. "I'll see if I can find one."

There are at least 20 cars in the drive-thru line, so I pull into the one open parking space. "Who wants what?"

Jeanette: "Double cheeseburger. Large Coke. No fries."

Ma: "Oh, Mc-fish. Is that what it's called? And French fries. But hot coffee instead of coke. Make sure it's hot, though."

Inside, McDonald's is a summer suppertime madhouse. There must be two families within thirty miles of here that are eating dinner at home around a table; everyone else is right here, or somewhere else along this boulevard, lusting for salt and grease, thin meat and air-puffed white bread. At first glance, almost everyone in the place looks overweight: the kids are rolly-polly, chipmunk-cheeked, gray-skinned. Some of them look like they're prematurely balding. The adults, too, look super-sized, not to mention frenzied: you can see brown and blonde and black hair turning gray before your eyes.

I've noticed a few grays myself in the better-lit hotel bathroom mirrors. The five or six lines to the counter are so long that they run out of room at the condiment table and turn into a milling crowd. This disturbs me. Mostly because somebody just coming into the place now from the opposite door could wind up getting served before I do, because there's no system here to insure that things proceed fairly and in an organized fashion. Where's the manager? Why isn't this set up correctly? I find myself subtly using my shoulders and elbows to maneuver in the crowd. I don't want to get ahead of anybody unfairly, but I also don't want somebody who came in after me to get served first. Now, I realize I could take a more Zen-like, don't-try-to-control-things, trust-the-universe, blah, blah, blah approach to this, and in fact I would like to be able to rise above the pettiness that situations like this always seem to bring out in me. So far, though, no luck.

When I'm finally on a discernable line behind nine or ten people, the woman standing in front of me, dark haired and pretty, 30-ish, with, I can't help but notice, a firm and shapely behind, turns and looks toward the door. While turning back, she smiles at me. And just like that, I'm a happier man. Oh, the power of a pretty smile. I'm rejuvenated. I feel attractive. I've still got it.

Does Marie smile at attractive men when she's looking for deck furniture at The Home Depot? Oh, probably, a little. So what? There are so many attractive people in the world. So many ways to be attracted. It's the man across the street from us that I have concerns about. Is Marie turned on by that guy? And, like, how much?

A short, muscular man with dark, slick-backed hair wearing a black shirt with shiny silver buttons squeezes past me and joins the woman with the nice butt.

"Hey, cutie." The guy playfully leans his broad shoulder into her petite one.

"Well, hey," she says, sexy-like. She lowers her voice. "How'd you do it?"

"Told her some of the coaches were getting together over a hamburger to talk about the all-star squad."

"She believed you?"

"Hell, yeah. Yesterday I told her the word gullible wasn't in the dictionary. She believed that, too. She says, 'Really, Gun? I wonder why not.'"

The woman laughs, places her small hand on the man's triceps-rippling shoulder. "Dan's down in the basement fiddling with his new wrench set. Surprise, surprise. I told him I was going to the mall. He calls up to me, 'Don't break the bank.' I swear he says the same thing every time I go out the door. Get a new line, why don't you?"

Now, I know, abstractly, that people all over America are cheating on their spouses. But to be this close to it disturbs the hell out of me. And their seeming lack of conscience about what they're doing *galls* me. I mean, shouldn't they at least feel torn, even tortured, about having an affair? It's true, I don't know anything about *why* they're doing it, the problems, the root causes. The ethnographer in me (hell, the flawed human being in me) knows they could probably offer some compelling reasons. *He drove me to it.* But all I can think about is the guy down in the basement who still thinks he's got a solid marriage, and the gullible woman whose heart old Gunther here is sooner or later going to break. And by the sound of it, there's a kid or two in the mix, as well. Suddenly, the pretty woman with the nice rear end in front of me looks a lot less attractive. As for Gun, well, he's bringing out *my* ugly.

And just as I'm thinking these uncharitable thoughts, Gun, turning casually, catches my eye (a good eight inches above his) and smiles a conspiratorial smile. *Hey, hey, hey. Got me some extra.*

It amazes me how often people assume you go along with their way of looking at things. For instance, in my early days at Rutgers everybody in the department assumed I was as casually hostile toward religion as they were- *Western* religion, that is; it was perfectly hip to be, say, a Buddhist. Sympathy for Muslims was high, too—which is all good by me. (Some days I aspire to something like non-denominational Universalist Buddhist Christianity.) For a while I let it go, but it began to bother me, you know, burying my faith, such as it was, under the proverbial bushel basket. So finally one morning before a department meeting, I mentioned to a colleague, loudly enough for half the room to hear, that I'd signed up to teach Religious Ed to the second graders of my parish. From the stares I got, you'd have thought I'd said I just came back from having breakfast with my old pal Dick Cheney.

Anyway, when I don't return Gun's smile, his eyes harden and linger on mine. And though I'm beginning to feel a tad concerned that this could turn out to be one of those incidents that spiral out of control—*Rutgers Prof Shot and Killed in Arkansas McDonald's*—nevertheless, my being a proud and stubborn working class male at heart, I harden my eyes too, and fasten them onto his.

The woman says, "What's the matter, Gun? What are you looking at?"

He smiles one of those movie tough guy dismissive smiles. "Nothin' much."

I shake my head and frown. I don't want to fight, but I damn sure want to register my disapproval. Finally, he turns back, and eventually they order their poison and I order mine, and life goes messily on.

In the car I distribute the food rations. I pull back the tab on Ma's and my coffee covers, hand Ma hers, watch and wait while she sips.

"Ooh, it's good. Hot as you could want."

When, a decade or so ago, some woman sued McDonald's for serving coffee that burned her when she spilled it on herself, Ma was not only incredulous that somebody could win such a suit for being careless, but deeply concerned. "Does this mean they'll only serve lukewarm coffee from now on?" Fortunately, it didn't turn out to be quite that bad; you can still get coffee plenty hot. Only now, there's a warning on the cup. "Ridiculous," Ma says, sounding much like her departed husband. "You should *expect* your coffee to be hot. They shouldn't have to warn you about it. Save the warnings for if a bomb is coming."

Jeanette and I share a smile, and maybe even an understanding: God, our Ma is a gem, isn't she?

Oklahoma in twilight. The rolling deep greens of the east are gradually morphing into the flatter browns and pale greens of the west. Dusk spans the horizon, toward which we hurtle like dreamers. Like questers.

I can hear Ma breathe deeply behind me and say, "Somebody better call Debbie and tell her we're going to be a little later getting there."

To my great and pleasant surprise, Jeanette immediately pulls out her cell phone.

"Debbie? Jeanette here. Look, we're going to Aaron's. We'll probably be in Flagstaff on Tuesday night, God willing."

She listens, rolls her eyes, sighs. "Because he *asked* her to come, that's why. You think *I* want to go there? No, he says he's going to Alaska or some godforsaken place. Hey, don't yell at me. Hey, you know what..." and she jabs a key on the little phone with her middle finger and drops her arm into her lap.

"What on earth?" Ma says.

"She's getting all pissed at *me*. I hung up."

I say, "She doesn't like when things don't go her way, Ma. Never has, never will."

"Oh, my goodness," Ma says. "It's only one or two extra days. She knows I hardly ever get to see Aaron."

"Probably Clint reminded her about what one day costs in that place," Jeanette says.

"I don't think it's about money," I say. "Debbie just wants you there, Ma. She wants you there *exactly* when she planned for you to be there. Remember when you had to postpone her high school graduation barbeque for one day because it rained?"

"Didn't she throw one of your favorite bowls through the window?" Jeanette asks.

Ma doesn't respond.

"Good luck with the small matter of living with Debbie," Jeanette says as she pushes her phone back into her pants' pocket.

"Well, she's not exactly going to be *living* with Debbie," I point out.

"Close enough."

"What do you...," Ma hesitates, "what do you have against Debbie, Jeanette? Did she ever do anything to you? Anything that hurt you?"

"Look, it's nothing."

"It can't be nothing."

"Well, if you really want to know, it isn't any one thing. It's watching her get everything she ever wanted. From you. From Da. From teachers. Her friends. Everybody. Getting you to move out to Arizona is the final straw, that's all." Then, softly, "Look, I'm not blaming you."

Ma blinks, looks out at green-going-brown America. "Yes, you are. And maybe you're right." There's a quaver in her voice. "You try to treat each one the way you think they need to be treated. You...you try your best to make everything work out for everybody..."

"And that's impossible," I say. "We want to do the impossible and we're outraged when we can't do it."

"Or we just feel sad," Ma sighs. "I still can't believe I'm going to live in Arizona." Her tone is one of wonder. Deep, sad wonder.

"It'll be great for those kids to have you there," I say. "You still have so much life in you."

"Oh, it *will* be nice to be able to spend more time with them," Ma says, maybe just a tad too sincerely.

* * *

We've covered another five hundred plus miles today, and still we drive. Jeanette drives, that is; I've finally given in to the fatigue in my eyes and the beam of pain down my back, and she's game for doing something besides ruminating. Reservations have been made at a hotel in Oklahoma City, which is an hour away. We cruise along the flat, straight, taillight-led highway toward the city best known these days for having one of its federal buildings blown apart by home-grown terrorists. In the wake of big-league September 11, Oklahoma City can feel like a Single-A game. Not, though, I'm sure, to the people around here, especially to those who lost loved ones. Especially those who lost kids.

Jeanette flicks on the radio. She gets old-style honky-tonk country music, and *switch*.

"....if you don't think Abraham's faith was as solid as a rock, you don't understand fatherly love, my friend....."

Switch.

"Next item: a 1988 John Deere 950 Compact Tractor for just four hundred and fifteen dollars. It's a steal, folks. At that giveaway price it won't last. Call us at...1 800 ..."

I suppose this fare is pretty much what you'd expect on Oklahoma radio, which, in 2002 is not what I would have expected. Frankly, I'd have expected the radio to pour forth the sounds of American homogenization. I'm glad to hear the twang of country music, and the twang of an Oklahoma preacher's voice, and that a John Deere 950 is available to the highest bidder.

Switch. "Intelligence on loan from God!"

"All *right*," Jeanette cheers. "Rush. They must replay the shows at night."

"You actually listen to this blowhard?" I say.

"Damn right I do. You could learn something if you did, too."

"Anything I could learn from him I don't want to know. He's one of the most hostile people I've ever heard. Full of hatred. I'm trying to shake off some of the hostilities I'm saddled with, not reinforce them."

Jeanette shakes her head and turns up the volume.

"You like this guy, Ma?" I ask behind me.

"I agree with him about quite a few things, but I wish he wasn't so sarcastic. Or, what's the word? Mean-spirited. I don't like meanness."

"Look," the windbag is saying in response to something a caller has just said, "why not legalize, and hence legitimize, human-animal marriages while we're at it? Why not let people legally marry their dogs and cats? This way they too can get all the many entitlements Americans have come to expect. I mean, animals are as valuable as humans, aren't they? Animals are people too. We're all animals, aren't we? If some old archaic document like the Holy Bible says man with man is an abomination, and if it says man has dominion over the animals, well, both of those statements are just meaningless mumbo-jumbo, aren't they? We're enlightened now. We know better than to pay attention to some old so-called holy book."

"Oh, come on, Rush," the caller, a male, says. "You're mocking an important issue."

"Hey," I say to Jeanette, and gesture toward the radio, "we don't have to listen to this. Let me see if I can find..."

"No," Jeanette says. "Why should we change it?"

"Because this guy is a fucking moron," I shout. "Sorry, Ma."

"Let me ask you something, friend," windbag says to the caller in a pompous, condescending tone. "Are you yourself gay?"

The caller hesitates at the bluntness of the question. "I don't apologize for that."

"Who said anything about apologies? Tell us about your family, will you? My own guess is, your mother was the force in the family. My guess is your father was diffident, secretive, somewhat mousy..."

The caller hangs up.

"Well," windbag gusts, "I guess that tells us all we need to know..."

I lean over and shut the radio off.

"Why did you do that?" Jeanette says, though without much conviction.

"I can't take him right now, Jeanette. Sorry."

She drives, staring straight into the blueblack west. Gazing at her shadowed face in profile, I ache for her. Gay, conservative, forty years old, in the thick aftermath of yet another relationship gone south, haunted by a jilted lover. Oh, my sister, beautiful misfit, God help you. God help us all.

A few hours later, in a motel in Oklahoma City, I lie alone in a queen-sized bed, the book of Flannery's letters open and resting on my slowly rising and falling bare chest. If I were truly a man of faith almost everything about me would be different. My relationship with Jeanette would be marked by patience and understanding, my feelings about Ma's move (and Debbie's desire for it) by generosity and understanding. I'd be looking forward to seeing my brother, not dreading it. I'd have complete trust in my wife's fidelity. I mean, she wouldn't... with *Brandon*? And, aware of the beam in mine, I wouldn't be yelling at every other stranger I encounter for having a mote in his or her eye. Somewhere a long time ago I learned that in the original Aramaic, the word sin means *to miss the mark*. How many times have I missed the mark? Answer: too many.

Chapter Four
Sunday, June 9, 2002

The Jesus Dream

The priest, a Father Baylis, tall, gauntly dignified, perhaps seventy, looks out over the large congregation of which Ma, Jeanette and I are part. "Thus," he says, "we see that Einstein's declaration that you cannot solve a problem with the same consciousness that created it is indeed highly compatible with the admonition of Jesus that unless a person be born again they shall not see the Kingdom of Heaven. In both cases nothing short of a transformation of consciousness is required." He pauses, allows us to absorb the point, which he's been artfully making for a riveting fifteen minutes: to become genuinely, deeply conscious *is* the golden key, *is* the answer to life's thorniest questions, *is* the most vital way in which we can receive God's grace.

Sitting there next to my mother and sister at sermon's end, I realize that I've been applying Father Baylis's words to *them*: *Jeanette* needs to wake up and see herself more clearly, *Ma* should not repress her emotions. *Marie*, too, if she is in fact attracted to Brandon, is not being thoughtful about what—and who—really matters in her life.

But then, oh, what's that thing about removing the beam in your own eye before attempting to remove the speck in the eye of the other?

"It's a difficult charge, isn't it?" the priest is saying as he gathers up his notes. "While a few may experience sudden enlightenment, ala St. Paul, most of us require enormous patience with ourselves while maintaining a persistent determination. Some of us will only truly awaken," and here he brings his right hand heavily down to the lectern, "when a hammer slams into our skulls."

Heaving the sigh of a man who's been shouting to the deaf all his life, he pauses and smiles. His expression appears more maternal than paternal. "Beloveds, God's grace is abundant upon the earth, but we have to cooperate with it. Let's begin right now the task of becoming truly conscious, shall

we? In the name of the Father and of the Son and of the Holy Spirit."
Amen.

The closing hymn is "Now Thank We All Our God," and the congregation sings it with a gusto that we back at St. Mary's in New Jersey sorely lack. I'm caught up in it and sing full-throated. Ma's giving it her all, too; slightly off-key, her voice trembles with sincerity. Jeanette murmurs along.

Though it seems now good fortune that we did, we had a hell of a time finding the church. Jeanette had told us over breakfast that she'd looked into Catholic churches in the area and that Christ the Redeemer would be our best bet. She'd downloaded the directions but apparently we took a wrong turn somewhere and drove along several desolate-looking outer Oklahoma City streets that were not mentioned in the directions. At one point I said to Jeanette that there had to be a church closer to the hotel than this one, to which she replied, "There is, but I want to go to this one." I asked her why, but she didn't want to say, and I didn't want to argue. Finally, at a crossroads of small bodegas, pawn shops and gas stations, Ma, looking over the tops of the low buildings, said, "Oh, I see a steeple over there!" We followed it into a neighborhood of dilapidated but brightly-painted one story houses and, with five minutes to spare, found the large, old, red brick church on a corner lot, complete with a rectory and small elementary school on the grounds.

Last night Sheri called me from a truck stop in Little Rock. "I don't think I want to live anymore, David."

"Don't say that. Don't think like that," I implored. "You don't get a second chance if you do something rash. You'll never know how good your life might have become. You'll never know how right the next person might have been."

"I can't get there, David. I just can't get there. It all sounds like bullshit."

Gripping my cell phone so tight that my fingers ached, I paced around the little hotel room. "Look," I said, "sometimes life just sucks, Sher. You're not the only one who suffers. We all do. You have to fight it. Because if you fight for it, you find out that sometimes life is pretty damn good, too."

She began to weep. "She won't even answer my calls. I try and try and she just lets it ring. I need to talk with her, David. I need to at least *talk* with her. We used to talk about everything and now she won't talk to me at all. It's torture. It's absolute hell."

"Why don't you see a therapist, Sher? If it's a question of money, I'll be happy to help you out. Go and talk with somebody who has expertise in relationships."

"I don't want to talk with someone who's being fucking paid to sympathize with me. I could be anybody saying anything as long as I'm paying for her fucking ear. Fuck that, David. I'd rather just..." She sniffled, and her breath pulsed through the phone like a heartbeat. "It's like making love," she said finally. "It doesn't mean shit unless the other person loves you back. Look, thanks for trying to help. I'm finished. I hope you have a good life..."

Scared, guilt-ridden, exasperated, I asked if she'd be willing to drive to Vegas. We could talk a little more. At least she'd have something to focus on besides doing herself in. She said she'd drive anywhere for a little hope.

"Hope for your*self*, for your future, for your *own* life, you understand that's what I mean, right?"

"Yeah, yeah, okay. I need you to help me, that's all.'

So, she's going to meet me in Vegas to talk rather than kill herself, and I think I may be an idiot.

And that's what I was dwelling on as we climbed the stone steps toward Christ the Redeemer's huge red wide open doors. I hoped it would be one of those get 'em in, get 'em out masses, forty-five minutes max. But when we stepped into the dark, cool nave, I felt a palpable quieting. In a pew ten rows from the modestly adorned altar, I knelt and closed my eyes and prayed to God in shards of barely coherent thoughts for sanity, mercy, relief, rescue.

From the first sung words of the opening hymn, it was clear that this was a congregation filled, as they say, with the spirit. Soulful, heartfelt singing, practically shouted communal responses. No sense that the congregation was here because they vaguely believed there'd be hell to pay if they weren't. Father Baylis' sermon held me from his first utterance: "Is there anyone here today who suspects that they need to make some changes in their life?"

I was moved by the profound dignity with which Father Baylis celebrated the Mass. In the deep silence of the enactment of the transubstantiation—a point in the Mass at which, according to the church, mere bread becomes the living body of Christ, a point at which I often drift away and have struggled to accept intellectually—this time my skin rose in goosebumps. For a few transcendent moments, I was as far away from myself and my troubles as heaven is from hell.

When the closing hymn ends in a crescendo of glorious notes from the pipe organ, the congregation turns and applauds the organist, a thirtyish man in a squint-inducing yellow suit who stands and bows with an exaggerated flourish. People file into the aisles to greet friends, the level of chatter high. Taking in the scene, I find it easy to conjure myself as a charter member of this parish, coming here happily every Sunday with Marie and the kids, joining the parish council, becoming a lector or ushering or teaching religious education. It would be easy, I sense, to truly *belong* to a parish like this, even as a partial, restless skeptic.

That's when it dawns on me that the demographic here is different: this congregation doesn't consist primarily of younger families and elderly women, as most do. The congregation for this Mass consists largely of professional-looking men and women of working age, most of Caucasian or Hispanic descent. Many of the men are here with other men, and women with women. I feel like hitting my head and making that annoying "duh" sound kids make.

I turn to Jeanette to ask just how she happened to find this particular parish, but she's being chatted up by the rather attractive woman with black-rimmed spectacles and dark, shoulder-length hair who's been sitting in the pew in front of ours. The woman smiles and introduces herself to me as Mia Perez and offers her hand.

"You know," I said, grinning, "it just now occurred to me that this isn't a typical neighborhood congregation."

Mia laughs. "Very astute. The nine o'clock at Christ the Redeemer is known far and wide as, among other things, the 'notorious' Mass and even the 'queer' Mass. People come a long way to be here. I drive down from Enid. It's worth every mile." She turns her attention back to Jeanette and asks what she's doing in Oklahoma.

"Passing through," Jeanette says. Then, to my surprise, she says, "If you really want to know…" and actually begins to elaborate.

My eyes linger on my sister. It's not *that* obvious, but in the presence of pretty Mia, Jeanette morphs into a blushing schoolgirl with a brand-new crush. As a girl, Jeanette had girlfriends over the house all the time. But at some point, that all stopped. She went to their houses but they never came to ours anymore. By the time she was thirteen or fourteen, Jeanette's life had become a mystery to me.

Ma taps me on the shoulder. "Wasn't that a beautiful Mass?" Her face glows. Her head lowers a little when she adds, "I feel a little funny with it mostly being gay people and everything, but it really felt like God was here with us. Didn't it to you?"

"It did feel that way. It feels like she's still here."

"Oh, you. All my life I've been taught to believe in a God who's a father to us. So don't try to change my mind about *that* too. Besides, 'Father' comes right out of the Bible."

"'He created them in His own image,'" I quote. "'He created them man and woman.'"

Ma raises her finger. "Right. *He* created them."

I raise mine. "But his own image must include the female, right?"

"Hmm. Well, that's probably the part that takes care of the feeding and the cleaning and everything."

"And the nurturing."

Ma blushes and I turn to see Mia scribbling something on a business card and handing it to Jeanette.

* * *

Outside, Ma the documentarian snaps a few pictures of the church, and a few more of the small, carefully tended garden along the side of the rectory: impatiens, begonias, the usual. She takes one of Jeanette and me standing in front of a life-sized crucifix with ivy curling around its sturdy wooden beams. Then we're back in the van, and heading up the highway entrance ramp, reunited with our old friend the interstate, which at some point will bring us into North Texas, and, by early evening, I hope, to New Mexico.

Blood red spray-painted words on the glinting red, white and blue I-40 crest: *The Highway of Spirit and Bone.*

There's a poet a-loose in these here hills.

"So," I say, "what did you guys think of that sermon?"

Ma, who's behind me in the pilot seat, doesn't respond. Jeanette is perusing the parish bulletin.

"No comment, Ma?"

"I'm still thinking. It was very good. He's such a distinguished-sounding man, that priest. It's just that his homily…it made me think about your father."

"How so?"

Jeanette glances back and sighs. Then, as if to shield herself from the conversation, lifts her shoulder and shifts her body so that she's pressing herself into the passenger door.

"Well, you remember how he used to hit you kids quite a bit when you got in trouble, don't you?" Her tone is uneasy, perhaps defensive.

"Yeah," I say. "I vaguely remember that."

"Well, David, you didn't get it nearly as much as Aaron did. Or even…"

Suddenly it feels very hot in the van, and I throw the AC to max.

When Ma can't seem to continue, I say, "I remember one time, I must have been around eight or nine, when I took all the World War II stuff he had in the basement, some of his old uniforms and a medal or two, and that helmet he took off a dead Nazi, and I set it all up on the front lawn and was going to have a yard sale and sell everything there for, like, twenty cents apiece? Do you remember that?"

"Oh my gosh," Ma says.

"And Da drives home from work and sees me out on the lawn, sees this big sign I made that says, like, '*Real War Stuff! Cheap!*' and he jumps out of the car and starts chasing me around the yard."

Ma giggles. "He caught you, too."

"He sure did."

"Oh, he was angry about that. But you couldn't blame him. He fought in that war and he almost died more than once, and there you are selling all his mementos."

It shames me now to think of it, but, hell, being a kid, what did I know. It was all thrown into a big cardboard box in the back of the basement, seemingly forgotten. "He hardly ever *said* anything about the war."

"Oh, he didn't like to talk about it," Ma says. "I remember one time—this was before you kids were born—he said to me, 'Lilly, I saw things over there that I wouldn't want my worst enemy to see.' I said, 'Like what, hon?' Well, he turned and pointed his finger at me and narrowed his eyes and said, 'Don't ever ask me that again.' And I never did."

"And yet the artifacts had to be preserved." I glance over at Jeanette, who avoids looking at me. "Anyway, you were saying, Ma."

"What was I saying?"

Jeanette sighs.

"Some connection between the sermon and Da hitting us."

"Oh, yeah. I was going to tell you about his Jesus dream."

"His *what*?"

"His Jesus dream. Well, he had more than one, but I was going to tell you about the one that made him finally stop hitting you kids."

Jeanette lowers the bulletin and stares out the window.

"It was one of the happiest days of my life, to tell you the truth. Because all those years that he hit you, well, I didn't like it. I just thought he was, you know, 'Spare the rod, spoil the child.' That comes right out of the Bible, you know?"

"Yeah, but..." I decide to shut up.

"Anyway, he came down into the kitchen one morning like always at five o'clock. I always got up a few minutes before him to make the coffee, you know. We liked to sit and sip our coffee and chat a little before you kids got up and the house turned into a madhouse. It was always the nicest part of my day. He was at his best at that hour. Not aggravated about anything yet. Anyway, that morning he came in and we sat down at the kitchen table with our coffee and I noticed he looked funny, pale and, you know, spooked-like. 'What is it, Bern?' At first, he just said, 'Nothing, I'm fine.' And I said, 'You sure?' Finally, he said, 'He don't want me to hit the kids no more.'"

Jeanette's gazing out at the ever-deepening brown, sometimes butte-dotted earth (we are indeed westward ho!). Though she's the youngest sibling, Jeanette got her share of beatings. Debbie probably got even fewer than I did. When she did get them, they were usually for dereliction of duty. The thing was, when Debbie got a beating, we all had to watch, or at least listen from an adjoining room. A warning to the rest of us. Listening to Debbie take a beating because she didn't watch me close enough was unbearable. I mean, isn't that what terrorists do? Highjack the plane, then kill one or two people in the front of everybody so that nobody misses the point and everybody gets nice and compliant?

With real urgency, I ask, "Did he describe the dream?"

"He said Jesus looked a little like Johnny Carson." Ma laughs, and so do Jeanette and I. "I know, silly right? Anyway, he came up to daddy, I forget where, I think on the golf course, and he said, 'Don't hurt my lambs anymore, okay, Bernie?' I remember daddy saying that Jesus didn't sound *angry* or mean or anything like that. It was more like, 'You know what, Bernie, you can stop doing this now.' He never said it to me, but he was relieved. Oh, he hated hitting you kids. After he hit you, he always had to go for a drive or disappear down in the basement and fiddle with some broken thing." Ma leans up from behind me. "That really bad time with you, Jeanette, that day he...."

Again, Ma stops. I peer into the rearview and see she's turned beet red and her chin is trembling.

What "really bad" beating?

Ma doesn't start up again, and each of us floats, a little numb, into our black and blue pasts.

Finally, minutes later, when she's recovered somewhat, Ma says, "Grandpa Stepenski was a rough man. Your father got a lot of beatings when he was little, too. So that's what he thought was the right thing to do. My father didn't hit us." Her voice trails off. "He kept to himself."

We ride in a silence full of the ghosts we're supposed to be intimate with—ourselves as little children, a Johnny Carson Jesus—until, several miles further on through the mud-brown landscape, Ma says, "After he told me, he dropped his head onto the table and started to cry. He cried and cried—the only time in almost fifty years that I ever saw him really cry like that. Finally, I said, 'Bern, oh, come on Bern, don't cry. Please.' And he stopped."

"You asked him to stop crying?"

"Beg your pardon?"

"Why did you ask him to stop?"

Jeanette's head twists toward me. "*David*."

I ignore her and turn halfway around. I try to modulate my voice, but it comes out harsh anyway. "Why didn't you just let him cry, Ma?"

"Oh, gosh." Her voice quivers. "It was so..."

"He probably needed that cry in the worst way."

"*David*," Jeanette shouts. "Shut up right now. You're upsetting her." She turns around to Ma. "It's okay, Ma." To me, pointedly: "What's wrong with you?"

Now, there's a question.

"I'm sorry, Ma. I just know sometimes letting out what's been bottled up for a long time is a good, healthy thing to do."

Ma nods. "I understand that. I shouldn't have..."

"Anyway, that dream. Wow. And then, he really never hit us again after that?"

"Never."

"Amazing. I wish I knew about that."

"Oh, boy. I guess I should have told you. Another mistake."

"No, Ma, I'm not saying that. Not at all. You did fine. Better than fine."

We drive on. Many silent miles later, I find myself saying out loud, "I think that's what the priest must have meant by 'cooperating with grace.' Da was offered grace in a dream, and he cooperated."

Peering into the rearview, I see Ma's eyes widen and glisten.

* * *

As we hurtle through the last flat sprawling miles of western Oklahoma and cross into Texas, both Ma and Jeanette have fallen into early afternoon, post-lunch naps. Thus, no picture will be taken of the sign reading "Welcome to Texas, the Lone Star State." In the hush, memories come to me; they're seemingly random ones, but who can say why the unconscious sends certain memories back to us at particular times? I'm sure it has its reasons. I recall a time when I was five years old and we were at South Beach, one of the beaches on Staten Island that used to be a place for families, though now mostly only teenagers use the place, to get high or laid or into brawls. Thirty-five years ago, bathers swam in the waters without worrying that they might sprout new body parts as a result. Our family was there frequently, spread out on a couple of old blankets, a Styrofoam cooler full of peanut butter and jelly sandwiches and thermoses of homemade lemonade. I'd be trying to build a deep, high-walled sand fort for my plastic soldiers, frustrated that the walls wouldn't hold; the sand kept slipping into the moat.

One particular summer day, Ma, who'd been reading *The Advance,* suddenly lowered the paper and said, "Where's the baby?"—meaning Jeanette, who was three at the time.

Da was lying on his stomach listening to our portable radio, to Bing Crosby or that ilk, his idols. He lifted himself up onto his elbows and asked Debbie, who'd been put in charge of us, "Where's the baby?"

"She was right there a minute ago. I just saw her."

Ma was already running down toward the water.

"You were in charge, Debra," Da said in a grave but unpanicked monotone. He seemed more concerned about the violation than about where Jeanette might be.

Debbie began to cry.

Aaron looked out from behind his *Boy's Life.*

I scrambled up from my failed fort, partly because I didn't want to be around when Da slapped Debbie in the face, which I nevertheless heard as I ran toward the water. *Crack. Crack.* Ma stood in the tide, knee deep, looking down into the water calling out, "Jeanette, Jeanette." To anyone in ear shot, she said, "Please help me find my little girl. She's blonde. She's wearing a green and yellow suit."

People tended to swim together in pockets, and I scanned the pockets for my sister's long blonde hair and striped bathing suit. I looked down the beach, and there, quite far out into the water–or so it seemed to my five-year old eyes–I saw a big white Styrofoam raft, one we'd found on the beach and had all been floating on earlier in the day –and her little body lying on it, bobbing in the waves. "Ma," I shouted, but she'd already made the same discovery. She was no swimmer, Ma, no athlete; she didn't even wear a bathing suit to the beach, just shorts and a shirt, but she dove through a wave and for all the life in her started swimming out toward that raft with an awkward but determined fury. Now Da was at the water's edge, too, and he dove into the tide and swam like some great lean fish through the waves. He arrived at the raft just as Ma had begun to tug Jeanette back in. Right away he took over the tugging. When they were a little ways from shore, I swam out to meet them. Jeanette's skin was ghastly white and her lips were blue and she couldn't control her shivering. Da looked in determinedly at the shore, tugging and tugging. Ma's eyes were latched like ropes to Jeanette, her free hand caressing her back. I'm not sure any of them even noticed that I was there, too, but I thought, thank you, God. Thank you, God.

I take a swig of coffee and drive, my heart slamming against my ribs. Too much caffeine, you know, will do that.

* * *

At a little after two o'clock we spot, from many miles away, a giant cross superimposed on the horizon. Although it is probably intended as a symbol of salvation, the thing makes for a chilling sight. As we get closer, I estimate it's two hundred feet high, constructed of concrete, painted confederate gray. It stands a hundred yards or so off the highway, apparently on somebody's private property. Not far off, in the scrub grass, cattle and horses graze. The blue north Texas sky gleams.

Ma, awed by the sight, asks if I'll stop so she can take a picture.

I exit the highway and pull up to a six-foot high chain fence. As Ma snaps away and Jeanette waits in the van, I stand in the afternoon heat and stare up, trying to get at just what it's making me feel.

That's when a Volvo wagon with North Carolina plates pulls up beside my van. A thirtyish couple, well-dressed and good-looking, and their two kids, a blonde boy and girl, get out and stand a few feet from us and gaze up at the cross. The little boy says in a southern drawl, "They ought to put swings on the arms."

The woman says, in a lowered voice, "I wouldn't want to be the daughter of the guy who put that thing up."

"Huh?" the man says. But he doesn't want an explanation. He pats his kids on the back. "Okay, we've seen it. Let's go."

Ma snaps one more picture. "Boy, I can't wait to show this one to Edna. It's something, isn't it?"

"It is. It is something."

The bigger the cross, the greater the doubt?

At a little after three we drive through Amarillo. Commotion on the highway slows us down.

"Hay," I say, and point out at the road.

"What?" Jeanette mumbles from behind the screen of her laptop.

"Hay."

A small pickup truck has lost its load of hay bales. Ten or so of them lay scattered like giant tan fuzzy die all over the highway. On the shoulder an older Mexican guy stands beside the truck with his hands on his hips.

"Oh, the poor man," Ma says from the back where's she's knitting away.

A mile later I realize that I didn't even consider stopping to help him. Da would've stopped. He would have pulled over and told us kids to wait and be still, and he would have helped the poor guy gather up his hay bales, even if it meant risking getting pancaked by an eighteen-wheeler.

Your parents never really die, do they?

On the western outskirts of the city, we pass a sprawling cardboard factory, a sprawling electricity grid, a billboard that reads "Genuine Historic Route 66 Souvenirs," a series of auto dealerships, a small Baptist church with a plastic-encased sign: "Before You Do It, Ask Yourself What Would Jesus Do?" This, of course, is a fashionable question in certain Christian circles these days (though not so much in the Catholic Church). Jesus wouldn't call in sick when he had tickets to the ball game. Jesus wouldn't try to get that woman he just met an hour ago in the bar into his bed. Jesus would help the Mexican man gather up his hay bales.

But one of the things I love about Jesus, one of the things that I find most compelling and convincing about him, is his *un*predictability. Beyond saying and doing things nobody else said or did, the so-called meek and mild

Lamb of God threw tables over, got pissed off at his hangers-on, spoke in brilliant riddles to the frustration of those who would have it plain and simple and blunt. When I'm at my most receptive, contemplating the life and words of Jesus never fails to knock me on my ass.

What would Jesus do, I think as I glance at my slouched sister. He'd understand why she is the way she is. He'd love her unconditionally. Mind you I'm aware that there's nothing simplistic or necessarily predictable about love. You don't read the Gospels and get the feeling that Jesus' brand of love is any touchy-feely soft sell. As far as I can tell, the word love is the linguistic container for the most complex, far-reaching, penetrating, challenging, misunderstood, mysterious idea—*force*—in all of existence. How could it be otherwise when we're told that God *is* love? How could it be otherwise when for the sake of love people willingly endure excruciating physical, emotional, spiritual and psychological pain. In transcendent moments, people stand in front of bullets for love, rush into flames (or into the ocean) for love, endure childbirth for love, give their organs to strangers for love, decide to pull the plug for love, resist all manner of temptation for love, forgive all manner of violation and transgression for love. Yet what I've mostly seen outside this speeding window is "You'll love our new crunchier fries." "Destroyer X, The Movie—I loved it." "Try *Samantha de Sade's Sadistic Love Potion*." Seems we've settled for very little where love is concerned. What would happen if I said, "I love you, Jeanette"? I don't think I ever have. When we were kids, Jeanette would get mad at me for barging into her room or for randomly turning the tuners on her guitar, and she'd say something like, "Get lost, you insect," and I'd tell her that I hated her guts, stupid moody jerk. Even when things were good, like, say, Christmas eve, when she and Debbie and Aaron and I would all be playing some board game, all of us brimming with anticipation of Christmas morning and the gifts we'd be receiving (although, led by Da mostly, we really did at least try to acknowledge that all this good stuff came about because we were celebrating Jesus' birthday), even then, even in high spirits, all of us drinking eggnog and listening to carols and playing Monopoly, selling property to each other for practically nothing because we felt generous, not insisting on the other person paying if he or she landed on Park Place with a hotel and even as Da hummed along with Nat King Cole and flirted with Ma, even then, I never told Jeanette that I loved her.

What if I did it now? Would it change anything? What if I gave my sister a hug? She might haul off and break my nose.

I have to believe she knows I love her, in the fashion of our family. You don't say it, you take it for granted. You *might* consider saying it if you found out the person was dying of brain cancer, say, but not a moment sooner. I've said it a million times to my kids, to Marie. Too many times, probably. Too indiscriminately. When we're just sitting around watching T.V., for example. These days I say it to Ma a bit more frequently too, and listen for her awkward, *I love you, too, David*, which sometimes comes. I was thirty before I could say it to Da, and he was in intensive care. In reply, he said, with a kind of resignation, even slight annoyance, "I love you too, David." As if it need not have been voiced. Almost as if the verbal declaration somehow *diminished* the fact.

If that's what he thought, I think he was wrong.

* * *

I'm seated three empty bar stools from two women a little younger than me in the otherwise empty hotel bar. The bartender, a soft-spoken, twenty-something-year old black man with small, wire-rimmed glasses, sits in a corner behind the bar reading a book called *Philosophy in a New Key*. (I like the sound of that!) Every once in a while, he looks up to see whether one of us needs a refill. We're east of Albuquerque and it's eleven-twenty p.m., and I should be in bed because we're on the road at five tomorrow. Going to try to make it all the way to Vegas, spend Monday night and Tuesday with Aaron and head back to Flagstaff on Wednesday morning. Ma should be in her new home by Wednesday night. And with any luck, by Saturday night I'll be soaking up the faces of my own kids and then sleeping in my own bed with my own wife.

I take a sip of my second cognac. The silk and sting are just right slipping down my throat. I feel punch drunk from driving for four days straight. I feel like the whirring particles that comprise my flesh are about to break apart and disperse, leaving me nothing but pure spirit. I feel like calling Marie and asking her how the hell, of all the guys in the world, she, a beautiful, accomplished, even-keeled, generous, wise woman, could possibly have chosen to marry a borderline obsessive-compulsive, spiritually haunted, unsettled rag of a man like me. But I've already spoken with her tonight. She's got a headache and though she tried her best to be engaging, she clearly just wanted to get off the phone. She did tell me that Ted and his "girlfriend" had a fight this afternoon and that Ted has been moping around the house all day. "I talked to him about it a little," she said, "but I think you and he should have a good man-to-man when you get home. I think he needs that."

Man to man? How did that happen? He was a boy when I left.

When I was Ted's age, I think as the burn of the cognac coats my tongue, my own father's idea of a man-to-man was to wink at me when a pretty woman walked by. I never liked it. Even as a very young boy I saw it as a violation. I can't imagine seeing some well-endowed woman go by and then winking at Ted. Would I like it if Marie did that, in a few years, with Genevieve, when some good-looking guy walked past them? Did Da think that doing it would make me feel more grown up? What it made me feel was angry. *I'm not in on this.* All I could do when he winked was look away, pretend I didn't notice. I liked it when he helped strangers on the highway. I liked the fact that he always gave poor people money, even though we didn't have much of it ourselves. I liked that in the car on the way home after Mass he would ask us if we understood the point of the gospel, and that we'd have discussions about it (well, lectures is probably more accurate, but I guess I didn't mind hearing them). But when he winked and smiled at me after a woman walked by, that felt wrong.

I take a long, stinging sip of cognac and glance at the women who are quietly chatting beside me. I have gathered that one of them is Jen but I haven't heard Jen use the other's name. Both are in their mid-to-late thirties, I estimate. Both are what I'd call "ordinary attractive," which, I suppose, is how I'd describe the vast majority of people I see. Probably how most would describe me. They're dressed nicely, both in skirts and blouses, a few tasteful accessories. Stylishly cut mid-length hair: Jen's is amber and not-Jen's light brown. Marie, I'd bet, would feel at home with these two. They seem down-to-earth, comfortable in their low-heeled shoes.

"Hi, there," not-Jen suddenly says to me.

"Hi."

"Care to join us? You look so all alone over there."

"Do I?" Only when I speak do I realize that I'm half-drunk. I don't in fact want to join them, but I gather up my bills and my drink and carry them over to where the women are sitting.

"Hi," not-Jen says, putting out her hand. "I'm Judith. This is Jennifer."

"Hi. I'm...uh..." and for a second, during which I may or may not be having a telepathic vision involving Marie and Brandon, I forget my name. "...I'm David."

"You're sure now?" Judith says, and shakes her hair back and laughs.

"I'm not really sure about anything."

"Rough day?"

"A lot of driving."

Prompted by a few sincere-sounding questions, I tell them, bare-bones, what I'm in the process of doing. As quickly as possible, I change the subject to them. They're both elementary-level reading specialists, in town for a workshop on the latest method for seducing kids who'd rather be playing video games into opening up a book instead.

"My God," Jen says, bringing the subject back to me. "I love my mother dearly, but she and I could not last in a car together for five hours, let alone five days. One of us would not make it there alive. Either you or your mother must be a saint."

"He looks kind of saintly, doesn't he, Jen?" Judith says. "In a manly kind of way, of course." She touches my arm and laughs.

Does it mean something that she touched my arm? "I don't think either of us quite qualifies for sainthood," I say. "But my mother's a lot closer than I will ever be."

"Well, that's as it should be," Judith says. "Let me buy you a drink, David. That one is almost all gone."

A button on Judith's blouse that I'm pretty certain was fastened a moment ago is unfastened now, so that a healthy bit of very pretty cleavage is revealed. The guilt machine begins to rev, but so does another engine— the one between my legs.

I have never, in all the years I've known Marie, cheated on her. And I never will. So why is there another glistening drink in my hand? The script says, *No thanks, I've got to get back to my room. Real early morning coming fast.*

The bartender, as he turns to go back to his book, catches my eye. If I'm not mistaken, he's thinking something to the effect of: *guys are so predictable.* Or maybe, *so weak.*

"Cheers," Judith says. "Here's to David's mom."

"And here's to yours. And yours." I lift my glass a little higher.

Judith rolls her eyes and touches her glass first to mine and then to Jen's.

For the next half hour, we talk parents. Jen's are deceased, but she thinks of them fondly—"more fondly with every passing year." She says she complained too much as a kid. If things could be magically reversed, if you could somehow *be* a parent *before* you were a kid, she says, all of life would run smoothly. "Why is it," she wants to know, "that we understand almost everything that's important only in retrospect?"

"Ask me tomorrow," I say, and both women laugh. I realize I feel good sitting here. It feels good to feel good.

Judith describes her father as "a tough old nut who won't admit he shouldn't be living alone anymore," who argues incessantly with her about everything from the fact that her marriage failed to the way she dresses, to the urgency that she remarry and become somebody's normal, happy wife.

When it's my turn I say, "My father believed in doing things by the book. And there were no ambiguities or subtleties in that book." When I say about Ma, "She's not real comfortable showing affection," they respond, "Oh, that's a generational thing, David," and "As a woman of that time, she was given lots of messages to keep her feelings to herself."

At exactly eleven-fifty-nine p.m., the bartender stands up and starts turning off lights. "I close at twelve," he says in little more than a mumble.

"I for one haven't had such stimulating conversation in three days," Judith says. "And, personally, I'm not ready for it to end. How about we continue the party in my room?"

Chapter Five
Monday, June 10, 2002

Some Things Can't Be Fixed

Nothing is going to happen here.
Sunken in the lounge chair, I glance around the room: two queen beds;
a small, mauve sofa on which both women sit; a desk with a stack of books
on the teaching of reading, all still in shrink wrap; on the walls above each
headboard, two identical paintings of a fat, green cactus; various sections of
USA Today lying open on the floor and on top of the bureau. We're drinking
wine they brought along from home "for just such an occasion." Because
I'm quite drunk, and despite the fact that I know nothing is going to happen,
my body seems to be experiencing a pre-sexual tingle. *No,* I tell myself and
try to participate in a conversation the women are having about the most
romantic places they've ever been: a little beach in San Juan; a small suite
in the Chateau Frontenac in Quebec; almost anywhere in Paris, of course; a
cozy, darkly lit, slightly-dangerous-in-a-mafiaesque-sort-of-way Italian
restaurant on First Avenue in New York.

Outside, close by, a police car or ambulance, siren shrieking, hurtles
through the dark toward some Texas tragedy. The urgency of the sound
momentarily gives us pause. But as soon as it has faded into the milky-aired
night, Judith sighs and says, "I feel like I've been in this outfit all day. If
nobody objects, I'm going to change. Is that okay?"

Jen shrugs and I slur "Sure." Judith stands, walks over to a dresser
drawer and pulls out two or three items that look a lot like sex, then walks
languidly into the bathroom.

My heart begins to thrum and sweat beads emerge along my hairline.
The skin on my face burns. When Judith closes the bathroom door, Jen
smiles coyly.

"I believe that's my cue."

"Look, no, don't leave. There's no need."

She takes her purse out of her lap and stands up. "It's really okay, David.

You deserve this. And so does she." Confidentially, she says, "She's had a *hard* life. Really. So this will be nice for her. Just be gentle with her, okay? She's a delicate person." And with that, she goes.

As soon as she's gone I stand, put my hand to my jaw and squeeze. *Leave. Now.* But I don't. I stay where I am, standing. When the bathroom door opens, Judith emerges wearing a silky robe that's loosely fastened at the hip and reveals a little off-white teddy-type thing, and a pair of lacy panties of the same hue. She seems unsurprised that Jen has left the room. "Is this okay, David? My wearing this?"

I know what I'm supposed to say. I notice and fix my eyes on a single, delicate, loose thread from her panties that rests like a spider's leg against her upper thigh.

"David?"

"Sorry. Yeah. You look…. But I, uh, I can't."

"You *can't…*?"

"Can't. I came down to the bar to have a quick drink. The three of us had a nice time chatting…" I sound adolescent.

Judith smiles, but she's hurt, embarrassed, and rightfully pissed off.

"I'm sorry, you know, if…"

"*If?*" Judith says, raising an eyebrow. "I'm generally pretty good at reading male signals. Not that I do this kind of thing very often. I do not."

"No, I know. We're both a little drunk. Signals got crossed…" By now I've backtracked and have my hand on the iron doorknob.

"Did they?" She holds her chin up in a slightly unnatural way. "You know, you strike me as someone who perhaps isn't completely honest with himself."

"You know something," I say and let my hand fall from the doorknob. "That's probably true. I'm not *completely* anything. So, let me give honesty a try. It's not the case that I didn't know what might happen up here, but at the same time, I didn't really think about it. I think, well, I think I came up because I wanted to feel excited, instead of worn out and run down. I mean, you're an intelligent, witty, attractive woman, and… but nevertheless, I'm, you know, *married.*"

Judith's expression has changed slightly, though I couldn't say for better or worse. "Honorable."

"Even for a guy who may not be honest enough with himself," I stammer, "that feels pretty close to the truth."

"Okay," Judith says, weighing.

"Doesn't make my coming up in the first place right, though. I should've said goodnight when the bar closed."

"I wish you had. But, then again, this is nothing either of us won't get over, is it?"

"Mine is the tougher part. Because it's part of a pattern."

"Hmm."

"You know, I never realized this before, but I think, somehow, Judith, I got the message that I'm supposed to be a saint. Like, *or else*. And obviously I can't do it. It's more like, I'm damned if I do something and I'm damned if I don't."

"You sound very confused."

"I sound like an idiot."

"Well, how about you leave now, David? I'm sleepy. Happy trails to you and mom."

Back in my room, I pace, then stand still and stare at the carpet, where I find a sordid history of faded spills of God knows what.

I don't think I will sleep.

On hotel stationary I write this: *I hope someday to outgrow my neediness. I am so sorry.*

I take the elevator three floors, back up to Judith's room. I slip the note under the door.

An hour ago, I told myself nothing was going to happen in there, but something happened anyway. And a note doesn't fix it.

* * *

In the dream, I have to escort Ma across a rickety, rotted wooden foot bridge over a landscape reminiscent of the Grand Canyon. Fog covers the rim we're heading toward. Marie and the kids are watching from a helicopter that hovers very close by. Against the bubble glass of the copter my daughter Genevieve holds up a piece of paper on which she's written *Mommy Loves*

?????. The pilot looks familiar, though I can't place him. A gust of wind comes up and the bridge sways and creaks. Ma says, "I hope they take our picture," to which I respond, "It'll have to be black and white, won't it?" "Yes, but it will prove I got you over this."

My eyes blink open and I stare at the red digits: 9:33. *Nine-thirty-three?* I roll across the bed and call Ma's and Jeanette's room. Five rings later, Ma answers, tells me she and Jeanette just got up a few minutes ago, that they both slept through the alarm and why didn't I call and wake them. After I tell her that I'm not even sure I'm awake yet, she says, "I guess we're all a little overtired, huh?"

We agree that, to save time, we'll eat breakfast on the road.

In the groggy shower, I'm relieved to remember: *nothing happened last night*. Though it doesn't quite feel that way.

A long ten minutes later, I step out of the shower and dry off with a stiff, bristly, overused towel, wondering what the hell my unconscious meant by "Mommy Loves ?????" I comb my hair and shave. I can clearly see the five question marks on Genevieve's handwritten note. Brainstorm: ????? = D-A-V-I-D.

B-R-A-N-D-O-N. Seven.

"Lord," I pray as I step into my shorts, *"get me back home. Please. Get us all home."* I sound like Dorothy from the Wizard of Oz.

* * *

Ma: "New Mexico sure is a lot different from Staten Island."

The earth here is a kind of overexposed moonscape: cracked and creviced, rust-colored, scrubby. Huge, sliced mounds reveal, casually, vast geological epochs. In the cloudless heat of noon, we're able to gaze across a distance of many miles, maybe hundreds of miles. It feels like we're seeing through time. Deep time. The crowded, progressive, civilized east coast existence we are still traveling away from strikes me, eerily so, as temporary and flimsy, a kind of fleeting respite from reality, a brief stage; this place, in its great emptiness and elementality, feels permanent, raw and real. It's what was before and what will be when human life, for whatever reason (take your pick), no longer is.

As we drive on, I feel myself floating in a keen, tingling stupor.

I have decided to tell Marie about the episode last night with the women from Kansas. With a light touch, of course, something to the effect of: "Wait till you hear the situation I got myself into last night." Marie's got a sense of humor. And she knows I'm hers for life. Whether she likes it or not.

Nothing happened, and that's all that counts.

And what about Brandon? If Marie isn't interested in him and I insinuate or, worse, make accusations that she is, will I only be pushing her closer to him? Will I be helping turn him from just the divorced neighbor across the street into an object of desire? Have I been doing just that for the last four or five years?

In the early afternoon of the day we moved into our current home, right after the big Mayfair moving truck pulled away, Marie and I sat on the front stoop, exhausted but happy to finally begin our new domestic adventure. The kids were squealing around in their big new backyard with Ma playing right along with them, and we sat there drinking tall glasses of ice water. A Lexus approached, slowed, and pulled into the driveway across the street. A few seconds later, a trim, good-looking man got out, saw us sitting there, and came over to introduce himself. We chatted for a while, though I don't remember many details. Maybe Brandon told us he was a T.V. producer, and that he lived alone and that he was divorced. Maybe Marie told him she was a freelance graphic designer but was taking time off to raise the kids. Maybe I told him what I did. I do remember thinking, this guy, for better or worse, *exudes* self-confidence. This guy likes himself a lot. I also remember, after he left, Marie saying something to the effect of, "What a cool guy. Looks like we've got ourselves a great neighbor, don't you think, David?"

I'm sure I said I did.

Ahead, a large, bright, blue and yellow sign stands proud in the sun, waiting to welcome us to Arizona. As I ease my foot off the gas, Ma asks me to slow down and readies her camera.

"Edna will love seeing these. She doesn't travel much but she reads about all these places."

"I hope she'll come out and visit you."

"I doubt it. She's afraid to fly, too. Especially now, after last September.

And it would be hard on her legs to sit on a bus or a train all this time. She's eighty-two already."

"That's okay," Jeanette says from the back, "David can drive her."

Gazing out at a series of billboards that announce the sale of genuine Indian jewelry at the next exit, Ma says, "I can't get it into my head that this is my new home state. It feels funny. I'm a Staten Islander, not an Arizonian..."

"I think it's Arizonan," Jeanette corrects.

"I know what you mean, Ma," I say. "After I took the job at Rutgers, it was about a year before I could admit to myself that I lived in New Jersey. It was my deep-rooted New York elitism."

"This is different though."

"We'll be driving right through Flagstaff in a couple of hours, Ma," Jeanette informs us. "Sure you want to keep going through to Vegas? You've been in this car for five days. We can call Aaron. I'm sure he'll understand." Under her breath she adds, "Probably be relieved."

"I want to see my son."

"Okay. Just making sure. I guess I should find us a hotel up there."

"I think so. He only has a one-bedroom apartment."

"So, Ma, MGM Grand? The Sands? What do you want?"

"We're not going there as high rollers, Jeanette," I say. "How about a Comfort Inn or a Hampton or something like that? Something on the outskirts, maybe."

"That okay with you, Ma?"

"Fine. I just want to see Aaron." A few seconds later she adds, "Debbie says they have a bus ride to the casinos at least once a month. I can go anytime I want."

"Which will be at least once a month, I'll bet."

"You know, if I ever win big..." But she stops, mid-sentence.

"Yeah?" I say, "what if you win big?"

"Never mind. I'll get used to this. David, could we stop in one of these little Indian shops that are coming up? I wanted to get something for Aaron. A little birthday gift."

"Sure, but you know, I think all they sell are things like arrow heads and beads and turquoise jewelry and dream catchers and that sort of thing. And of course, tee shirts. I don't know what you have in mind."

"I don't know either. A tee shirt or a sweatshirt would be fine. Just a little something. What's a dream catcher?"

"Well," I say, "take Jorge Posada for example. On the Yankees. Has a good arm, good bat, big in the clutch."

No response.

"Joke. It's an ornament. I mean, I don't know the mythology behind them. I suppose they keep dreams from slipping out of your memory. (*Mommy Loves ?????*) Or your grasp. But for non-Natives it's mostly a decorative thing. They look kind of like fancy, man-made spider webs with feathers hanging off them. Debbie sent some to the kids once."

We roll along a potholed service road toward a shabby, adobe-type restaurant/souvenir shop called *Sun and Moon Trading Post*. It looks forlorn, half-dilapidated, lost in time.

I dread seeing Sheri more than I dread seeing Aaron. What good can I possibly be to her? What can I say to her that can make the slightest difference? Really, all I've done is teased her, haven't I? Teased her with the idea that driving out to Vegas might hold some hope for her. Not unlike what I did last night to Judith. I knew damn well I wouldn't cheat on Marie, but I let it go pretty far anyway. What did I want? The ego gratification of knowing I *could* have had her if I wanted? No. It was trying to find out if she might want me. Why though? Because sometimes I feel invisible?

The van crunches to a stop in front of the trading post. While Ma and Jeanette head inside, I sit a minute in the driver's seat, rubbing my eyes and picturing myself out on the deck of my house on a warm summer afternoon, Marie beside me in her modestly sexy one piece, both of us chatting, sipping some ridiculously colorful summer drink she's concocted for us, the kids splashing away in the pool. When Marie goes inside to fetch some munchie or other, the kids call, "Daddy, watch this! Daddy, watch me!"

What is it about the word *daddy* ringing out of an excited little kid's mouth? Sure, they say it a hundred times a day (*mommy*, on that scale, is uttered about three times as often), but only once in a while do you hear it in a way that it hits you with the full force of its meaning. That meaning, of course, is almost too immense to bear. *Daddy, take care of me. Put a roof over my head. Show me what love between a mommy and a daddy is supposed to look like, daddy. Show me how to behave with my siblings, how to love them. Show me how to find and keep friends. Show me how to pray, daddy, and how to believe in the God I'm praying to even after the inevitable bombardment of doubts and questions comes. Show me how to tolerate mystery and unknowing. Show me how to express my emotions. Show me how to control my desires. Show me how to use money and material things wisely. Show me how to live, daddy.*

When I'm finally ready to step out of the van, it's into a hot, bone-dry breeze. I stretch and inhale the blowing heat, which keeps on blowing in the hollow of my chest. Idly, I look at the state of the exterior of the van: a mash of bugs splattered across the grille and fender and a thick coat of desert dust caking the body, front to back. The filthiness bothers the hell out of me, and I wish there was a car wash right here, right now. I'd even settle for a bucket of soapy water and a few rags.

When I turn back toward the shop, I find a little girl in a dirty pink and white dress standing a few feet away, staring at the van just as I'd been doing. A Native American girl of seven or eight, with bronze skin and intense brown eyes and raven-black hair that blows across her face with the hot gusts.

"Hi, there," I say.

"Hi. Where's New Jersey?" Her voice rings like bells.

"Oh, it's far, far away from here. Near the Atlantic Ocean. Do you know where that is?"

She lifts her arm, points east down the highway.

"Yes, New Jersey is many days in that direction." There's something silly-sounding about my putting it that way. *Me come long way on solemn journey from Piscataway to evil Las Vegas, and then beyond.*

"My grandmother had to go to Washington, D.C. once," the girl tells me in a lilting cadence. She pushes her hair away from her face, but it blows right back. "She didn't like it there."

"Ah."

"She cried when she came home. Now she stays here all the time. We live over there." She turns, points past the store and restaurant, past a sagging, barbed-wire fence and across a distance of four or five hundred yards of sagebrush and dry clay, to a small compound of white concrete dwellings. I can make out three older model Ford pickups, one with the hood up. There's a scattering of rusty metal barrels, heap of tires, a lopsided swing set, and what I'm guessing is a corrugated tin chicken coop. Beyond the compound lay sage-dotted hills. A spotted horse ("a paint" I believe they used to call them on *Bonanza*) grazes near a twirling, half-formed dust devil.

"Do you like living here?"

She shrugs her frail shoulders. "I'm glad I don't have to live in Washington, D.C."

I scan the landscape, try to conceive of what it must be like to be an eight-year old native American girl living here. I've read the major ethnographies, of course, but they didn't make so great an impression on me that I feel I know what this little girl's life is like. A thought: I could get a grant. Come back here for a season, or several seasons, and find out for myself. All my work has been on the east coast in the inner city. I should expand my scope. But I won't undertake that kind of project until the kids are older. We have certain established family rhythms, and I don't want to disrupt them.

"I need to go find James," the girl tells me.

But I've fallen in love with her voice and want to hear her talk some more. "Who's James? Is he your brother?"

"He won't stay still," she says. "He's hard to find. He only stays still if you hold him."

"Some people are like that, aren't they?"

The little girl says, "Are you coming here just to pee, or to really buy something?"

"Boy, David," Ma says as I climb back into the van. "You sure got a lot of stuff in there. I'll bet they were sorry to see you go."

"Well, I wanted to bring something back for the kids and Marie. Marie's going to like that necklace. And some of the tee shirts are really cool. Are you happy with what you got for Aaron? I think a Baja jacket is a great idea. Very cool. And he can probably use it up there in Alaska."

"Oh, I hope he likes it. I can't believe how cheap it was. You'd pay a lot more for something like that in Macy's." She leans up to the front and taps Jeanette's shoulder. "And that was so nice of you to fix their refrigerator. I couldn't help thinking how proud your father would have been. That's just what he would have done."

"I just tightened some screws." But for just a second, at the invocation of Da's pride in her, Jeanette's eyes twinkle. Twinkle, then go dark.

A few miles east of Flagstaff. Higher elevation now, lush pine forests, cooler air, and ahead a stretch of the southern spine of the Rockies. Such extremes out here. A little while ago I stared down at desiccated fissures; now, in the middle of June, I'm looking up at a snow-capped mountain ridge.

My cell phone sounds its mini-Mozart. I expect to hear Marie's voice, but it's Debbie. "Have you come into the city limits yet?" Somehow she calculated that we'd be just about where we are at just about now.

"Just about."

"Is she still insisting on going to Vegas?"

"Yeah. We'll be there tonight."

"Does she realize she could be out of that van and sitting in her beautiful suite in a little more than an hour? We're just off the highway and up the mountain."

"Deb..." I glance at Ma, who frowns and looks back out the window.

"I know, I know," she says—which could be her motto: *Debbie Knows*. "She wants to see Aaron. I wouldn't mind seeing him once in a while myself, but he makes no effort whatsoever, and we're only five hours away."

"You ever go up to see him?"

"I'm a busy woman, David. Quite a bit busier than I imagine he is. Listen, are you making sure she's taking her blood pressure pills every day?"

"Of course," I say, though I haven't actually thought of it, even once.

"God, I really wanted her here today. This has thrown off my entire plan."

"Look, it's the way things worked out, Deb. Can one or two more days really make that big a difference?"

"I know you don't want to understand this, David, but I've waited a long, long time for this. Okay? And not only that. I have a lot of people to take care of over here. I blocked out today to take care of getting mom moved in. I don't think you realize all the things Clint and I had to do just to make her coming here possible. We've got a waiting list for this place that's years long. The fact is, she should have come out here years ago. And if mom lived here, maybe we'd get a visit from you guys once in a while, too. My kids hardly know our side of the family, and that bothers me. It shouldn't be that way."

"You don't take too many trips back east to visit us either, Deb. The highway runs both ways, no?"

"That's true. But I've *got* to be the busiest one of us by far. You don't understand. I don't get summers off. I don't have a month off in the winter between semesters."

"Which is a choice you make. Maybe you like to be busy. Maybe you *need* to be busy."

"Okay, look, I didn't call so you could play shrink with me. I *am* busy. Another word for it is productive. Responsible. Getting things done for a lot of people."

"We'll be there sometime on Wednesday. Here. Say hi to Ma."

I thrust the phone toward Ma, who takes it but holds it a foot away from her head for a long few seconds before finally bringing it to her mouth and saying hello. Then I exhale some of the anger-steam that's built up in my gut, tell myself to look out, look up, enjoy the beauty of this place.

Ma listens, and once in a while gets in a polite, "Wow, that's nice." Debbie must be prepping her for all the fun she's going to be having from now on. When the conversation ends, Ma hands the phone back to me. "Okay," she says, meaning I don't know what.

"You *are* taking your pills every day, aren't you, Ma?"

"Of course." She sounds insulted.

"Just looking out for you, that's all."

* * *

Late afternoon. Road work has us creeping at ten or fifteen miles an hour, single file, down a road that feels mercilessly eternal (maybe Hell is a highway that gets you nowhere). We crawl past a gang of shirtless workers gathered around a jackhammer; they're white, black, brown, red, muscular and sweaty, and most, if not every one of them, as we pass, takes a glance into the van. A few, when they lay eyes on my sister, lewdly grin. Naïve thought: if the urge to do real good in the world had even a tenth of the strength of the sexual urge, life on earth would be glorious.

I stare through a drifting haze of desert dust at a procession of eighteen wheelers and RV's, though the vehicle just ahead of me is an impatient-looking red Ferrari, a flyer forced to crawl.

My thoughts wander around; I can't seem to steady a thought long enough to see it through: the article I'm doing on a thumb-sucking, violence-prone 8-year old girl whose family I studied last year in Newark; Marie's fine, silky pubic hair; the day Aaron left for college.

The day Aaron left for college. A hot, humid morning near the end of summer. Ma, Da, Debbie and I stood outside the house with him waiting for his ride to come. He'd gotten a scholarship to be part of some special new Humanities program at SUNY Oswego, which is way the hell up on Lake Ontario. In the image my memory offers, nobody is saying much. Aaron's looking down the street, tapping his foot. When his ride finally comes, he gives Ma the old, awkward Stepenski semi-hug and peck kiss. He shakes Da's hand but doesn't look him in the eye, and Da says something like, "Okay then, son." Which I take to mean, *we've had a lousy relationship, and I've had to hit you, but I love you.* Maybe though, in light of the story Ma told about Da's Jesus dream, what he really meant was *I love you and I'm sorry I hit you.* I'm sure Aaron took it as, *okay then, son, looks like you've finally managed to slip out of my grasp.* He turns away from Da and gives Debbie and me a half-wave, gets into the car and it drives off down Old Richmond Path. Jeanette, of course, is up in her room, though I feel her bitterness toward Aaron pulsing through the heat like a ghostly presence.

Once Aaron was gone, he rarely came home. He'd visit at Christmas for a week or two, but almost never in the summer, choosing instead to get a job in the town of Oswego or on campus. Or he'd stay at a friend's or a girlfriend's house for the summer. He always had girlfriends –smart hippie chick types who, despite their feminist leanings, tended to mother him. One summer he hitchhiked around the country. I remember getting a postcard from him from Rocky Mountain National Park, up in Colorado. It said, *Pretty cool out here. You should see it if you can. -A.* Right after graduation he went to Iowa to get an MFA in Poetry. Started right up with a summer session so that we didn't see him for more than a week or two that summer either. And then after Iowa he turned into the enigmatic gypsy poet adjunct that he is today.

* * *

At Kingman, we leave I-40. First time we're off that road in three days. Before we get onto 93, which will take us up past the Hoover Dam and into Vegas, we stop and eat dinner in a Pizza Hut. It's only six-thirty but almost everything in the salad bar has already turned brown at the edges. I eat a heap of it anyway. I've got it in my head that I ought to get myself as healthy as possible to survive these next few days, and a heap of brown lettuce and some tough-skinned cherry tomatoes is the healthiest thing they have.

"Has anyone called him to let him know we're almost there?" Jeanette says between bites of a chicken wing. "Knowing him, we'll go all the way up there and he'll be gone to Alaska already."

"Oh, he wouldn't do that," Ma says.

I sigh, take out my phone, dial.

"Hello," a young-sounding female voice says.

"Hi. I'm calling for Aaron. Stepenski. Do I have the right number?"

"Just a second," the woman says curtly. The sound goes muffled but I can make out her voice saying, "It's some guy."

Then, "David?"

"Hey. Yeah, it's me. Who was that that answered?"

"A friend."

"Ah. Well, listen. We're close. We're in Kingman. Be there in a few hours, I guess."

Jeanette's phone rings. She pulls it out of her shirt pocket, turns and whispers into it. Our pretty, chubby, intelligent-eyed waitress comes to ask if we need anything else. Ma is trying to listen to both Jeanette's and my conversations, and doesn't notice the waitress.

Aaron says something I don't quite hear. "Say that again."

"Would you like anything else?" the waitress repeats.

I shake my head no.

"Where are you staying?" Aaron asks again, with an edge of impatience.

"Uh, the Comfort Inn, I think. It's on Paradise Avenue, but not down in the center of town. A little ways out, it looks like on the map."

"I know where it is. You probably won't get settled in until after ten or so, if you're still in Kingman. You're probably exhausted. How about I come over in the morning?"

"Hold on." I feel a thud to the side of my brain when I remember again that I've agreed to meet Sheri. Why the hell did I do that? I glance at Ma and start to convey Aaron's suggestion. But Ma seems to be praying. In any case, her head is bowed and her eyes are closed.

"You know what," I say, "I think Ma would like to see you as soon as possible. And we've got to head back to Deb's early Wednesday morning anyway. So, why don't you come by tonight for a little bit?"

Long pause: "There's a lounge on the first floor," he says. "I'll meet you there around ten, ten-thirty."

"Good. See you then."

"Hey, David."

"Yeah?"

"Is Jeanette planning to hang out with us?"

"I don't know," I lie. "Why? You want me to ask her to come?"

"No, no."

"You want to ask her? I can put her on."

"No. See you later."

I put the phone down on the table and tell Ma that things are all set. We'll get together with Aaron tonight.

"Good," she says. The muscles of her face shift as she screws up her resolve.

The waitress has returned for one more attempt. "Dessert, anyone? Our Death-by-Chocolate is heavenly."

I hear Jeanette say into her phone, "I'll have to give that some serious thought. Can I call you Wednesday?" She sounds, by her standards, almost giddy.

"So?" the waitress says, when once again none of us responds to her question.

"Death-by-Chocolate, did you say?" Jeanette asks and she pockets her phone. "I'd love some of that." She *smiles* at the waitress, who beams back at her.

Ma says, "Oh, I guess I could stand a piece of that, too. It isn't too big, is it?"

"It's pretty big," the waitress says, more to Jeanette than Ma.

I, too, agree to indulge; I'll experience a little death.

"So, Jeanette," Ma says when the waitress heads off to retrieve the killer deserts, "who was that you were you talking to?"

"Oh," Jeanette replies, "that was Mia. From the church we went to in Oklahoma yesterday."

"Oh, yes," Ma says, and bravely smiles. "Very nice woman."

I remember Father Baylis slowly lifting his pointer finger and saying, *You cannot solve a problem with the same consciousness that created it.*

* * *

Before we're allowed to approach the Hoover Dam, we have to take our place at the end of a long line of vehicles waiting to pass through a security checkpoint. Thankfully, the line's moving at a pretty good pace. When we finally arrive at the makeshift checkpoint—a few barricades, some trouble lights set up on a scaffold, two police cruisers—a thin, crew-cutted policeman takes a cursory look at the van. He tips his hat and winks at Jeanette, who frowns, and waves us on.

A thick, floating mist fills the night air as we drive the switchbacks of the Hoover Dam. The whole scene feels so unreal that my fingers tremor on the steering wheel. Lack of sleep, the imminence of seeing my gloomy brother, Marie and the kids so far out of my reach. Sheri. I'm not sure that I won't, at any moment, drift into incoherence. Or worse, drive into the damn Colorado river.

"Wow," Ma says, snapping pictures at the haze and the unfathomable wall of concrete and water and dark sheets of rock. "It's amazing what man can do when he puts his mind to it, isn't it? This is incredible."

Her voice, making its awed observations, locates me. Drive. Stay on the road.

But now I'm picturing terrorists in a cockpit, that haunting Atta guy, the darkness surrounding his intense and intent eyes. As the plane is about to slam into the tower, he's muttering praise to Allah. At the same instant there's some young Catholic, Staten Island secretary, somebody I might have gone to school with, now engaged to a Staten Island, bar-hopping, Giants-fan fireman, glancing out one of those tall, narrow World Trade Center windows and realizing, half-consciously, that she's about to be incinerated.

Praise be to Allah.

Dear Jesus, save us.

I can't go there myself, but I do understand the simplicity of atheism.

Full-blown, lavender night; we drive along a dark, bending mountain pass until, finally, we come out of a long final curve and behold a sea of lights in the valley below us. At first, I think it's Vegas, but I see from a road sign it's Henderson, a Vegas burb, I guess. Fifteen minutes further down the highway, which is suddenly teeming with traffic the likes of which we haven't seen since we left the east coast, we enter the city of Las Vegas. I take a deep breath to see if corruption and greed have an odor. Jeanette leans up from the back and reads out directions. There are frequent exit signs and alternative routes and cars flying by at ninety miles an hour, and I feel like I'm taking three lives into my own hands (not to mention the ones at home that will be changed forever) as I try to steer us across four lanes in time to get off at our fast-approaching right-lane exit.

We make it, somehow, and then it's a matter of creeping along a congested boulevard bordered by hotels and shops and second and third-tier casinos (we can see the big ones all lit up in the distance) until finally we spot the lesser neon sign for the Comfort Inn.

When I pull into an empty spot in the lot, it's exactly ten-forty-one. I breathe a long breath and shut off the engine; the trusty van shivers down to stillness like an angered stallion.

"I'll go check us in," Jeanette mutters and hurries ahead of us toward the front doors.

Ma and I walk slowly across the lot together, bags slung over our shoulders, not knowing quite what to say in the face of our impending reunion with prodigal Aaron. Ma stops suddenly, says she thinks she's left her camera in the van, but after a bit of digging around in her purse, finds it.

"Well, at least I haven't lost this, right? Can you imagine?"

"You're doing great, Ma. You haven't lost a thing."

In the lobby, Jeanette emerges like a spy from a little phone cubby behind the continental breakfast bar. She hands me a key. We see the doors to the lounge over in the far corner of the lobby, but we all head toward the elevators, Jeanette in the lead.

"Shouldn't we check and see if he's here?" Ma says.

"Let's throw our stuff in our rooms and wash up first," I suggest.

As we wait for the elevator, Ma says to Jeanette, "Are you sure you won't come? Just for a minute? Just to say a quick hello to him? It's not asking that much, is it? No matter what, he's still your brother."

"Sorry, Ma. It's more than I can do."

Why? Why is it more than you can do? I want Ma to say to her. I want to know. Maybe I'll get some insight into why it's so hard for *me* to see him.

In the elevator Jeanette pushes a square plastic button with a lighted number 5 on it. D? A? V? I? D?

"You could come," I say to Jeanette as we begin to rise, "and just say something like, 'I can't stay but I wanted to say hi.' Then he'll say hi to you and you can go. Just make one simple gesture, Jeanette. Even something like that might open the door a little, lead to something."

"I don't want anything to lead to anything."

"Okay, fuck it then."

"*Da*vid."

"Sorry, Ma."

At the fifth floor a small tone sounds and the doors slide open. We start walking, but Jeanette stops.

"Look, David, since you don't know anything about this, you shouldn't try to fix it. Okay? Some things *can't* be fixed. I finally realized that with Sheri, and it's just as true with Aaron. And you know what, I can live with it. And you'll be a lot better off when you finally learn to live with it, too. And, Ma, I'm sorry that's the way it is, but it's okay. It isn't the end of the world."

"How do you know?" Ma says.

We all gaze down the yellow-tinted hall full of yellowish doors, and go find ours.

Agitated, I flip on the T.V., surf, stop at the local news. A chiseled male face with perfect hair and a deep voice finishes his report on the winner of a teen beauty pageant and moves on to a report about a news conference held earlier in the day by the mayor of Las Vegas in which he and the chief of police assured the public that, despite persistent rumors, the odds of an imminent terrorist attack on the city are "slim to none" due to unprecedented security measures.

As I'm about to go out the door, I realize I've forgotten to call Marie this evening. Back home, it's after midnight. I wonder why she didn't try to call me?

Ma's ready to go when I knock. She's wearing clean white slacks and a pretty aqua sweater that she must have been saving for a special occasion. "You look beautiful," I tell her.

She makes a face.

"Accept a compliment, Ma."

"Okay."

Waiting for the elevator, she says, "If I could do it over again, I would do it a lot differently. We would all talk more. If two of you were having a problem with each other, I would sit you down together and make you talk it out, and not just let it...just..."

"Fester?"

"Yes. And I would have us all pray together about it. That's what you and Marie do with your kids, isn't it?"

"Well, we used to. We've kind of gotten away from that."

"And there wouldn't be all that hitting," Ma says emphatically. "My goodness. The hitting made everything so tense. Sometimes it was like walking on eggshells the whole day. I hope he's in a good mood. I hope none of the kids does anything that upsets him. I should have asked him to stop when you were all still little. I should have said no hitting after the very first time he did it." Her eyes are plaintive, childlike. "In those days, the wives didn't tell the husbands what to do and the husbands just did whatever they learned from *their* fathers."

"Yeah. But things are changing now. For the better." I'm about to say something to the effect of, men have had their chance and blown it. Let's give women a chance to run the show. But the elevator arrives and, hesitantly, we step in. A small, bent, old man with tubes in his nose and a canister of oxygen on a transom stands counting bills in his gnarled, quivering hands. Covering his small head is a red, white, and blue baseball cap that says *God Bless America.*

"At least," Ma says softly, "I hope you kids have learned from some of the mistakes we made."

"In some ways. We don't hit our kids. I don't think Debbie and Clint do either. But we make so many of our own mistakes, Ma. And I feel the same way as you do: I hope our kids when they're grown won't repeat them. New generation, new set of problems, new set of mistakes. But mistakes or not, I love you. We all love you. You're a good mother and even better grandmother."

"I love you, too," she says. She says it almost easily, and it's lovely to hear. "I just wish your father and I had been better at showing our love."

I put my arm around her shoulder and press her body into my side as we come to a halt at the lobby.

"*Finally,*" a burly man looking into the opening elevator door says. He's wearing an orange, pelican-themed Hawaiian shirt and a thick, gold necklace. "Jesus Christ, I been waitin' a friggin' hour. What the hell took you so long?"

Ma and I stare at the man. Then we hear a weak voice behind us say, "I got the shits, Tommy. Gimme a break, will ya?"

"Give *me* a break. You ate too much Mexican at the friggin' buffet again, din ya? Come on. We're wasting the whole friggin' night here." He turns and walks away toward the doors.

The old guy stuffs his billfold into his front pants' pocket and stutter-steps through the lobby, pulling his life source behind him. Ahead of him the burly man shakes his head and glances at his watch as he holds the door open and waits. "Maybe you shouldn't of come on this trip, pops. You been a big pain in my ass."

"Poor man," Ma says. "Can you imagine a son talking like that?"

It's twenty past eleven, and Aaron's not in the lounge. All the tables are full of Vegas revelers, so Ma and I find a pair of tall stools at the bar. Certain that even a sip of hard booze will sink me, I've ordered us both mugs of Corona Light.

"What time is he supposed to meet us?" Ma asks, watching her wedge of lime float in a thin golden foam.

"I think we said ten-thirty. Might have said eleven. I'm sure he'll be here soon."

I check my cell phone to see if I somehow missed a call, and just as I'm looking at the little grey/blue screen, the thing rings. "Hello?"

"Where are you? Are you in Vegas yet? You said you would call me."

"Sheri. Hi. Where are you?"

"I thought you'd call by now."

"We just got here, Sher. Like, five minutes ago."

"You're not bullshitting me, are you, David? Don't, okay? Not you, too."

"We just got here. Look, hold on a minute." I cover the phone. "Ma, it's Sheri. I have to talk to her, but I can't talk here. Do you mind if I go out into the lobby for a few minutes? You'll be okay?"

"I'll be fine. My goodness why does she keep calling you two?"

"Because she doesn't know what the hell to do with herself. Listen, order yourself something to eat." I tap the bills on the bar. "I'll be right back."

The lobby is bustling and there's no quiet place to sit or stand, so I head for the doors, telling Sheri to hold on. Outside, the night air is warm and still; I can't find any moon in the sky. I do spot a small, lighted pool in which nobody appears to be swimming or lounging, and head toward it. I have to go through a gate to get into the pool area, which requires that I use my key card, so I tell Sheri to hold on one more minute. Desperate impatience oozes from the phone.

"Okay. I'm good now, Sher. So where are you?"

"Some dumpy Motel Six. It's just down the street from the casino that looks like the New York skyline."

"Are you okay?"

"Oh, David."

"Are you drinking, Sher?" I drop into a plastic lounge chair under a three-quarters open umbrella.

"No, I'm not okay, and yes, I'm drinking. Johnny Walker Red, to be specific." She lets me hear her slosh the bottle.

"Maybe you've had enough for tonight, though, huh? Look, we're about to meet with Aaron. Which is a little tense, so..."

"Jeanette's not there. Jeanette doesn't want to see Aaron."

"True."

"I know she doesn't," she says with drunken conviction.

"You probably know more about it than I do."

"I know Jeanette better than anybody. I know her life and I know her soul. And I know...a lot, David."

A man and a woman roughly my age, in their bathing suits, stroll out from a side door of the hotel and come through the gate. They look at me, smile, take seats on lounge chairs at the opposite side of the pool and kick off their sandals.

"Oh, David, if I could only sleep with her again, even for just one more night. At least I could be happy one last time."

"Sher, that wouldn't make you happy. Not if you knew it was the last time. It would be torture."

"She doesn't like sex very much."

"What?" Though I don't mean for her to repeat it; I have no interest in hearing about my sister's sex life.

"Her libido isn't that strong," Sheri says. "Mine's out of control—when it comes to Jeanette, anyway. Sometimes she liked it. It depended on her mood. She's so moody. But, oh, David, when I knew we were going to make love on a certain night, all that day would be magical. I'd be all smiles and I'd give people a break when I pulled them over for speeding or whatever, and it would just build up and my heart would pound and I could hardly wait for night to come. I'd bring home flowers and wine. I'd always get home first and be waiting for her. I liked to be in the bed when she came up to the room. It was like our little dance, you know? You can't imagine how exciting it was."

"No, I get it." I hear a splash and look up to see that the couple has taken to the water. I watch their bodies glide, side by side, under the glimmering, underlit blue. They come up together mid-pool and laugh.

"All day I'd dream about her beautiful perfect body beside mine, the way it would feel to run my fingers down her back, her tiny, shy kisses." The more she talks, the more she sounds like she's under hypnosis. "...until finally it was really happening. I'd think to myself, this is too good to be true. But we were really there in each other's arms, naked, free, in love. Oh, God, David. It has to happen again. I have to have her again."

I can't help it, thinking of Marie, her face, her eyes, that body. I have to have her again.

"Sher," I say. "It will happen again, just with someone else. Someone you love just as much as you love Jeanette. Even more. It's going to happen. Trust me. But, look, right now I've got to go see Aaron. Don't drink anymore, okay? Get some sleep. You have to take care of yourself."

No reply; just a palpable disbelief that I intend to get off the phone.

"We'll talk tomorrow," I say. "Okay? I'll call you first and then I'll come over and we'll talk."

I hear the alcohol swashing down her throat. "When you see Aaron," she says, "tell him he's a bastard for what he did."

"What? What do you mean?"

"Your father would never even have wanted to know. Why else would he beat *him* up too, if he didn't do anything wrong? I still don't understand why Jeanette loved him so much. He was a bastard, your father. Aaron was a bastard, too. I could be her whole family for her. Why doesn't she see that?"

"Sheri, I'm not following this. I don't know what you're talking about."

"Jeanette said you and your mother were out somewhere. Your father didn't want your mother to know. Or you either. He made them swear not to tell. He was always trying to protect her from the truth. Like Jeanette being a lesbian was such a great sin. *He* was the sinner."

"What are you talking about, Sheri? Were Jeanette and Aaron doing something? Something sexual? Is that it?"

"*No*. No, David. Jeanette never had any desire to be sexual with any guy. You're mixing up the bastards in your family with the bastards in mine."

In the far corner of the pool, the man and woman are cuddled, murmuring. I see mostly the man's muscular back. Then I notice the woman's bikini top floating in the water beside them.

"Sheri, I'm going to call you tomorrow, okay? We can talk about all these things. Put the bottle away now, please. You're only going to make yourself sick."

"David, I need you. I need you. Don't go yet."

"Look, it's close to midnight and my mother's in the bar and probably so is Aaron. I've got to go."

I hear swigging.

"Sheri?"

"I am so fucking alone, David. I don't have a soul in this world. You're the only person in the world who even gives a shit. But maybe you don't either."

My eyes close. "I do. And I'll help you, Sher, any way I can. I'll come by tomorrow and we'll have a good talk. In the meantime, please get some sleep. Please. Put the booze away and rest. Okay? Good night."

They're making love right there in the corner of the pool, right there in the rippling water like I'm not even here. And really, I'm not.

* * *

I wrestle with whether I should go find Sheri at the Motel Six tonight or just hope to God she's okay when I see her tomorrow. I know I can't take this much longer, and Da's voice, garbled through a fat cigar, answers: "Can't take it, huh? What choice do you have, mister? Stop complaining and *do* something." And he's right.

Before I step back into the hotel, I stop, take out my phone, dial home. It's eleven-fifty here, almost three back east, an insane time to be calling.

As the phone rings I cringe, knowing that anyone on the other end who hears it will feel that awful alarm a call in the dead of the night has to trigger.

When a male voice says "Hello," I'm speechless for a second. I don't seem to know the voice. "Hello?" it says again.

"Teddy?"

"Who's this?"

"It's me. Daddy."

"Daddy?" His voice sounds a little less foreign using the word.

"Yeah. It's me. Were you expecting a call from your...from Alison? At this hour, buddy?"

Defensively, "No."

"Be straight with me, Ted."

"I am, dad. I'm not ex*pect*ing her to call me."

"But you were *awake*?"

"Yeah."

"It's so late, bud."

"I can't sleep."

"Is everything okay?"

"Everything's fine."

I hear my sigh amplified by the great, sudden silence Teddy and I create. "I hope you know you can talk to me. I'm here for you. Wherever I am, whatever I'm doing, if you need me, you're the priority. You understand?"

His "I know" betrays doubt.

"Listen, Teddy, I love you. I love you and..." and I wish this hotel room provided a manual for how to speak with a troubled, beloved kid who sits a couple thousand miles away and is suffering through maybe his first big emotional crisis.

"I know you do, dad," he says. "I know it."

"Good," I say. "Don't ever forget that. *Never, ever* forget that."

"Okay."

"So, is Mommy all right? Your sister? No problems with the neighbors or anything?"

"Wait. You *know*?"

"Know what?"

"Nothing."

"Tell me what you're talking about. Is it something to do with the neighbor? Brandon?"

What I feel is an untenable cocktail of rage and helplessness. But I have to be solid.

"Is he... like what's going on with him and mom?"

"Oh, mommy always liked him," I say. "In a neighborly way. You know, he's basically a good guy. She's a pretty good judge of character."

No reply.

"Anyway, do you and Alison sometimes call each other late at night?"

"*No,*" he says as if the idea is unfathomable.

"Look, if it makes it any easier for you to be straight with me, I'll tell you that I used to do that kind of thing. I used to call girlfriends at all hours of the night. It felt exciting, you know. Mind you, I wasn't *twelve.* Not even thirteen. But I used to do a lot of things, Teddy. Some of them were fun and more or less harmless and some of them, honestly, were stupid and dangerous and make me cringe when I think about them. My parents didn't know what I was doing or thinking about. We didn't talk much. And I guess, to tell you the truth, I'm a little afraid you won't want me to know half of what you're up to, either. Or even what's on your mind. You know what I mean? And I'm really afraid I won't know how to ask. So, just so you know, I want us to be able to keep in real touch with each other. Be as straight with each other as can be reasonably expected. I want you to feel like you can talk to me about anything."

There's silence, then, "Alison broke up with me. She likes some other kid."

At the sound of the dear boy's quivering voice, my own shaky heart pangs. "Ah, Teddy. Ah, you poor kid." I hear all the cliches of comfort in my head but I don't speak them. I shut up. And when I don't speak, the kid tells me, in his halting, awkward way just how bad it hurts.

I listen. I know he needs me to listen. Except, after a minute or two, I can't help telling him that I miss him. And that I love him like crazy. Which, damn it, shuts him up.

Into the thick silence I say, "Hey, sorry, Ted. I'm talking about myself, aren't I? How much I miss you, how much I love you. Blah, blah, blah. I'm sorry. I know it hurts like hell. I wish I could be there with you right now. I so wish that."

"Dad," he says, and he's crying now, "I saw mommy kiss that guy. That asshole, Brandon. Not like a real long kiss or anything. They were in the kitchen and they thought we were asleep but I was in the living room on the couch with the lights out. Why did she kiss him, dad? What is she *doing?* She's *married.*"

"Whoa, whoa. Hold on. What did you see?"

"He came over at like ten-thirty at night and fixed that drip in the faucet she's always complaining about. Then he stayed like another hour after he fixed it, just talking. I think they drank a bottle of wine. Then when he got up to leave, they just started kissing and then they saw me and got like freaked out but they tried to play it cool like it wasn't anything."

"It *wasn't* anything, Teddy. Adults kiss each other all the time. You know that. It's a sign of gratitude. I didn't get that damn leak fixed before I left and it bothered her. Look, please don't worry about it. I'm not concerned at all. But I've got to go. Uncle Aaron is waiting for me. I'm coming home soon. We'll have a good, long talk. We'll go to a ballgame. Right now though, try to get some sleep, okay? Please?"

"Okay."

She wouldn't. No way.

***

I do understand how men kill other men over love. If love is even what we're talking about.

Chapter Six
Tuesday, June 11, 2002

Revelations

There he sits, my hulking brother, hunched at the bar beside Ma like a human beast of burden. The sight of him floods me with a sudden, explosive love, a desire to run and embrace him, prodigal though he may be. I want to forgive him, ask his forgiveness, erase the history of our pain in a word or gesture. *Get at least this one thing right.* But before I quicken, I halt. Thirty feet from the bar, I stand and take in the sight: Aaron's wearing a ratty denim shirt; worn, gray (probably originally white) shorts; frayed low-top sneakers; no socks. I used to think of him, of his physical presence, as suggestive of an ancient willow tree in winter, with his hanging swirls of bark-brown hair, his thick limbs and broad, drooping shoulders. Ma looks tiny beside her eldest son, a delicate pastel perennial. She's fidgety as a toddler, head bobbing in answer to Aaron's soft-spoken questions and murmured replies.

I walk to the least crowded corner of the lounge, where there's a little leaning space along the wall.

"Say, fella, you all by yourself?"

A wiry, bald-headed man with a hearing aid looks up at me through his pink-tinted bottle glasses. The tan leisure suit he's sporting is just a tad big for him, but it works with the glasses in a naive, 70's kind of way. Before the towers fell, nobody would have thought of the 70's as an age of innocence.

"Let me buy you a drink why don't you?"

"No thanks," I say. "But thank you."

"Come on. I just won three grand over at Trump's place. *Three grand.* Swear to Christ." He glances around, bobs a few times on the balls of his tan, Rockport walking shoe-covered feet. "You here with somebody?" He looks to the left, looks to the right. "You ain't here with nobody, are you? Let me buy you a drink. We'll celebrate. Have a good time."

"Actually, I am here with some people. And anyway, I'm not drinking tonight. But congratulations on the windfall."

He inclines his head toward me. "Pinball? You want to play pinball? I'll play pinball. What the hell do I care?"

"I said *windfall*. Congratulations."

"Graduation, huh," the man says with a bemused smile. "You ain't got some free time right now? Ain't no graduation at this hour. Hey, I just won five friggin' grand. Let me buy you a drink, for God's sakes. Celebrate with me."

"I don't drink," I say, "I'm in recovery." The statement is, apparently, loud enough to cause patrons in the immediate vicinity to turn and, by the look in at least some eyes, pity me.

"Hey, I understand, I understand," the man says. "Everybody got their problems. That's no shame. Come on, I'll buy you dinner instead. I know a good place right down here on Paradise. We'll grab a cab. Unless you got a car maybe?" He eyes me up and down, with a little too much emphasis on down. "Tell you the truth, you look like a guy could use a little fun. Come on." With a grin, he breaks into a little three-step shuffle. "I still got it, if that's what you're wondering."

"No, that's not what I'm wondering."

"Look, I'm just trying to be a nice guy here. You rather be alone? Fine. Suit yourself. Go get yourself a nice glass of milk, why don't you?"

I don't want to retort with equal mean-spiritedness, but what comes out of me is "God bless you," though it may be the most hostile utterance of those words in the history of human conversation.

"What's that, fella?" the guy says. He's up on his toes, inclining his hearing-aided ear toward my mouth.

Now I feel obligated, to God if not to this man, to repeat the words. In a neutral tone, I say, "I said, 'God bless you.'"

"Up yours, buddy. Ya fuckin' freak ya." And shaking his head, he walks off.

I am a man in the middle of a career that involves observing, documenting, and trying to make sense of *"a range of complex human behaviors in familiar environments."* But really, I don't get it. Though colleagues in the field occasionally blurb me as an "expert" (which simultaneously strokes my ego and makes me wince; it's called imposter syndrome), what I am is an eternal novice. One colleague in the department, Mary Jean Nunn, who does her primary work in the homes of families of women who are sent to prison for violent crimes against children, says her mantra to her grad students is simply, "Let nothing human beings are capable of surprise you." I, on the other hand—and maybe it's willful naiveté, maybe a failure of imagination—I find far too many of the things human beings are capable of—myself included—downright baffling.

Ma glances around the lounge; I've been gone too long. Or maybe she needs rescue from too much one-on-one with Aaron. After a long, calming breath, I head to the bar. Both Ma and Aaron turn at the same instant.

"Is everything okay with Sheri?" Ma says straight off.

"She'll be all right. She's still upset, but she'll be okay."

"Did she make it home yet?"

I shake my head to avoid the outright lie, then with a quarter-turn, face my brother. The first thing, the very first thing, I notice is the pale, inch-long scar over his left eyebrow. I see myself slash him with the razor edge of my crude walking stick and quickly, guiltily, drop my gaze straight *into* his eyes. For a pain and love-mingled instant, we are a pair of dark reflecting pools.

Aaron's eyes drop away first. "How are you, David?"

"I'm okay." I put out my hand to shake his, and he brings his toward mine cautiously, as if I might be playing a trick on him. But before our hands clasp, I drop my hand and lean up to give him a hug instead. This is not something he and I do, and although I'm a little surprised at my gesture, Aaron, judging by his slow-motion lurch backward, is scandalized. I keep coming though, press my chest into his, put my arms around his shoulders and squeeze all the more tightly for his resistance—the equivalent of: *fuck you, bro; I love you and you're going to let me show you.* He taps my back a few times with an open palm, then eases himself away. I drop my arms, step backward, and look down the bar at the long row of silhouetted heads all ringed in smoky, slightly diabolical-looking halos.

"So," Aaron says, "life's okay by you?"

"Life's okay."

"Ma's been telling me about the trip. Good times." He presses his big finger into a drop of condensation that quivers on the lip of his glass. "Hey, look, thanks for bringing her up here. I know it's a huge hassle."

"She insisted. And, you know, I wanted to see you, too."

"Right." The first appearance of his trademark life-weary smile. "Didn't mean to imply you were merely playing chauffeur." Lifting a glass of murky, blood-colored wine, Aaron sips. He says, "Let me buy you a drink."

"I'll get it."

"Those are your tens on the bar, David," Ma says. "I got myself a bowl of soup by the way. Turkey noodle. It wasn't very hot but tasty. A little too salty. Thank you."

"You could have asked them to heat it up, you know. Are you sure that was enough?"

"Oh, sure. It came with nice fresh hot bread. The bread was hotter than the soup. I'm good and full." She climbs off her stool. "Boys, I'm going to the ladies room. Don't let him take my wine away."

"Over our dead bodies," I say.

"Good." She takes a few steps and stops. "Oh, you know what I mean."

When the bartender comes by, I order a Corona Light.

"She looks good," Aaron says. "Sometimes, when I haven't seen her for a while, I expect to find this really old, feeble woman. One foot in the grave, you know? I braced myself for that. I was pleasantly surprised."

"Guess I see her often enough that I don't experience that."

Aaron scratches his earlobe. No earring anymore, I notice.

"So," I say. "Alaska, huh?"

"Yeah. Kotzebue. Ever hear of it?"

"Way up north, isn't it? Coastal? I read a study somebody did up that way with the Innuits. Sounded like a pretty grim place, to tell you the truth. Though you'll never hurt for wild salmon."

Smirk. "You've been in Vegas for what, two hours now? You must be getting that feeling about this place, too, huh? Anybody hit you up for money yet? Or tried to sell you a piece of the desert? Offered to share a disease?"

"Just a minute ago a very friendly older gentleman invited me to dinner. I don't want to judge anybody prematurely, but I think he had some strange plans for us."

"It's either pathos or bathos here. The twin gods of Vegas. They dress up in neon and polyester and take turns running the show."

My beer arrives and I take a small sip. "A place like this must be desperate to keep its poets, Aaron. The fact that there's going to be one less of them offering a modicum of lyricism, of...*soul*—that can't be a good thing."

He eyes me, possibly suspicious of my use of the word soul. (My colleague in the English department, Rich, claims that poets in the postmodern era may only use the word ironically. Talk about a self-damning rule of thumb.) "I've got no soul left to give to this sinkhole," Aaron says. "Anyway, there's a pile of compelling reasons for me to leave, which I won't burden you with. Plus, I'm just restless. The curse of my existence. One of them, anyway."

I can almost feel the romance of Aaron's restlessness, his lifelong affair with wanderlust. Or should I say escapism? To travel down that old highway of spirit and bone one more time into the great unknown, into this year's promised land. And away from whatever unpleasantness you leave in your wake. I mean, how poetic can you get, right? Straight out of the textbook for high romantic living. Except lives are affected when the troubadour decides to move on. People get hurt. There's certainly a trail of wounded lives in Aaron's wake: three ex-wives (at least two of whom were devastated by his departure), us. Who knows who else? For a long childhood decade, I was the biggest fan Aaron had in this world. And so maybe I expected, as we were growing up, a little more big-brotherly direction about looming adulthood from him.

"Mind if I ask who that was who answered the phone before?"

Aaron sighs. "A woman I've been seeing."

"She got a name?"

Deadpan: "No, actually."

"Names are overrated anyway."

"Some."

"Is it serious?"

"What kind of name would that be?" This, followed by the weary smile.

"She's not going north with you, I take it."

"No. That wouldn't work."

"How'd you meet her?"

"I helped her out of a jam, I guess."

"But you used a little too much force?"

"That's an unfortunately truer statement than you realize."

When Aaron lifts his wine glass to his lips, I lift my beer to mine. Here's to caustic riddles that never get resolved.

"I was straight with her about who I was, what I was and wasn't capable of. How many times can you make the same mistake, after all? I thought I made it clear to her that we'd be wise to think of ourselves more as friends than lovers. I thought she was in basic agreement with that."

"Until you told her you got the urge for going, right?"

"Truth be told, it was more than an urge. Let's just say I received a sign that it was time to hit the road."

I raise my eyebrows. "A sign?" Like Da's Jesus dream. Of course, in order to receive such a dream, you either have to be receptive or it comes as one of Flannery's annihilating blasts.

"You don't want to know, David. Trust me."

Where have I heard that line before? "May I ask how long you've been together?"

"Two, two and half years. There are complications. I'm not going to go into it."

"Fine," I say. All these cryptic remarks are making me weary anyway. "Your business is your business. But I do feel for her. I mean, if you're in love with somebody for two and half years and they suddenly announce they're up and moving to Alaska...."

The skin around Aaron's lips tightens like the purse strings of a miser. "Look, David, it's nice of you to sympathize with Sue Ellen, but let's be frank: you don't know anything about her or about us, so you're really in no position to take a position on this, are you?"

He's right, of course. And, yes, I see the theme emerging here, slow learner that I am.

Ma returns from the ladies room, her face bright with animation.

"Can you imagine what just happened to me?" Before we can even try, she says, "A man offered me three hundred dollars to let him take my picture holding up my middle finger at the camera. Can you imagine? He said it's for some magazine advertisement he's doing. He said all I had to do was sign a release and he'd pay me the money in cash."

"Did you do it?" Aaron asks.

Pure incredulity. "Aaron!" Ma says, "That's disgusting. Three hundred dollars would be nice, but I'm not doing something like that for anybody or for any amount of money."

I live in a country where people bare their deepest, crudest secrets, not to mention most of their flesh, in front of howling, hooting T.V., on-line, or other sundry audiences, a country where athletes who rape women or beat their girlfriends half to death get worshiped for their on-field statistics; where, for a fat paycheck, people are willing to get married on prime time to louts they must know are louts but what the hell is a vow but a bunch of gibberish anyway so why not? And here's Ma refusing to lift a finger to contribute to the culture of greed, crudity, and vapidity. I mean, like so many things these days, it makes me want to cry. "Thatagirl, Ma," I say, voice cracking, and give her a soft love-punch on the shoulder.

Ma blushes, looks away, takes her seat at the bar.

Aaron hands her her glass of wine, which trembles in her hand as she tries to sip.

"Yeah, she won't sell her soul for three hundred bucks," Aaron says to me in a low voice, "but she'll leave the place she loves for free to please her demanding daughter."

I look coldly into my brother's eyes and say under my breath, "Don't push this, Aaron. This ordeal has been trying enough on everybody. The decision's made. Nobody's thrilled with it, but she agreed."

"Stop whispering, you two," Ma says. "Boy oh boy, I'll tell you, this has been some trip. Wait till Edna hears about it. She won't believe half of it. Oh, and that reminds me, I want to take a picture of the two of you together. Okay? Do you mind? And can we do it right now, while I remember?" She rummages through her bag for her camera. "I know it's in here. And before you leave me in Arizona, remind me to take one of you with Jeanette, too, okay, David?"

At the mention of Jeanette, Aaron's head drops off an invisible shelf.

"Oh, thank God, here it is. I know I'm going to leave it somewhere. I'll never forgive myself if I do."

"That's a nifty little camera," Aaron says. He takes and looks it over.

"I've got a whole documentary of our trip in there. You can put hundreds of pictures on one of those tiny little disky things. Go over there. Get close together boys."

Aaron and I stand up, side by awkward side.

"Wait a minute," Ma says. "I can't fit you both in yet." She has some difficulty with the zoom feature, so she takes a few steps backward instead. Just as she does, some guy turning suddenly from a conversation takes three strides and smacks into her. She manages to stay upright but the camera fumbles out of her hands and hurtles to the floor. In the second or two it takes me to realize what's happened, Aaron has already lunged at the guy and grabbed and lifted him by the collar.

"*Whoa*," I say, and slap my hand down hard on my brother's arm before it can spring forward and shatter bones in the guy's skull.

"Sorry, man, sorry," he pants. "Total accident." His hands rise up as if he's surrendering. He's in his late twenties or so, with long, slicked back hair and a black leather camera bag strapped over his shoulder. "My mistake. Totally sorry."

"Damn right it's your mistake. You almost knocked down an old lady, asshole." Aaron's face has blossomed to crimson; I can feel the cables of muscle in his arm throbbing under the skin.

"Let him go, bro. He's sorry."

But Aaron tightens his grip on the guy, literally lifts him off the floor, then drops him free. As he hurries away, patrons' eyes linger on us.

Ma checks the camera for damage. "It doesn't look like anything broke," she says to me; she's afraid to look at Aaron.

"You know, that was the same man who wanted to take my picture for three hundred dollars," Ma says.

"If I'd known that," I say, "I would have let Aaron break his face open."

"Oh, you would not. Anyway, never mind. Let's take the picture now, okay?"

But Aaron needs more time for the ice to melt, so for a few uncomfortable moments Ma and I make small talk about the camera. *So well built, to get knocked around like that and keep working.*

When we sense that Aaron's ready to resume the photo shoot, Ma again takes a few cautious steps backward. She looks into the LCD screen as Aaron and I resume our pose in front of the bar. I sling my arm over my brother's shoulder and feel Aaron's body stiffen as if I've injected him with strychnine.

"That's nice," Ma says. "Oh, darn it. Wait, hold on. Don't move." She lowers the camera and starts to fiddle with it. "Oh, no, I hope the shutter thing didn't get broken."

I keep my arm where it is while Ma repeatedly presses a button that doesn't respond. I can hear Da saying with barely-controlled patience, *Don't force it, Lillian. Take your time and figure out what the problem is.* But Ma never quite got with Da's program in that way. She did, and *does,* try to force things, not being nearly as patient with the physics of the objects of the world as Da was. Maybe that was 'unconsciously on purpose,' as they say—her small act of rebellion. Maybe it was the fact that in so many important ways, she was nothing like him; a match made in Purgatory. Still, a match that lasted unto death.

Aaron's shoulder is literally twitching where my hand rests on it, and I know I should offer to look at the camera, but I doggedly hold my position. The old man who'd invited me to dinner walks by, still alone, a little more hunched than before. Muttering, he looks at me with my arm around Aaron's shoulder and shakes his head like I've betrayed him, like I've made an incredibly stupid choice. And it dawns on me that my *forcing* myself on Aaron is perverse, a selfish attempt to satisfy my own need for some kind of connection with him, even if only in this superficial way, even if it isn't what he wants. And for whatever reasons, in his life and in his body, Aaron clearly doesn't want it, doesn't need it like I do. So I lift my arm off of him just as Ma lifts the camera back up to her eyes.

"All set," she says and waits for us to resume our pose. When we don't, she says, "Oh David, do what you were doing before. That made such a nice picture."

"It's alright, Ma," I say. "This is good enough."

She frowns, refocuses, and finally snaps a picture. She tells us to stay there and snaps another. "Good. These will be beautiful."

With comical immediacy, Aaron and I both reach for our drinks. Ma examines her camera one more time and puts it back in her purse. Sipping my beer, I make fleeting eye contact with a woman standing alone a few feet away. She's older than I am but not much, with a hair color, metallic orange, that nature didn't produce. Her nose is long and crooked, her eyes, behind the long lashes and dark shadow, are sad, and her very open blouse reveals too much of her need. When she smiles at me, a smile full of melancholy, it takes no effort to mirror her smile.

"So, how's your sweet Marie?" Aaron asks.

"Fine, fine." I'd rather not think about her until I can talk with her, get this Brandon business straightened out. What Teddy saw, of course, was a thank you kiss, a peck.

"Hmm."

"Hmm?"

"No. You sound tentative, that's all."

"Long, unresolved story, to be honest. More later? Maybe?"

"Okay. Kids good?"

"Yeah, for the most part. They're going to miss Ma something awful though."

"Well, at long last you have a legitimate reason to take the family out west."

Does he mean that as a dig? That having him in the west hasn't been enough to motivate us to come out? I don't bother to point out that he's never formally invited us. He certainly wouldn't want us to stay with him. And we did come out to visit Debbie once, four or five years ago, when she and Clint were still in the old, less luxurious place. Debbie invited Aaron to come down to Flagstaff while we were there, but for some under-explained reason, he couldn't make it.

"We do what we can," I say.

"Certainly."

"So, how goes the writing?"

"Sill doing it. Another of my bad habits."

Ma, who I'd somehow forgotten was right there, says, "Are you publishing a lot of your poems, Aaron?"

He frowns. Or maybe grimaces. He looks past me to Ma, whose eyes go bashful and sad and look away. His elbows rest on the bar, and he lowers his head like a spacecraft landing on the pad of his long, interlocked fingers.

"Once in a while." Shrug. "Heard any good jokes lately?"

"If I have," I say, "I can't remember. Never could remember a joke."

"Oh, I heard a good one the other day," Ma says.

Aaron and I look at her.

"Okay. Here it is. There were these three men..." she says. "No, two men. No, three. Oh, was it two men or three men? I can't remember."

"It's okay, Ma," I say.

It's not okay to her. "I just heard it last week. It's very funny. Father Jerzy told it at Bingo..."

"Ma," Aaron says, "if it makes any difference, I don't like jokes. I prefer spontaneous wit."

"Some of them are good, though," Ma says. "This was a good one. Nothing dirty or bad words or anything."

Coming up to the bar, a woman of sixty or so with a pile of white hair and a small jewelry store's worth of silver hanging from her neck and wrists, turns and says to everybody in the vicinity, "Did you hear? They're closing Harrah's. A bomb scare. Terrorists, they said. But then somebody just said it turned out to be a hoax. Who knows anymore, right? Excuse me. Bartender. Oh, Jesus fucking Christ, he can't hear me. *Bartender. Yoo hoo.* God, I need a scotch."

Aaron mutters, "Blow the place up, for God's sake. That wouldn't be an act of terror, it'd be an act of mercy."

I raise my glass.

"Oh, Aaron," Ma says. "Don't say things like that." She adds in a lowered voice, "And what if there's an F.B.I. agent in here. They're arresting people for saying things like that nowadays. You have to be careful. They might not take it as a joke."

"All right then. I take it back. Hey, listen, I better get going. I'm still packing. That and getting rid of stuff."

"If you need storage, I've got plenty of room in my barn," I say. "I could take some things back in the van."

"Nah. Thanks anyway. I think I'll just have a bonfire. You want to meet me in the lobby tomorrow, around ten? I can show you guys around a little. There's some real pretty back country not too far away. Unless you were planning to play craps, Ma."

"I don't understand craps," she says. "I don't even like saying that word. I like the slot machines. But sightseeing would be even better. And I'm taking you both out to lunch. My treat."

"You have a car?" I ask Aaron. "Because if you don't we could come to your place."

"No, don't do that. I use Sue Ellen's car."

"Oh," Ma says. "I was hoping to see where you live."

"It would only depress you."

I picture second-hand books standing in a hundred crooked piles, covering half the floor space of some tiny, overheated or overcooled apartment, and old newspapers, beer and wine bottles, paper plates stained with the remains of the sauce of General Chao's Chicken. And handwritten drafts of long, complex poems about how nothing much matters in the godless universe.

We finish our drinks and collect our cash, minus three or four singles for the bartender.

In the lobby, I keep my hands in my pockets so Aaron can see that I'm not going to attempt anything foolish by way of sentimental displays of affection. In fact, after announcing that I'm going to go out to the van to see if I left my toiletry bag there, I simply give Aaron a wave and a "See you tomorrow."

Ma, though, rocks her body backward, thrusts it forward, and wraps her arms around his waist. At first Aaron looks flummoxed, but as I walk toward the doors, watching them over my shoulder, he appears to give in; he envelopes her into his big, gawky, sullen willow tree self. I come close to allowing myself the sulky, boyish thought: *when's the last time you hugged me like that, Ma,* but manage to nip it in its childish, when-are-you-going-to-get-over-it-David bud.

As I scuff my way out to the van, the night air silky and lukewarm, I feel like a man dreaming of himself walking across a parking lot in Las Vegas. How unlikely a setting for a man like him, who can't settle into a mode, a philosophy, a point of view, who wants everything about himself and everyone else to be at least a little bit different than it is. Overhead, he hears the parking lot lights buzz like trapped mosquitoes, and the louder buzz of a low-flying helicopter. And beyond the helicopter, he's pretty certain, he can hear the buzzing of the stars. He has a premonition that just beyond the visible depths of black, an asteroid is heading this way.

Movement in the little white Corolla up ahead startles me out of my gloomy sleepwalk. The dome light is on and my glance simply slides inside. A woman sits in the passenger seat, reading. She's got generous lips and long, dark, thick hair, and she's wearing a muslin blouse and a necklace of turquoise beads. As I pass, she looks up from her book and our eyes make fleeting contact, a completely expressionless exchange, like a cat looking at itself in a mirror. Nevertheless, intuitively I know she's the woman I spoke with on the phone when I called Aaron. His Sue Ellen. I'm certain she knows who I am, too. Beside her, lying curled up in the driver's seat, thumb in mouth, is a small body in pajamas. I think a boy.

When I get to the van, I linger by the driver door, watching the Toyota as I try to remember what I came out here for. Sure enough, Aaron comes lumbering through the lot toward the waiting car. When he arrives, he glances around before he opens the driver door. I duck a little, though I'm hidden anyway; he doesn't see me. Lifting the child, he lays it across the back seat, then climbs into the driver seat. The dome light goes off, the headlights and taillights come on, and away they go, into their mystery.

* * *

They're showing video of the bomb scare. Hundreds of people—dolled-up women in slinky dresses, elderly women with canes, tire-bellied men in NASCAR tee-shirts, young guys with gold chains and baseball caps on backward—everybody streaming out of the mammoth casino with eyes round as plates while policemen and firefighters jog grimly toward the building. We have seen this nightmare before. Except this episode turns out to be a false alarm: Sin City lives to sin another day. Nevertheless, for dramatic effect and just so nobody forgets what *could* happen, they cut to video of the first plane flying into the unsuspecting tower against a luminous September sky. I stare again at an image everybody in the universe has seen too many times, think again of the secretary who lifts her head from an inter-office envelope to see the huge gray nose of the plane about to obliterate her and slash a planet-wide scar into the psyche of the oblivious, benumbed, and contented masses —one of whom is me. She's muttering her last words again, *Oh, my God*. I shut the T.V. off.

My bones feel old as I walk to the window, but my soul feels older. In the immediate distance, Las Vegas, lights flashing and bells ringing and whistles blowing, parties on. But I stare at the shadowed outline of desert hills beyond the clamorous city. They loom, eerie and foreboding. I turn, glance at my cell phone, which lies recharging on the coffee table. The tiny envelope icon indicates a missed call. How'd that happen? I push the appropriate keys and hear Marie's voice. "Hi, honey. I just wanted to talk. I'm feeling kind of...I don't know. (Sniffle.) I...never mind. We'll talk. I need to talk about something. Call me tomorrow, please? Bye. But, look, don't worry. I want you to sleep, okay? You need your sleep. I...I love you, David. Please don't worry."

Please don't worry about what, damnit?

Tomorrow is a long time.

Settled into the bed, I open my Flannery O'Connor and reread this uplifting gem, which I'd read this morning but which didn't quite register: *I don't know if anybody can be converted without seeing themselves in a kind of blasting annihilating light, a blast that will last a lifetime.*

Oh, Christ.

* * *

The knocking on the door somehow gets incorporated into my dream. I'm driving through a scene of devastation: smoke, the guts of buildings, a few tattered, zombie-like people wandering through the wreckage. From the passenger seat somebody starts knocking on my head with his or her knuckles, but I'm afraid to turn and see who it is. That's when I realize that the knocking is coming from the real world.

"Just a minute," I call out, relieved to be rescued, for once, by real life. I climb out of bed and pull on my shorts. Daylight glows behind the curtains. I've been in the deep precincts of sleep, and still feel like I'm lingering on its outskirts.

Jeanette, wearing chinos and a mint green tee shirt that says "Free Trade Makes $ense," nods good morning.

"Hi there, sis," I mumble. I haven't called her "sis" in approximately thirty years. "Come on in."

"No thanks. Listen, after we drop Ma off tomorrow I'd like you to take me to the airport."

"What? Why?"

"Change of plans. I'm going to Oklahoma City for a few days. You don't mind driving back home alone, do you? I figured you'd be happy to be rid of me."

I sense that in her muted way she's thrilled to be telling me about this: the thrill of finding (yet another) new lover.

Although I assure her I can handle it, I do, in fact, feel some ambivalence. Call me a fool, but I was beginning to think she and I were starting to get somewhere. I don't need to be best friends with my sister, but I want more than what's been. On the other hand, being alone for a few thousand miles strikes me as awfully appealing, and maybe even healing. "May I ask, what about Sarah?"

"David…"

"Sorry. None of my business."

"Thank you, really. So, you'll drive me then? My flight's at eleven o'clock tomorrow morning, out of Flagstaff. It was the only direct flight to Oklahoma City. It's a regional airport."

"We'll have to have Ma all finished at Debbie's by nine or so, right? That means we'll have to leave here really early."

"Or you can take me to the airport first and then take her to Debbie's. Or we can leave tonight if you want. Or now. The sooner the better, as far as I'm concerned."

"We've got plans with Aaron. And Sheri's going to…."

"*Sheri?*"

"I don't know why I said that. Never mind."

"No more about Sheri," she says emphatically. "Let her solve her own problems from now on. I'm not doing it. Enough is fucking enough."

"Okay. Right."

"Good."

"Okay, see you later."

She unleans from the doorway, half-turns, turns back. "Hey, David, are you okay?" And she looks *right* into my eyes. I search hers for sarcasm, for judgement, but what I find is concern. "I know it's all the stress of this move, but is there something else?"

"No. I'm…fine." Her eyes, though; have I ever seen them this soft? "Well," I say, "to be honest, I'm worried."

"About?"

"Marie, actually."

The wispy blond wings of her eyebrows lift.

"I think she might be into another guy. A neighbor of ours. I've semi-suspected for years that she's attracted to him, but, you know… never enough to act on it."

Jenette's eyes are still wide and receptive, except now they're blinking rapidly. "Whoa," she says. "I'm sorry, but that is the last thing I expected to hear."

Where's the right starting point for a conversation like this? How far back do I go? How much do I say about Marie's attraction to men who exude confidence, about my own insecurities, about how I now wonder if I've somehow driven her into Brandon's arms. When I start to speak, unsure of what I'm going to say, a gut-deep sob lurches up through my throat.

"Oh, David," Jeanette says, and she steps into the room and wraps her arms around my lower back. "Oh, David."

I stop the sobbing almost as soon as it starts, though I think I've cracked my ribs in the effort. I don't know why I don't let myself go; for five seconds, I felt like I was experiencing the release I've needed for, oh, thirty years or so.

In a voice that sounds damp and strange to my own ears, I say, "It might be nothing. Just, you know…"

"I bet it's just flirtation, David. You know, that's not a crime. You do it, too, right? Almost everybody does."

I think of Jen. Of the need I felt to be noticed, affirmed, to be found desirable.

"I guess I do. I do."

"You used to flirt with Sheri *a lot*, and like you meant it."

"Yeah, but, I mean, that wasn't going to lead anywhere."

"*I* didn't know that for sure."

"Wait. Did that bother you, Jeanette?"

"A little." She looks down at her feet. "Probably wise," she says, "not to assume the worst."

"I could use as much wisdom as you can spare right now, sis."

It's only when Jeanette's arms drop away from my body that I re-realize she's been embracing me this whole time. Now she takes three steps back into the hallway. "If I did," she says, "you'd be the first person I'd give it to."

That may be a dig, but I don't care.

My sister smiles, oddly, sadly, sisterly. "Get some sleep, David. That'll help. Maybe you'll have a dream that gives you some answers."

I watch from the doorway as she heads down the hall to her room. At her door, she halts, turns and comes back.

"I just remembered something Sheri—of all people, Sheri—said to me once. 'It's not who you flirt with, it's who you stick with.' Kind of true, don't you think?"

* * *

Because the hotel restaurant has a forty-five minute wait for a table, Jeanette, Ma and I walk across the street and eat breakfast at Denny's. Jeanette looks well-rested and alert and is practically talking Ma's ear off about how the market is not only going to rebound within, at the absolute most, two years, but how it's going to move into an unprecedented period of bullishness—so long as the Republicans retain control of congress. Not being a stock or bond holder, Ma certainly won't benefit much, at least not directly, although she emits the occasional "Wow" and "Great" as she chews her blueberry waffle.

"So, Ma," I say when Jeanette pauses to slice into an almost burnt-black sausage, "since Jeanette's got that flight tomorrow, do you mind if we start the drive to Debbie's tonight? I thought we could spend the day with Aaron, have a meal with him in the late afternoon, then take off by, say, five or six. Sometime late tonight we could get a hotel room within striking distance of

Flagstaff, drop her off at the airport in the morning, then go get you settled at Debbie's. It's not ideal but…"

"I'll do whatever is easiest for you two. But Jeanette, are you sure you want to make David drive all the way home by himself? That doesn't seem fair."

"It's okay, Ma," I say. "I'll be fine. I like being alone sometimes. She's not being unfair."

"You're going all the way to Oklahoma to see somebody you only met for ten or fifteen minutes? Doesn't that seem a little crazy?"

Jeanette's face flushes. "I've been talking with her on the phone a lot these last few days, Ma. We're getting to be pretty good friends. I'm actually going to do some financial consulting for her."

Ma nods, then blurts, "Come with us today to spend some time with Aaron? Just a few hours? Will you do that for me? Please."

Jeanette looks stunned. "You don't know what you're asking me."

"Yes, I do. To spend the day with your two brothers and me."

"I can't. Please don't ask me again, Ma."

Ma wipes her mouth with a quivering napkin. She lifts her coffee cup to her lips but can't steady it enough to sip. She looks at me with pleading eyes. So, I'm shocked to notice, does Jeanette.

I sip.

* * *

Aaron's due to pick us up in half an hour. Leaving Ma in the lobby with a newspaper, I walk out to the pool to call Marie. Nine-thirty in the morning, it's already eighty degrees, naked sun burning through the blue screen door of heaven. A helicopter thrums low and loud up above, like a machine whose mission is to chop the sky into small, blue pieces.

"Hello?"

"Hey. It's me."

"David? Oh, it's so good to hear your voice." Hers sounds strange, though; half an octave off normal.

"Sorry I missed your call last night. I had the cell phone with me so I don't know how that happened. Maybe I was in a dead zone."

"In Las Vegas?"

"What, there are no dead zones in Las Vegas?"

"Well, you'd think not."

"I did try at one point. Late. Teddy picked up. We talked a little, poor kid. Did he tell you?"

"Yeah. He told me this morning."

"Told you everything we talked about?"

It's probably a cruel impulse, but I want my silence to urge her into whatever confession she's going to make.

Finally, she says, "I don't know what you said to him, but I think it may have helped some. He sounded ever-so-slightly more upbeat this morning. He wasn't whistling out the door or anything, but he might have been slouching a little less."

"A small, good thing." It occurs to me that Teddy may be showing some budding Aaronesque qualities. God help him. "A twelve-year-old kid," I say, "shouldn't be worried about rejection. He shouldn't be worried about anything. He should be enjoying being a twelve-year-old kid."

"This particular kid's really love sick."

I look into the little holes on the phone as if Marie's face were there. "Guess it can happen at any age, huh? Love sickness."

Silence.

I shake my head, sigh, stare at the unshimmering blue pool water. "So, why did you call yesterday? I mean, was it anything in particular? You sounded kind of upset."

"I was. I... Look, Teddy told you what he saw, right, with Brandon? I want to explain."

Another chopper cuts the sky. I raise my voice a little. "Please do."

"He's been coming over a lot these last few days, since you left. I think it's mostly kind of knowing you aren't around…I think, I thought, he was being protective. Making sure we're okay. Typical guy thing."

"Go on."

"*Listen*. Last night he came and fixed that damn tiny leak in the faucet…" Her voice begins to falter… "that nobody in our house cares about but me. That drives me crazy. You haven't even tried to fix it, David. You, who fixes *everything*. And so when he finished and there really was no more little *drip drip drip*, I was so happy I gave him a hug. I didn't know Teddy was in the living room watching, misinterpreting."

"But you kissed him, according to Teddy."

"I didn't...I didn't initiate the kiss."

"It's pretty obvious he wants to fuck you, Marie. I know you must know that."

Silence.

"Seems like you've been giving him some indication that he might have a chance?"

"Oh, God, David..." She's weeping now. "He...Oh, I can't talk about this now."

"Marie, if it's all innocent, why is it so hard for you to talk about?"

"I can't right now," she cries. "I can't think. I'll call you later."

Swearing, grimacing, I pace around the empty pool. The temperature feels like it has risen twenty degrees in the last five minutes. Once I'm able to collect myself, somewhat, I begin rehearsing my call back to her: *I'm sorry, honey. I'm so sorry. I'm a fool. And maybe I just create problems myself. I have to give that some serious thought. In the meantime, all of the sudden over the last few days, in addition to everything else, I'm worried that I'm going to lose you to our slimy bastard neighbor. I might as well be locked up in a padded room if I lose you. Might as well shoot me if I lose you. Hell, I feel like I'm losing everybody. I can't lose you, too.*

I punch in our home number. *Ring, ring, ring.*

A plodding helicopter eclipses the sun and casts its dark shadow over me. Military. Soldiers in the sky: soldiers with weapons, soldiers of fortune, holy warriors. Would it be all that tragic if one of their bullets were to target my heart?

There's ringing, but no answering.

* * *

Amid a scatter of granola bar rappers and coffee cup lids, I sit in the back seat of Aaron's soon-to-be former girlfriend's white Corolla, circa '85 or '86. My feet rest on several layers of dog-eared books: *Native Son, Hamlet, The Waste Land and Other Poems, Ariel, Grimm's Fairy Tales*; *The*

Berenstain Bears: Too Much Pressure.

"I drive out here all the time," my brother is telling us. "It's one of the most beautiful places I've ever seen. Probably the one thing about Nevada I'm actually going to miss."

Aaron has taken us into a desiccated, rocky hinterland, far from the "civilization" of Vegas, a place where the skin of the earth has been lasered by the sun into stale gray-brown cake. It may be the starkest landscape I've ever seen. Nobody on the road out here; we haven't encountered another vehicle, another human being, for over an hour. Ma, transfixed in the passenger seat by the terrain, keeps saying things like, "This is like another planet." Twice she's asked Aaron to stop so she can get out and take pictures: boulders spilled along the roadside like enormous mutant fruit; cracked-earth craters; a squat patch of cactus with tiny, delicate, hyacinth-blue flowers.

"You don't come out here alone, do you, Aaron?" Ma says. "Goodness gracious, I wouldn't. What if your car was to break down? I'll bet you a person could die out here before anyone found them."

"Something like that did happen to me once," he says matter-of-factly. "Car just seized up on me. I didn't have a cell phone. Still don't. An elderly Latino couple from Needles stopped and drove me into town. Nice people. Retired dentists both."

"Did you have to wait long? Were you afraid?"

"I waited a couple of hours. Just before I got desperate enough to say a prayer to St. Jude I saw their little Volvo coming down the road."

St. Jude, tell me Marie has not been unfaithful.

As Ma talks about the power of prayer, my foot slides over a small hardcover and I casually glance down. The jacket is comprised of mostly plain white space with black lettering near the bottom which I have to lean down to make out.

a conversation with judas over cognac and cigars

poems by *aaron stepenski.*

"Speaking of prayers," Ma says. "This is just what I picture in that gospel story where Jesus gets tempted by the devil in the desert. You know the one where he goes out there and the devil tries to get him to say things and do things he doesn't want to do?"

Aaron nods. I think, Jesus doesn't give in. Maybe he was tempted to, though.

"I wonder why," Ma says, "there had to be a devil in the first place?"

"Wow," Aaron says. "That's one profound question, Ma."

I think, from the way her head tips, that Ma is flattered. Surreptitiously, I lift Aaron's book and rest it in my lap.

"This *is* a stark place," he says to Ma. "You could film that scene here pretty effectively. In fact, from some of those hilltops I'm sure you can see the kingdom of Las Vegas in the distance. But what would a guy with love and peace and justice on his agenda want with Las Vegas?"

"Now you sound like him." Ma bends her thumb in my direction. I cover the book with my hands and feign offence.

Aaron chuckles. "I just doubt Jesus would be tempted by the thought of having Vegas for a kingdom. Tempt him with something worthwhile, for Christ's sake."

"He cares about the *people* of Las Vegas," Ma states firmly. "He loves them just as much as he loves the people from the east coast."

While they theologize, I open my brother's book and flip a few blank pages until I come to the table of contents. Among the twenty or so titles are these: "Alternate Ending #3"; "The Second-Best Beating" (cringe); "In Lieu of Flowers"; "The Next City Is My City"; "Offer It Up;" "That is Not What I Meant, At All."

"Besides, I think Las Vegas *is* part of his kingdom," Ma says. "One of the fun parts of it, as long as you don't overdo it. Some people overdo it, but some people are too serious about every single thing. I think God wants us to have fun sometimes. You agree with that, don't you, David?"

"What?" Again I cover the book with my hands and look up. "Fun? Fun is good. I'm pro-fun." Except when it involves destroying a marriage.

Aaron glances back, notices the book in my lap and his eyes go water to ice. "Where'd you find that?"

"It was on the floor."

"Put it back down there where it belongs, okay? That's hers. That's private."

"What is it?" Ma says.

"Nothing," Aaron says. "Just an old book."

"I didn't know you published a book," I say. "I knew you'd published a lot of individual poems. I never knew you published a book. That's fantastic, Aaron. Boy, there are a lot of things about you I didn't know."

"That's because they're not worth knowing. Just drop it back on the floor, okay?"

I don't. I push: "Who's reading the Berenstain Bear book?"

"Wait a minute," Ma says. "You've published a book, Aaron? And you never even told me?" She sounds incredulous, wounded. I share both sentiments, and I feel a few others, but since Ma's voicing the insult, I won't pile on.

"No, listen Ma," Aaron says, "that particular book I don't like to show to *any*body. I don't.... It's way too personal, and dark, and...you wouldn't care for it, believe me. If there's ever a next one, I'll send you a copy. I promise. I'll dedicate it to you. But this one is to be avoided, trust me."

"If my son wrote it," Ma says firmly, "then I'm not afraid to read it."

I steal another peek. On the blank page after the table of contents Aaron has handwritten these words:

Sue Ellen,
You say you don't know who I am.
Well, this is a taste of what it's like.
-A

The road turns, rises, dips: a wall of orange dust, clusters of sage, a mountain peak the shape of a withered hand. Before I put the book back on the floor I flip another page, wanting to get a look at the title poem. But the page I turn to is blank, except for the printed dedication:

For Jeanette

My life is my apology and my penance

My God, what the hell did you do to her, Aaron?

"Now listen to me, Aaron," Ma is saying, even if you don't want me to read your book, I want you to know I'm proud of you for writing it and getting it published. That's a fantastic accomplishment. You always were a good writer. Very creative. The teachers said that about you from the second grade on." She adds, "And no matter what you might think, your father would be proud of you, too. Very proud."

Aaron curls his lower lip around his bottom teeth and sinks the upper ones into it. He says to me in a chilly, even threatening voice, "Put it on the floor, David."

This time I do.

"Oh, goodness," Ma says, "look at this place, would you." It's a curving, washed-red mountain wall, sheer, full of shadowed crevices and cave mouths, sharp crags and dry brush. "Can we stop so I can take a few more pictures?"

"Sure, but this isn't so different from where you took the last ones."

"Well, it's very different from Staten Island."

Neither Aaron nor I can argue with that.

"Don't get me wrong," Ma says, "Staten Island's beautiful in its own way. This is just so different."

"You do have a refined sense of beauty, Ma," Aaron says, and pulls into a space against the side of a building-sized rock where there's level ground and room for a car.

We step into vast silence and pulsing heat. Ma heads toward a particularly striking aspect a good fifty yards away, a series of caves of varying elevations in the rock wall, and Aaron and I lean against the doors of the car. "Tell me something," I say. "Why did you have to apologize to Jeanette?"

The look he gives me is one degree below utter contempt.

"Hey, am I completely deluded to think that as a member of this family I have a right to know at least *some*thing about why two of my siblings don't talk to one another?"

"I don't know if you're deluded or not, David, but I don't want to discuss it. I've let all that go. Anyway, you see her all the time. Ask her."

"Think I haven't?"

"She won't say?"

"Does that surprise you?"

"I don't get surprised."

"I'm asking for too much, I know." My hands come up from my hips and my fingers splay out. "But, look, I'm not asking out of some prurient interest."

"Why *are* you asking? Why do you care?"

I kick at the dust. "You want the truth? I ask because sometimes I just don't feel like I'm part of my own fucking family, that's why. And now…even at home… Never mind that. But believe me, Aaron, I know how messy families can be. It's not getting at the messy stuff in our family that scares me. It's avoiding it forever that scares me."

Aaron hears me. I know he hears me. And suddenly he turns and faces me, pokes his long pointer finger into my chest. The intensity in his eyes just about freezes mine. "Okay, here you go, bro. You ready to get messy?"

"Damn right I'm ready."

"Okay then. When Jeanette was twelve, I caught her—well, saw her—in the shed making out with some girl, a girl who was quite a bit older than she was: I'm talking seventeen, eighteen. Not anybody I recognized from the neighborhood. And I don't mean they were giving each other little experimental kisses, either. It was way more than that. I mean, this older girl was being really fucking aggressive with Jeanette. Needless to say, I was dumbfounded, shocked, mortified. Etcetera."

"Wait a minute. Wait. Back up here. Let me understand this. Where were you? What were *you* doing there?"

"I was going out to smoke a cigarette behind the shed, like I always did in those days. They were in the shed. I always went quietly for obvious reasons, and they didn't hear me. I heard grunting in there and I peeked in the window."

"Did you say Jeanette was *twelve*?" This detail mortifies me. "Twelve is a little girl," I say.

"I agree. At least it was back then."

"It still is, Aaron. Except to fucking Madison Avenue and fucking Hollywood."

"Yeah, I know, I know. Anyway, I was stunned. Terrified. I mean, it wasn't an out-and-out *rape*—if I'd witnessed Jeanette being raped I'd have gone in there and flung the other fucking chick through the window, believe me. But I wouldn't say it looked consensual either. The older girl was all over her, and Jeanette looked nervous, though…kind of passive, too." He looks over to see what Ma's up to, and so do I. Still exploring, snapping away.

"Jeanette was *twelve years old*," I say. "How fucking consensual can it be if one person is twelve and the other is a fucking legal adult? That's just wrong." I feel knots tightening in my shoulders, my hands forming fists. "And I *do* call that rape. You saw Jeanette get raped, Aaron."

Thirty yards away, Ma looks over at us, having caught my tone, though thankfully not my words. "Everything okay, boys?"

"Everything's dandy," Aaron says. "Look, relax, David. Calm down. This is news to you but it's also ancient history."

"I'm relaxed," I say, though I'm so agitated I could bite one of these boulders. "So what did you do?"

"The first thing I did was make some noise so they'd get scared and stop, and then I walked by and pretended I didn't see them. I guess the girl took off as soon as I went inside. Then I moped around the house for hours trying to think what to do next. Because I had to do *something*. I'm a fucking Stepenski. Problem arises, fix it."

I close my eyes. The vision of Jenette being raped tangles with a vision of Marie in Brandon's arms.

"I wanted to tell *her*"—Aaron nods toward our shutter bug mother, who has actually put her camera down and is examining a small, green/blue bush that appears to be growing right out of a boulder—"but she wasn't around. I think she'd taken you to the doctor's that day. I think they were worried you might have a heart murmur. Remember that? That scared the shit out of me, too, but that's another story."

It scared the shit out of you that something was wrong with me?

"I should have waited," Aaron says, "but it felt really urgent to me that somebody else know about this. Somebody who could *do* something about it." He moves his foot around in the dust. "You want to know what I think it was, David?"

I don't know what the "it" is that he's referring to, but I nod.

He spits this out: "The *taking advantage*. I could never tolerate that. People in a position of power taking advantage of people with no power. I just fucking hate it. I hate it. Of course, I've been an adjunct for twenty years, which is one of the great exploitations, and I allow it to happen to me. So…"

"I know. But what did you *do* that day? What happened?"

"Stay calm. Your face looks like it's going to go up in flames."

"What the hell did you do?"

"I decided to tell him."

"*Da*? You told *Da*?"

"That's how fucking desperate I felt. Because whatever else you say about the bastard, you knew he would *do* something. *Take action*. And that's what I *needed*." His gaze sweeps out over sheer rock to the bare sky. "Goes without saying it was the worst decision I ever made. And you're looking at a man who's made some doozies, as Ma would say."

"You told *Da*? Did you tell Jeanette you were going to tell him? You two were on good terms in those days, weren't you?"

He shrugs. "I got along with her as well as I got along with anybody. She didn't follow me around night and day like you did, but…" Brief flash of the weary, wry smile. "Of course, our good terms ended forever that day. Hey, enough. Now you know." He nods. "She's coming back."

Ma holds her camera in her hands like an infant. "I think I got some really good shots. I don't know what it is about this place. It feels… *spiritual*, don't you think? I wouldn't have thought I would feel like that in a place like this, but I do."

"It *is* a spiritual place, Ma," Aaron says. "Every time I come out here, a part of me wants to stay forever. I have to drag myself back home."

I repeat to myself what I think I just heard: Aaron saw Jeanette get raped and then told Da about it because Ma wasn't around because she was with me at the doctor's because they were afraid I might have a heart murmur. (That part turned out okay: I had something like a juvenile heart murmur, which we were assured I would outgrow. Have I?)

Gazing out the window on the way back to Vegas, out loud I utter, "The highway of spirit and bone."

Aaron turns. "What?"

"Oh, somebody spray-painted that on a highway sign somewhere."

"Hmm. I like it. I could use that."

"Yeah, well, I was thinking I might write a memoir of this trip," I say facetiously. "And that's the title. So I've got first dibs."

"Fair enough."

"It's either that, or 'What Mr. Fixit Couldn't Fix.'"

"I like that, too," Aaron says. "I can relate."

"I like the first one better," Ma chimes in. "Because it has the word 'spirit' in there."

* * *

By pretending to bend down to tie my shoe, I manage to read one short poem. It's called "In the Gallery."

We can see that her mouth
will say nothing.
Her nostrils
aflare
imply a long night
during which some
unsavory force
has disheveled
her wheat-gold hair.

In the next room,
a young boy
cries,
then gets dragged
through the room.
Skidding to stop,
he, too, stares

and says to his mother,
But where are her eyes?

* * *

When we return to the outskirts of Vegas at around four in the afternoon, Ma suggests we find someplace to eat an early supper. "Take us somewhere nice," she says to Aaron. "It's my treat."

I have no appetite. All I want to do is figure out how to get Ma away from Aaron and me long enough to hear the rest of the ugly story that a big part of me doesn't want to hear.

But for a well-dressed and stylishly groomed elderly couple at a corner table, the restaurant, called *Bella Costa,* darkly lit and tastefully decorated, is empty.

"Gosh, are we dressed okay for this place?" Ma whispers to Aaron as we wait for the maitre d' to seat us. Aaron and I are in shorts and tee shirts and Ma's in slacks and a yellow and pink short-sleeved pullover.

"We're fine," Aaron says. "The trick is to look really bored and really entitled when you come through the door. Almost never fails. They don't want to accidentally turn down some eccentric big shot."

After contemplating a follow-up question, Ma opts for: "I hope the food is good."

"I'm pretty sure you're going to like it."

Indeed, the food is the best I've tasted in at least a week, though, given all the McRoad food we've eaten, most anything would taste gourmet. The first glass of wine—a red Beaujolais—goes right to my head. The broken hours of dream-haunted half-sleep and relentless driving and too many drinks have made me prey to easy intoxication. And I've got to drive again tonight. And, oh God (how did I forget this?), I still have to go see Sheri.

"I need to use the ladies room," Ma says. "Don't say anything too interesting until I get back."

"That'll be easy," Aaron assures her.

As soon as she's gone I say, "I noticed—this is before you asked me not to look at your book—that it's dedicated to Jeanette. Does she know that?"

"You should have left that book on the floor. You can be real asshole sometimes, you know that?"

"I do know that. I now know that more than I have ever known it. But how was I supposed to know what that was? It looked interesting. So, does Jeanette know?"

"I don't know how she would. *I* never her told her. We don't talk, remember?"

"And yet you dedicate a book to her."

Weary smile.

"Why don't you give me a copy to give to her? That might matter to her. I mean, it must matter to you."

He raises his hand to stop me.

I lift my glass, tilt it, drain the contents. "I'll ask again: is this none of my business?"

"Are you your brother's and sister's keeper?"

"Unless I've misread, I think the implied answer is yes."

"I think you have to let your siblings have their problems and not think it's up to you to solve them. You must have a few of your own to work on, no?"

Ma comes back from the ladies room. She's smiling; there's a bounce to her step. Time in the desert has done her good.

But I don't want her here right now. "Hey, Ma, would you mind calling Debbie and letting her know the new plan? That we'll be there early tomorrow afternoon, after we bring Jeanette to the airport."

Ma makes a face. I hand her my phone. "Just punch the little telephone icon. I already have the number dialed. But, look, why don't you talk in the lobby over there? I think it would be more polite than to do it at the table."

"You're trying to get rid of me. All these big secrets." She frowns at my fake smile and goes off.

"Okay, so what did Da do when you told him about Jeanette? This is driving me crazy. I mean, how the hell did he react to that?"

"You really want to know?"

"No, but tell me anyway. This was after he stopped hitting us, no? It must have been, if Jeanette was twelve."

"That was one of the reasons I thought I could tell him. I figured she'd get a lecture and get grounded for a month. Which I actually believed might be a good thing. In case this older girl came back. Good God, I was stupid." My brother's eyes tick around my face and his mouth works into a grim smirk. "I knew he'd be pissed off. But you're right, for whatever reason, he wasn't hitting us anymore."

Not the time to fill Aaron in on the Jesus dream, though he ought to hear about it.

"Unfortunately, he had a relapse that day."

I stare at one of the curls falling down over my brother's brow, but he looks me in the eye. "I told him what I saw in the shed and he didn't say a word for a full minute. Just moved his jaw around, the way he always did when he was fuming inside. Then finally he says, 'Okay.' Gets up, goes and finds Jeanette up in her room. They passed me on the way back into the living room and, my God, she gave me a look I swear I'll see to my dying day. Incredulous. Helpless. Judas. How could you betray me? I'm talking bullet to the heart. Ten thousand deaths. Sometimes thinking about that look makes me wish I'd never been fucking born."

Aaron finishes off his wine as our waiter comes by to replenish. "So, he closes the door to the living room. Two seconds later he starts beating the crap out of her. This is *Jeanette*, mind you. His princess. The one who got hit like once a year, even in his big-time hitting days. She must have gone into shock or something."

I lift myself up a little to see what Ma's doing: standing in the lobby, laughing with Debbie. Laughter between two Stepenskis. Go figure.

"I sat leaning against the door listening to the whacks. Jeanette didn't make a sound; well, just grunts and groans. Finally, I couldn't take it anymore. I got up and opened the door and said—well, actually I was bawling my eyes out by that time, which is the only time I ever remember crying—I said, 'Don't hit her anymore, Da. Please stop it. Hit me instead.' He stopped and stared at me. I can see him staring at me. It was like he was very, very slowly coming out of a trance. His eyes actually went soft. It was the closest I've ever seen *him* come to crying."

"Oh, Jesus. Oh, the poor guy."

"*He's* the poor guy? Yeah, you're right, David. Da's the victim, here.

Jeanette's curled up on the floor turning black and blue and *he's* the poor guy. Give me a fucking break."

"He didn't *want* to hit her though. It was the only way he knew how to respond. And yeah, the hitting was scary, but the truth is he didn't hit us that hard. He..." I rake my hair at my inability to speak. "So anyway, what happened?"

Aaron shakes his sad, bemused head. "I'll never understand your loyalty to that man. Never. Except that you're hell bent to obey that great fourth commandment."

"I'm trying to be loyal to the truth. To how complicated a person's reasons can be. To their *reasons*, Aaron. I'm not justifying the hitting. That's the last thing I'd ever do."

"Bin Laden's reasons? Bush's reasons? Anyway, he finally, in this eerie monotone, tells Jeanette and me not to say a word about this, ever, to Ma or you or Debbie, and he walks out of the room and goes down to the basement. Stayed down there a long time. I tried right away to tell Jeanette I was sorry, that I was trying to protect her from a pervert, but she just stormed out, wouldn't look at me. She's barely looked at me in the thirty years since."

I hold my head in my hands and stare at my brother. "That's got to be killing you. That's got to be killing both of you."

"Like a slow, incurable disease."

"Doesn't have to be incurable," I say. Me, Mr. Pollyanna. "Things can change. They have to."

* * *

Ma's the only one with anything to say on the ride from the restaurant back to the hotel: there's a woman Debbie's dying for her to meet but she won't say why, it's a surprise; the desert is more beautiful than she could ever have imagined; she's taken 67 pictures so far and boy oh boy she can't wait to get them developed, or printed, or whatever you do with pictures these days.

Out of the blue, Aaron says, "Look Ma, if you don't want to go to Debbie's, you shouldn't go. Because once you do, you're there. You don't have to do anything you don't want to. Do you realize that? That you have a choice here?"

I want to shriek, *Shut up, Aaron*. She *did* have a choice. Right up to four days ago she had a choice. She made a decision. She shouldn't have to keep making the same painful decision over and over again.

Ma takes some time to form her response. "You know, Aaron," she says with trembling hesitance, "I think your attitude about changing your mind about things is a little different from mine. And I guess that's okay, everybody's different. Except, well, for example daddy and I believe vows and such should be kept sacred. We don't think you should change your mind once you make a vow. But..."

"Vows? We're not talking about vows here, Ma."

"Well, I am."

"Okay. Well look, with all due respect to you, I think people make some vows they realize they can't keep. And trying to keep them is only a bigger mis..."

"Well, I don't agree with you about that," Ma interrupts him. "When you work on keeping a vow, God helps you. He knows it isn't easy. But a vow *is* a vow. You being a poet who respects the meaning of words so much, you should know that."

Whatever Aaron might want to say, he doesn't.

"Anyway, about Debbie. I told her that I was going to live with her and I am. And I'm going to be happy there because I know how to be happy wherever I am. Most of the time, at least."

And even though I myself have been feeling as ambivalent as it is possible to feel about this whole matter, I want to lean up and kiss Ma for taking this stand.

"I only wish," she says, "that I was going with a little more peace of mind about you guys, that's all. That's the one thing I can't say I have, peace of mind about my children. My goodness, I have kids who won't even talk to each other and I don't know how to change it. And I've prayed and prayed about it, and I still don't know how to change it."

Change. The word bores deep into my gut. Ma, Marie, my kids, my life, their lives. Everything and everyone has to change. It's the way of things. And no one has to change more than I do.

Aaron pulls us into the hotel lot, three emotional zombies. Helping him look for a place to park, I half-consciously glance over toward the area where my van is parked and see that the hood is up. Of course, it has to be Jeanette, checking the fluids, readying things, anxious to get to her new love interest in Oklahoma City.

Which is when I get the idea. There's no time to think through its logic. What I do is lean up to the front seat and say, "Hey, Aaron, Ma, what's that up in the sky? Is that an eagle? Pull over a second. Right now, quick. You gotta see this bird."

"Are you kidding? Is this a joke?"

"No, come on. Quick. Up there, to the left." Aaron pulls over and as he and Ma lean forward to look up through the windshield, I pretend to look, too, but grab Ma's camera out of the top of her bag and slip it into the day pack resting on the back seat beside me.

"Where, David?" Ma says. "I don't see anything."

"What the hell are we looking for, David?"

"A bald eagle. I swear. Or at least it sure looked like one. Maybe it was a hawk. Some beautiful, majestic-looking bird. Something Ma could tell her friends she saw. Must have been a mirage. No pun intended."

"Beg your pardon?" Ma says.

"Mirage. Get it? There's a casino..."

"The whole city should be called the Mirage," Aaron mumbles.

"Oh, well. Sorry," I say. "Hey, Ma, can I see your camera for a minute? I want to check something out. You know, I'm thinking of getting one myself."

"Sure. It's right...oh, gosh. Oh, goodness gracious." She fumbles around in her bag, then looks side to side, behind her, under her, on the floor. "Oh, my goodness, don't tell me I left it out there in the desert. Could I have been that stupid? Did I leave it out in the desert?"

"Check all around," Aaron says. "I'm sure you have it."

"I *am* checking. It isn't here."

I pretend to look around too, say, "You know, I did see you put it down on a boulder at one point, Ma. The last time we stopped."

"Gosh, I don't remember doing that. Oh, my goodness, how stupid I am. You see? I probably *do* need assisted living, or whatever Debbie calls it. Oh, goodness gracious, the one thing I promised myself not to lose, and I lose it."

Grimly, Aaron says, "We'll go back out there, Ma. I know all the places we stopped. Between the three of us we ought to be able to find it. It's not likely anybody else has even been out there." He begins to turn the car around.

"Okay but look," I say. "I can't go. I've got to go see Sheri. I've *got* to go see her now. She's in a bad way and she could do something awful if I don't go now."

"Sheri?" Aaron says. "Who the hell is Sheri?"

"Sheri's *here*?" Ma says.

"Yeah, she's here. I'll explain it all later, but listen, Aaron, pull over to my van for a second, will you? It's right down that aisle. Over there."

Thankfully, from the angle of our approach, Aaron can't see Jeanette fiddling around under the hood. Until it's too late. When he stops beside the van and realizes that Jeanette is standing three feet away, I've already leapt out of the car and shouted to her, "Get in fast. It's an emergency. Ma will explain."

Jeanette, a Stepenski to the bone, jumps into the back seat, no questions asked.

"She'll help you find it," I say to Aaron and Ma. "I'll meet you guys back here in a couple of hours. Go. Hurry."

As Aaron drives off, all three of their faces look so bewildered it's almost comical. Almost.

* * *

"Sher, I'm on my way to the Motel 6. I'm driving now. I'll be there in, like, ten minutes."

"Ten minutes?"

"Yeah. How are you doing? You okay?"

"I'm...Who the hell knows..."

"Are you drinking?"

"You...am I what? What? If you drink this much, you don't feel drunk. I don't feel..."

"I'm coming over and we'll have a good talk, okay? We'll get you sobered up."

"You know what this reminds me of, David?" Sheri slurs. "She used to call sometimes, on, on the good nights, to tell me she was, she'd be, she was, you know, coming home soon. And I'd go and get ready. Take a shower, get into bed, you know, all warmed up and…and sweet-smelling and ready. And then she'd come home and, and, you know what she always did, David?"

She waits, so I say, "No, what did she do?"

"She would stay downstairs awhile because…I think she did it just to tease me, to get me, to make me, to get me excited, you know what I mean? And it did! It got me hot. Got me so hot, David. Does Marie ever make you, you, wait, David? To get you hot?"

Marie's name double-knots my already knotted gut. "Sometimes."

"And then *finally* she'd come up. I liked to be in the bed already. You know what I mean? She was so shy about *sex*. You know that? She was, she was so shy. Like a girl. But you know what she liked to do? Do you, David?"

"No, Sher. No idea."

"She liked to give me these little kisses. Baby kisses. Just tiny… And she'd make the softest little, like, you know, purring sounds. Oh, God, I can still feel the way she baby-kissed my eyes…"

"I see the sign for the motel now. I'm almost there."

"Wha…?"

"I'll be there in a minute. You're in 209, right?"

"2-0-9. Yeah. Room number 209. Been here two days now. Right? Two days?"

"Don't drink anymore. Please."

"Can't. Just finished up the last drop."

"That's good. Drink some cold water, okay? Or make coffee. It'll help. I'll see you in a minute."

"Okay. Okay, babycakes. I'm gonna get ready for you now. Don't make me wait too long."

It's only a few blocks from some of the big-deal, fancy casino-hotels, but this place is nothing but an anonymous, two-story slap-up job, like a thousand others all over America where there's a highway and an exit. It sits glumly in the middle of an acre of parking lot asphalt, baking in the late-afternoon desert sun.

After auto-locking the van doors, then double-checking that they're really locked (easy to picture bad things happening to nice vehicles in a lot like this), I walk toward the outdoor stairway that leads up to the balcony and the second-floor rooms, noting license plates: three or four Californias, a Utah, an Ontario, a New Jersey. I read bumper stickers: *M.A.D.D.*; *This Car Climbed Mt. Washington*; *He Gave His Body for the Sake of Your Soul*; *I'm NRA and I Vote.*

The black, wrought iron handrail is too hot to touch, so I plod up the stairs like Sisyphus pushing his big stone of troubles, my legs leaden and my balance not quite right. When I reach the top stair, I pause, figure out which way to turn, and because I'm scared shitless, take time to send up a prayer: *Lord, let this work out somehow.* I trod slowly: 221, 219, 217. Every door is shut, every curtain closed tight. 215, 213, 211. Okay, so what's the plan? Give her a big hug, one last pep talk with a dose of tough love: *You're beautiful, you're smart. Stop feeling sorry for yourself and get your life together.* Sober her up. Walk with her down to the restaurant and get her a bite to eat and a cup of coffee. Try to make her laugh. Make sure she's got enough money to get back to Florida. Check her oil. Say goodbye. Forever.

209. Deep breath; semi-hard rap on the thick door. Nothing. Five more raps, hard enough to hurt the knuckles.

"Sheri," I call into the door. "Hey, it's me."

Four guys, college age, pile out of a room a few doors down, laughing and insulting each other about the size of their dicks. Baseball caps with frayed brims on their short-haired heads, all muscle and swagger, they pass me, looks of suspicion, even scorn, in their eyes, the implication being, unless proven otherwise, we're enemies. In America, you may be innocent until proven guilty, but you're also foe until proven friend. There was a brief hiatus in that attitude right after the attacks, a grace period when people felt somehow more humane and united, but it's pretty much dried up. Still, I feel like screaming into their beer-fueled, MTV Real Life, I-got-to-get-laid-or-else skulls: *I'm not the enemy. Look the fuck around you, for God's sake. I'm not the enemy.*

I listen to the sound of thick legs thundering down metal stairs, this herd of wild American males. I glance over my shoulder to watch their four long, waddling, brutal shadows cross the steamy lot and tumble into a white, rented Ford Escort that sinks and shakes with the weight of them. The engine roars and away they go.

I shout into the door. "Sheri. It's David."

Nothing.

In one frustrated, impatient motion, I grip and turn the handle and shove my shoulder into the door, which swings open easily. I stumble into the room.

Sheri's lying in the bed all dolled-up: make-up, eye shadow, lipstick, hair combed out. She's propped herself up, bare shoulders showing, the rest of her is contoured under the thin white bed sheet.

"Sher," I say.

"Hey, lovergirl."

I can hear the drink in her voice. And her eyes are red-veined and swollen behind the powder and paint. "How are you doing? You okay? You drinking water?"

"Been waiting for you, sweetie."

The bathroom door is open and I see, and hear, that the sink's faucet is leaking. Or am I dreaming this? "I know," I say, and my voice sounds foreign to me, as if I'm an actor in a play and not me in real life. "Sorry. You know we've been visiting with Aaron. We took a long drive out to the desert and had an early dinner. Speaking of which, I was thinking we could walk down to the restaurant and get a cup of coffee and a bite to eat. We've got to get you back on your feet, girl. I see there's a little coffee shop/restaurant right near the office. Why don't you take a shower and get dressed. I'll wait outside."

She gives me a languid, drunken smile. "I got a way better idea, honey buns. Come on over here and I'll tell you all about it."

"Sher..."

"Don't be shy, little missy. I won't bite you."

Okay. We're not going to let this get weird. "Sher, I'm not sure what you have in mind, but I don't think I'd be much good at pretending, like, to be Jeanette or whatever, if that's what you're thinking. You know damn well she and I couldn't be any more different. And anyway, I'm..." Not about to do anything bizarre here. No way.

She tries, voice-wise, to keep the charade going and still respond to the actual me. "You're, you're the closest thing in the world I have to her. Do you understand that? Look at you: you have her eyes—the shape of them. And you have her, her blood, and her skin. Come on, don't let me down, babycakes. Make me happy one last time. I'll never ask for anything ever again, I swear to God."

I stand rigidly near the door, my legs turning to jelly. "Sher, please. Think about what you're asking of me. And maybe you're forgetting that there are anatomical issues."

"You're so shy, sweety. But I'll be real gentle. I promise."

I have not made love to anyone but my wife in fifteen years. I have never betrayed her trust. This is not going to happen.

"Are you...afraid of me, little one? Are you afraid I'm going to hurt you, honeysweets? I won't hit you anymore, I promise."

"You won't what?"

"You know I never mean it. I'm changing, I swear. I'll be sweet to you forever from now on. No more hitting. I'll be sweet right up to the very end. I told you I could change. Don't you believe me, baby?"

"Sheri." The skin on my face is a fast-spreading wildfire. "Sher, what would be the point of doing this?"

"Oh, God, Sugarbuns, why is it always so hard for you to give in to me? You always resist."

"Sher, I'm not following this. I came here so we could talk. As you damn well know, I'm David, not Jeanette. Come on, Sheri. Don't put me in this situation."

Her eyes turn porcelain doll. The dripping bathroom faucet suddenly sounds like a waterfall. When her right arm comes out from under the sheets, she's gripping her ugly little pistol.

"Sher, what the hell are you doing?"

"Give me a reason not to, David. My God, I never felt so, so, so. I can't see the point of... if she's not with me..."

My eyes are transfixed on the gun. "Sher, that thing's not the answer. Let me take that, okay? Then we can really talk. Okay?" I wait, don't move an inch. I am zen-level aware of the door behind me, of the escape it offers me.

"She doesn't want me." Sheri's voice is a moan in a cave. It feels surreal, as if she's leaving the world right before my eyes. "You can watch me go. You can tell her all about it." The gun is pressed to her temple.

I inhale, exhale. "I want you."

"What?"

"I want to make love to you, Sheri. Me, Jeanette. I really do. But let me take that away first. I mean, how can we, you know, have any fun with that thing cold, ugly thing right there in the bed with us?"

Her eyes tick over my face. "You still want me, lovergirl? You mean it?"

I nod.

I walk, slowly, to the side of the bed. An incoherent prayer silently seeps out of me.

"You wouldn't lie to me, sweetie." Sheri's eyes, battered as they are, open, wide and waiflike. "We never lie to each other, do we honeygirl?"

"I'm not lying to you. Let's just get that stupid thing out of our way."

She puts the goddamn pistol into my open, trembling palm, and I walk it back toward the front door, push my left sneaker off with my right foot, then my right sneaker with my left. I kneel down and place the gun inside one of the sneakers. I realize that I can run; I can take the gun and run out of the room. But that would only save one of us.

"You just love to make me wait, don't you, honeycakes? You know how worked up it gets me when you make me wait."

I walk back to the side of the bed, no idea what I'm going to do or how whatever I do is going to change anything. Because, really, this can only end badly. Sheri takes my hand and begins to caress my fingers. She brushes them against her face. When I close my eyes, I see my real lover's face. *I've never betrayed you,* I think to her. *Never. Please say you haven't betrayed me.*

Sheri inhales the skin on the back of my hand, trying to find her lover's scent. She lifts herself a little in the bed and takes my hand into her mouth and the sheet slips down, revealing her breasts. *This isn't real*, I think, staring at my sister's ex-lover. Her breasts *are* real: they're full and shapely and pale, risen nipples large and dark and dimpled. Real and unreal. I feel the oxygen leaving my head, leaving the room, the universe.

When Sheri takes my fingers out of her mouth they glisten. They don't seem to belong to me.

"Do your baby kisses," she whispers.

Baby kisses. I close my eyes and keep them closed, as if being blind will clarify all this, or better, transport me back to my living room in New Jersey, Genevieve on my lap with her subtraction homework, saying, *See, daddy: this take away this equals this.*

Yes, Spinning Jenny, I do see it now that you've explained it!

Sheri emits a groan of impatience. I breathe out, lean down and begin to kiss her face, as softly as I can; the kisses are whispers, feathers brushed against her skin, which reeks of whiskey and tastes of salt. As I kiss her, she takes my hand and places it on her breast. I can't exactly tell, since none of this is real, if I'm getting hard. *None of this*, I tell Marie, *is real.*

Sheri groans again. It's the sound of a soul dying. "Oh, baby," she moans. "My baby baby baby. I'm not going to hurt you anymore. I promise. Never again. If I hit you, just remind me that I promised and I'll stop. Okay, babycakes? Don't let me forget. Sometimes it just takes me over but it's not about you, baby. I just get so angry sometimes."

I press my hands against my legs to keep them from touching her. I kiss her cheek. "Why would you want to hurt me?" I say. My voice is not mine. I kiss her eyes, her forehead, her chin. Lightly, lightly. I try desperately not to be here, not to be me. I'm here, but I'm not me.

"I told you so many times," she says. "Don't you ever *listen*?" She sounds like a little girl on the brink of a meltdown. "It's what happens to me when, when it feels like you don't won't give me everything. You...you keep so much of you for yourself, and it's not fair. I give you everything."

"I know," I say, and kiss her hair. I think I finally understand how desperately Jeanette feels she has to protect herself. My arms come away from my legs, but I only let my hands stroke Sheri's strong, bare shoulders. I kiss her eyebrows. "You have so much to give."

"I don't even know what I'm doing when it happens, and then you misunderstand me and you get all sullen and distant and I can't get across to you how it feels to be me and you don't even try to understand, and...*oh.*"

Sheri moans; an anguished, guttural moan. "You aren't her," she blurts, and with both hands grabs me by the shoulders and begins to shake me. She punches my arms and my shoulders and my back with her fists. She hits hard and I can feel bruises forming under my skin, though I'm too benumbed to feel actual pain. She punches me and cries, "Why didn't she try to understand me, damn it? Why? She only cares about *herself,* the bitch. God damn her."

"Stop hitting me, Sher. That's enough."

She punches my elbows, my ribs. "All she cares about is her goddam self."

"Enough, Sheri," I shout and drop my torso onto her like a weighted blanket. I clench her wrists and squeeze. But she's strong and she frees herself and begins punching again. She punches and bawls into my shoulder, "God damn her for not loving me."

"For God's sake," I shout, "maybe she can't love you. Maybe you can't love her either."

Sheri's raw, wet eyes harden. She stops punching and tries to catch her breath. Even so, she wails, "You don't understand a goddamn thing, David. You're just as ignorant as everybody else." And suddenly her nails rip through my t-shirt and puncture the skin around my shoulder blades. The sting bites and I reach up, grab her wrists and thrust her hands down to the bed and pin them there.

"Stop it, damn you. You don't solve anything by beating somebody up. You shouldn't have hit my fucking sister, Sheri. You *abused* her." I'm seething, squeezing her wrists. "Why the hell shouldn't she leave you? You had no right to hit her. Don't you see that? Don't you see that? You had no right."

I squeeze her wrists until her hands blotch to pink and white. "It's your fault as much as hers. You don't abuse another human being. You don't take advantage… Jesus, we're all so fucked up." And my voice shatters into a cry as beads of blood crawl down my back like bugs and drop onto Sheri's arms and onto the white sheet beneath her.

"Oh, my God," Sheri weeps. "Oh my God, David. Oh, Jesus, what am I gonna do? What are we gonna do now, David?"

What we do is cry together. A long, hard cry that feels like it's bubbling up from a well so deep it has no bottom.

* * *

The sun hovers just above the lead-colored hills, lingering, hesitant to fall, like a drowsy child who won't admit he's on the brink of sleep, because sleep equals defeat. Our little Genevieve, for a brief period last year, became terrified of going to bed. This was in the autumn, just after the attacks. She'd scream for us to come, *please, please mommy, please daddy, I'm scared.* For the first week or so, we went to her and stayed until she'd spent herself crying and finally slept. But the problem persisted. One night as she screamed for help and I got up to go to her, Marie took my arm and said, "Wait, David. I think we have to let her learn to calm herself down. She has to learn that she can make it through the night." I could barely stand the thought of her facing her terrors alone, though in such matters Marie is almost always right. So I waited. It was absolutely nerve-wracking, hearing the child's anguish and staying put. But eventually she fell silent. After three nights of no rescue, the screaming stopped altogether.

Plenty of parking in the dusky hotel lot, but I'm not ready, so I drive the outer perimeter. We've been checked out of the hotel since this morning and our bags are laid out in the back of the van, courtesy of Jeanette. All I have to do is gather the troops, say goodbye to Aaron, and get the hell out of Dodge. For which I'll be ready in a minute—just need a little more time to gear up or decompress or whatever the hell my mind and body are screaming at me to do. Although I've never suffered a migraine, and I don't have arthritis, at the moment I feel both ailments, in a way that's borderline excruciating, except that it's also numbing.

During one of my circumnavigations, I spot Aaron's girlfriend's Toyota parked under a light pole. But I'm too spent to imagine that anything hopeful might have happened in that car between my siblings and mother while I had my bizarre rendezvous with Sheri. More likely there's new carnage to face.

* * *

Peering through the motel's coffee shop window from an angle that doesn't allow them to see me, I register, with a kind of surreal wonder, that Aaron and Jeanette are speaking to one another. Like a boy punished and locked in his room, I press my nose to the glass of the window. They are definitely speaking. True, they look as awkward and subdued as blind-daters, but, by God, they're speaking. Sitting between them at the little round table like a sun trying not to beam too brightly, Ma smiles and listens and nods.

A fine-grained darkness, a slight cool, the scent of the planets inching closer to earth, settles around me as I stand at the glass and watch them drink up, argue over who's going to pay (Jeanette wins), and walk through the coffee shop exit into the lobby. When Ma spots me pushing through the double front doors, she *runs* across the lobby and flings her arms around me. "Oh, thank God, David, thank God you're okay. I've been so worried about you." She presses herself into me, rewraps her arms around my back and squeezes, so hard that I feel the raw tenderness of Sheri's punches and scratches. But this is what the little boy in me has been asking for for years, for all his conscious life, but that little boy is nowhere in sight. The adult is taking mental notes: appreciate this later.

"Is she okay?" Ma says. "Oh, my goodness, I was so afraid something bad would happen. I just had an awful feeling. But then, as we drove out to the desert again, your sister and brother got to talking—to *each other, David! Do you believe it?*—and I was so happy I forgot about everything else. But, is everything okay? Are you okay? You look so pale. Is Sheri…?"

I activate the speaking muscle and my voice says, "I think she's okay." Though I don't know that. After we lay there a while and wiped our eyes and sighed to each other, she went into the shower and I went down to her car and checked the oil and belts, etcetera, bought a cup of coffee and brought it up to her. I forced her to take some money. "It's time to start over," was the last thing I said to her. I can't say for certain that the look in her eyes meant she agreed.

Her pistol is in the van, under the rim of the spare. She didn't ask me to give it back. I don't think she remembered that I took it.

"I'm just so happy you're here now," Ma says, and she leans up and kisses my cheek.

Jeanette and Aaron mosey over to us. Jeanette says, "So, is she going to live?"

"There's hope." My gaze holds on to Jeanette; she's doesn't look the same. Looks younger, more vulnerable. More beautiful. It occurs to me that the bruises on my body are hers, too.

"I can't believe you didn't tell me she came out here," she says, but it's in mock frustration.

Shrug, shake of head. "Some things are better unspoken."

"Hey, listen, guys," Aaron says, 'I'm going to have to say my goodbyes. I've still got a lot to do."

When he hugs Ma, her eyes fill with tears. "You take care of yourself, okay? And come to Arizona and visit me. Don't stay up there in Alaska forever, you hear me?"

"I never stay anywhere forever."

Loosely, cautiously, Aaron embraces Jeanette, and she stiffly reciprocates. He tells her he wants to send her something and she mumbles her assent. Good enough. Plenty good enough.

He turns to me, ready to tolerate, I suppose, one more hug, but I say, "I'll walk out with you, if you don't mind."

"Oh, David," Ma says, sniffling, "I didn't tell you. We decided to stay here tonight. We're just too exhausted. And we figured you were, too. Do you mind? We thought we'd get up really early and bring Jeanette to the airport, then you can take me to Debbie's, if that's okay."

It is.

"Would you mind bringing our overnight bags back in from the van?"

Not at all.

What she wants is one more embrace with Aaron, and she gets it. When they let go, they both have to dry their eyes.

I walk with my brother through the parking lot, a vestige of dusk still simmering at the bottom of the horizon to the west.

"We never found the camera," Aaron says. "Ma's being a real trooper about it."

"I have it."

"What? Where'd you find it?"

"I took it right before I sent you guys back out to the desert."

Aaron's bushy head lolls. "You mean you.... You're a son of a bitch, you know that?" He smiles. He's got a very fetching smile when he uses it.

"Son of a saint is more like it."

"There's no depth you won't stoop to, is there?"

"I can go pretty low."

He turns serious. "Hey, how are things on the home front?" He asks like he knows something. Of course, he's a poet. He picks things up in ways the rest of us don't understand.

"I want to be a good Stepenski and say everything's fine."

"Kids or wife?"

"A little of both. Mostly Marie. I think she's got some kind of attraction to a neighbor. I don't know how to think about it. All I know is, I have to trust her. I always, always have. I mean, if I can't trust *her*, I'm a goner."

"Look, she knows how good she has it, brother. You can be a pushy son of a bitch, and too guilty about everything for your own good, but, hell, you're a good man. A *damn good man,* in fact. Marie's not stupid. She's not gonna throw that away."

However far from the truth his words are, I'm overwhelmed with gratitude that he's saying them.

My legs are jelly by the time we arrive at his car. A phrase from some source that I can't recall comes into my head: '*Intimacy has never been this close.*' "Hey Aaron," I say, "don't answer if you don't want to, but do you have a son?"

His big old head tilts away from me. "How'd you come to that conclusion?"

"I saw a little guy sleeping in your car last night. Saw Sue Ellen, too."

He pushes an errant curl away from his eye. "He's not my son. He was already almost a year old when I met her."

For the sake of the boy, I'm relieved. "Is the father in the picture?"

"Sends a check every once in a while. He's not all that stable. Which I guess is what he and I have in common."

"You're more stable than you think," I say, though I don't know why. "You've raised this kid with her then, huh?"

"You could say that." He shuffles his feet. "Look, I know where you're going with this: you raise a kid for a couple of years and then abandon him and head off for Alaska? What a bastard, right?"

Right now I don't care to be the voice of anyone's bad conscience. "You have your reasons. God knows you don't have any obligation to explain anything to me."

"True, but since your conniving scheme helped fashion a bit of a reconciliation between Jeanette and me, I'll take a shot. Not that it's easy admitting this." He gives his unshaven chin a long rub. "A couple of months ago I come in from teaching, right, and the class has gone badly, nobody putting any effort in, nobody willing to revise their precious essays on the department-required ridiculous topic of why there ought to be more holidays in the year. 'I can't revise this, Professor Stepenski. It says exactly what I mean already.' Anyway, I come in from a long day of hearing that kind of crap and the kid's in the middle of a meltdown. We're talking maximum tantrum. Blood curdling screams, bulging eyes, foaming mouth. Total defiance. He's prone to these kinds of displays, but this was the worst one I'd ever seen. So, the second Sue Ellen sees me she says, 'I can't take this anymore today,' and storms out the apartment, drives off somewhere. So I gotta do something with the kid. I try everything I know, even though I'm in no mood to make goofy faces and sing stupid rhymes. Of course, nothing's working, he's oblivious, and inside me this murderous frustration is building and building." He pauses, swallows, looks away. Shame, or something very close to it, darkens his eyes. His voice unsteadies. "Finally, he says something really defiant and the next thing I know I'm picking the kid up and, I swear to Jesus Christ, David, I have every intention of flinging him through the window or into the wall or something that's gonna hurt him really bad. I am literally moving my arms backward so as to throw him with as much force as I can..."

He looks at me full and square and frank. "That, thank God, is when my arms go slack. That is when I have my darkest epiphany." He snaps his fingers and drops his arms to his side.

"Aaron, I...."

He gazes up at the sky, at yet another helicopter come plowing by. "I have that demon in me, brother. Hell, I could've killed the kid. I sure as hell would have seriously hurt him. I stood there, sort of outside myself, and I looked at myself and said, *who the fuck are you and what the fuck are you capable of?* That's when I knew I had to leave. I told her that night I was moving on. Going someplace remote.

"Want to hear the most ironic—if ironic is the right word—thing about this?"

I'm inside his bottomless eyes now.

"I love that kid," he says. "I love that little boy more than I love myself."

Your arms went slack, I want to say. *You didn't do it. It didn't happen. You love him.*

"That's it, brother. Now you know everything. And you should thank God you don't have the rage gene that I seem to have inherited from our dearly deceased daddy."

"I'm not so sure I don't."

"Nah. You're ninety percent Ma. Lucky bastard. Appreciate that." Weary, weary smile. "Okay, I'm going. For God's sake, don't forget to tell her you found her camera. You'll be her hero all over again."

I push my hands into my pockets, then pull them back out. "Good luck in Alaska. Keep in touch, okay?"

He nods. We shake hands. He gets into the car and drives away. Everything is just like always, and everything is completely different.

Chapter Seven

Wednesday, June 12, 2002
Home

In the glassy-blue predawn, I clutch a Styrofoam cup of steaming coffee with one hand and with the other steer the van out of the hotel parking lot. Beside me, Jeanette holds the printed MapQuest directions that will put us back on the highway; back in the pilot seat, with the overhead light on, Ma reads from a small prayer book. We ride down a garishly lit but deserted boulevard of small-time casinos, pawn shops, tattoo parlors and fast-food joints. Into this nightmare carnival midway, two young men emerge from what looks like a combination liquor/sandwich/porn shop. Both wear overly-large, hooded sweatshirts, hoods pulled up over their heads and halfway down their faces. They lurk along the sidewalk, and as we pass them I give them a quick perusal but keep the expression on my face as neutral as possible. One of them catches me in the act and I flinch when he pulls his hand out of his sweatshirt pouch, aims his fist at me, and gives his middle finger a flick.

Thinking, *I'm not the enemy, but how would you know that?*, I peek across at Jeanette—her eyes are focused on the road—then glance into the rearview mirror at my own worn-out face as if checking for a wound.

"Those poor boys," Ma says. "What a way to live. Can you imagine?"

"What," Jeanette says, "they don't have free will? Somebody's making them live that way?" She points ahead at an overhanging sign for south: *Henderson; Hoover Dam; Arizona.*

As we circle under a flag-draped highway overpass, I remember the family that crashed a few days ago, back in wherever. Today may be their burial day. Sorrow, sorrow, everywhere. We head up the ramp and onto the highway, I shift my body, settle in for the drive.

It's Ma who keeps the topic going. "Oh, come now, Jeanette. You have to feel sorry for somebody who's got a life like that. Walking around in an awful neighborhood like this at five o'clock in the morning. You have to pray for people like that. Do you think anybody would *want* to be in a situation like that? They probably have never had anything better."

"I understand, but in the end, we make our own beds."

"We need to thank God our own lives are so blessed."

I gaze up into the darker portion of the sky, away from the city lights, and think I see the tail of a shooting star flare and fade, though it may just be a spot floating in my weary eyes.

"You know what daddy used to say to me whenever we drove through a bad section of a town, or read about people starving in Africa, or any kind of tragedy like that? 'Count your blessings, Lilly,' he used to say. And of course, even though we didn't have much money, he insisted on tithing ten percent of what we had. And always to the poor."

It will take more than this lifetime for me to wrap my brain around my father. I hope I'm easier to figure for my own kids, but quite possibly not.

Since waking up this morning, an impatience to see Marie, to somehow get assurance that she's still the blessing I've always taken her to be, has been banging around my brain.

"You know," Ma says, "one time I was sitting with him—in the hospital this was, right near the end—and he started talking about you kids, how he tried to raise you..."

"How *he* tried to raise us," Jeanette says. "Did he forget that you were part of that?"

"Of course not," Ma says. "But he was talking about himself. How he wanted you all to be really good at understanding how things work and how to fix things when they broke. That sort of thing. I told him, 'It's good you did that, Bern. They can all take care of themselves in an emergency.' But do you know what he said then? He said, 'In some ways, I don't think I did such a good job. I made a lot of mistakes.'"

I hold my coffee cup up to my lips so that I don't blurt, *Why did you not tell us this before?* It also occurs to me that she might be making this up, except it isn't like Ma to fabricate a story for manipulative reasons, even well-intentioned reasons. If we were to drive another three thousand miles together, I'd probably find out all kinds of things I never knew, mitigating evidence, alternate versions, new interpretations. If we were to drive forever, I might find out everything I ever wanted or didn't want to know. Careful to modulate my tone, I say, "He said that, huh? What did you make of it?"

"Oh, I don't know. He had a lot of drugs in him and he would say things that made no sense sometimes and then say other things that seemed to make a lot of sense. His mind was kind of loosey-goosey by then. But I think he felt a little, you know, guilty about being too rough on you guys."

"Well," I offer, "after the, uh, the Jesus dream, he stopped the hitting, right? At least, mostly."

I catch Jeanette's eyes as they dive down to her feet.

"I know it." Ma's voice tremors. "I know it. But you know what I think? I think he wanted you guys to forgive him. I think he felt a little unforgiven. Except, he couldn't bring himself to ask. He was a proud man, your father. But if you want forgiveness, you have to ask for it, don't you?"

"It's okay, Ma," Jeanette says. "It doesn't matter anymore."

"It does, though, Jeanette," I say.

She sighs and folds up the directions.

"There's something crucial," I say, and again have to work to control my tone, "about actually *hearing* that you're forgiven. I mean, psychologically-speaking, that's what's so powerful about the sacrament of reconciliation. I remember reading Jung on that subject." Except I can't remember much. "How psychologically important, and healing, it is to *hear* it."

"If the help it gives you is only psychological," Ma says, "then the heck with it. It better be more than that." She emits a disgruntled harrumph. "Anyway, I'm finished." Though immediately she adds, in full earnest, "Look, he wasn't perfect, but God knows there was a lot of good in that man. More good in him than most of the men I've ever known. People remember a lot of different things about their parents after they're gone, but I want you two to never, ever forget…"—and here her voice breaks—"that he was a good man."

* * *

They're not letting anybody but ticketed passengers go out to the gates, so we stand, awkward in the face of Jeanette's parting, near a battery of metal detectors and x-ray machines. Ma has to use the ladies room, and Jeanette waits for her to walk away before she says to me, "Okay, so what the hell happened with Sheri?"

It's funny how many wait-till-Ma-can't-hear conversations I've been part of these last few days. I guess we think we're protecting her. Someday it will be my kids who wait for me to walk away.

I give her the facts; don't mention the weird role-playing business in the motel room, or the punching, or the scratches that are just beginning to scab over. I don't mention that I now know she was abused by Sheri, and that fact damn sure makes strangely fragile the way I view my sister right now.

"What kind of state was she in? Does she have any money?" Grim faced, she shakes her head. "I'll call her from the gate."

"She's all set with money. But I wouldn't call her, Jeanette. I think you have to let her get over you. Let her turn the corner. She promised me she'd go home today. I think she meant it. I think she hit some kind of rock bottom yesterday. Let's let her go home without any Stepenski intervention for once. See what happens."

Jeanette tilts her head to see if Ma's coming. She is. "I don't even know what home means for Sheri. Her family life is…you don't want to know. So, I mean, what the hell is *home*?"

This is disturbing. Yet another problem we can't fix. "Count your blessings," I say.

"Okay. Then what?" She shuffles. "Hey, look, whatever is going on with your wife, I hope you work it out. I really do."

"Thanks, Jeanette. I hope so, too."

Ma's nose runs, her head trembles; Jeanette's eyes dart and glisten. The two of them stand a foot apart from one another, heads drooped and slightly averted like two thirsty flowers side by side on a sill. Finally, Jeanette leans and gives Ma a quickie peck on the cheek. I take a step toward her, but she throws her bag on the x-ray machine's belt and quickly passes through the metal detector. Only after she's safely on the other side does she turn. "See you, David. Let me know you got home safe."

A couple of young business guys in suits stand a few feet away checking her out and taking their time putting their shoes back on.

"Have a good trip, sis," I say. "Say hi to Mia. Make sure she treats you like you deserve. And you get home safe, too."

She looks at me, not suspiciously, not knowingly, but as if she's relieved that we don't have to acknowledge something we're nevertheless acknowledging. "Thanks," she says. "Say hi to Debbie. Really, I mean it."

* * *

"Almost there, Ma."

"Already?"

Her hands fret over the little blue and green knitted object that for the first time fully resembles a child's torso. The bodies of Teddy and Genevieve float before my eyes, and I feel the full force of the ache, the craving, to enfold them, to inhale their skin and kiss their eyes. But I also long to fall, to collapse, into Marie's arms—if that's even an option now. Whether such a thing would happen before or after we have what will no doubt be the most painful and consequential conversation of our lives, I don't know.

So much I don't know. I could write a book.

"Next exit," I say, adjusting my voice best I can from wariness to optimism. "According to Debbie's directions, we drive through the town of Flagstaff a little while and follow the road up the mountain. You're going to live on top of a mountain, Ma. How do you like that?"

"Oh, I think it's grand." She almost sounds convincing.

As we curve down the exit ramp, a tremendous bank of iron-gray clouds, majestic and surreal, comes into view; I want to stop the van and stare at it, lose myself in it, but we curve away and just like that it's behind us and I'm following road signs through a nondescript section of bars and banks and places to buy cell phones and ammunition and french fries. Finally, the signs lead us up the mountain.

"Boy, we're really climbing, aren't we?" Ma says. "I feel it in my ears."

"Me too."

"You know, this isn't what I pictured Arizona to look like. This is more like Colorado or something." She takes a deep breath and blinks her eyes. "All of a sudden it got cloudy, didn't it?"

"Almost feels like it could snow."

"You know what, David?"

I watch her gather strength.

"I think God made that happen."

"Made what happen, Ma?"

"Made me think I left my camera out there in that wild place when all the while it was on the floor of the car. And then He put Jeanette and Aaron in the car together. It was like a little miracle the way it happened. And now they speak to each other again. Finally. I think they've forgiven each other for whatever they were so angry about." Her mouth crumbles. "I've been praying for this for years and years."

I smile and touch her hand. "God works in strange ways, doesn't she?"

Ma frowns but quickly brightens. "You know what else? Being on this trip...being with the three of you, and talking with Debbie so much on the phone, well, I know we've got our problems—all the things about daddy that everybody struggles about, and..."

"Ma, as far as that goes..."

"Let me finish, will you?"

"Sorry."

"What I was going to say is, the way I feel about you all is just how much...you know...that, even with everything that's not perfect, I still think we have a lot of..." Now Ma's mouth goes wiggly, but it won't release the word. Still, I manage to resist the urge to complete her sentence.

"You know. *Love.*" Hers is the face of the bashful girl who grew up in a home where diffidence and emotional restraint were default modes, where love was a verb, the doing of whatever needed to be done. "That's what I'm always going to remember. All the love."

* * *

Constructed at the edge of a depth of piney woods is a billboard-sized, rough-hewn sign with the words *Three Peaks* carved into the wood and painted forest green and outlined in gold; in smaller letters below: *Welcome*

Home. A Debbie touch. I wouldn't be surprised if, whenever it was that they had the sign made, Debbie was already thinking of the moment Ma would see those words. And I have to admit, it's sweet. Bittersweet for me, maybe, but sweet for Ma.

"Special for you, Ma," I say, pointing. "Want to take a picture?"

"Beg your pardon? Oh, that's their whatchamacallit, their motto. It's on all the brochures and everything. No, I put my camera at the bottom of the bag, where it's good and safe."

"I hope she's not mad at us for being late."

"She'll get over it."

"Okay, but don't you get all excited, David. All this is almost over and you can finally get back where you belong, with your wife and kids."

At these words I feel a complicated stab at the heart and I wheel the van off the two-laner and onto a gravel path. We drive through a dense, mostly white pine forest: fathoms of slender, smooth-barked trunks supporting a green scrim of needled limbs. All around, the dartings of small animals, the swoop of dark birds. Rolling down my window, I breathe in the cool, refulgent, wild, pine scent. "Smell the air, Ma. Nectar of the gods."

Peering around, taking it all in, I see Ma's Adam's apple rising and falling. I slow down, reach across, and run my hand over her arm.

"Gosh, I don't know how I feel," she says. "As long as we were only on the way, I didn't worry too much about getting here. But now we're not on the way anymore." She gazes out the window as if to gather the mental energy to comprehend what's happening, what's about to happen. "I've always been like that," she says. "Even as a little girl, if my mother was taking me to the dentist—oh, I hated going to the dentist—I would pretend in my mind we were going to the toy store. The whole way I'd think about the dolls and doll houses I was going to see, the pretty dresses and things. Right up until we walked into his office. Then I couldn't pretend anymore."

"Wow. Pretty healthy strategy."

"That's a nice way to look at it, David."

"I had a little epiphany last night," I tell her. "That if there's any way to see the good in a situation, even a bad situation, better to look for that. I don't know if it works, but I'm going to give it a try. And you know what else I realize, Ma. That comes from you. That's almost always what you do."

My mother blushes and emits some sort of maybe proud, maybe embarrassed, maybe astonished sigh.

Ahead and to the left we spy a clearing; beyond it lay a spread of large, white-with-black-trim Victorian-yet-rustic style buildings with grand rap-around porches, cupolas and towering spires. There's a white gazebo in a sloping field of grass so green it appears to glow and walking paths with old-fashioned wrought-iron lamps interspersed around the course. A gaggle of mallards make their way across a glassy pond, rustic wooden benches placed here and there along the paths. Just a few people out, sitting on the benches or strolling slowly.

"My gosh," Ma says. "Look at all this. It's a wonderland."

"It is."

A small wooden sign on a post, in the style and colors of the larger one out on the road at the front entrance, points us to a gravel parking lot and the main office. I pull into an open space, shut the engine off, glance around at the fairytale setting, disarmed by it.

The front door of the main building flies open and three children, their arms waving wildly, shouting "Grandma! Grandma!" come galloping down the stairs. Ma's eyes light up and she fumbles for the door handle, finds it, and scrambles out of the van. The children fly into her arms and she absorbs them in what looks like a state of pure ecstasy for all parties.

Behind the kids, Deb and Clint and an elderly, elegantly dressed Black woman step onto the porch. Debbie's wearing jeans and a pink, knitted sweater; her long, chestnut brown hair is pulled back in a loose ponytail. She looks younger than I remember her; she looks like one of the old T.V. commercial Ivory Girls. Clint's wearing a blue suit with a gold-green tie, and looks more silvery up top than I remember him, though his smile strikes me as disconcertingly boyish—and fully genuine. The woman with them has her grey haired arranged in a neat bun; she's slim, fairly tall, bright eyed, wearing a tailored green and silver paisley dress. The three of them simply watch the spectacle of the gang of giddy children smothering their grandma with hugs and shouted plans for all the things they're going to do together from now on.

My cell rings. *Home*. My heart bangs as I answer. "Hello?"

"David." Marie, sobbing.

"Honey? What's wrong? What is it?"

"Oh, David. I'm so sorry. I am so sorry."

I lower my head and walk toward the pond and away from the commotion of the reunion. "Sorry for what, Marie?"

She sniffles. "Oh, David. I've got to talk to you. I love you. I need you. I don't know what made me so weak. It was a huge mistake. It didn't go on, but still… You have to forgive me, baby. You have to. Or else… Oh, please come home now. Please, David. I need you to come home and I need to see you and I need you to forgive me."

"Marie…" But she's bawling and I can't think straight anyway, so I tell her I can't talk right now, we've just arrived this second, and that I'll call her back later. I *do* say, 'Look, it's okay, we'll talk,'" but I also, in effect, hang up on her.

I stand near the placid pond and pretend I'm still on the phone until I feel half-composed.

As I walk back toward Ma and the kids, Debbie, Clint and the other woman begin to climb down the steps. Debbie opens her arms and throws them around Ma, eyes glistening. They embrace for a good long while. I take a long lungful of the cool, woodsy air, then step up to my sister and give her a hug.

"Oh, David, thankyouthankyouthankyou," she weeps into my shoulder. When I offer my hand to Clint, he clasps it with both of his and shakes it with a vigor that takes me aback. "Thank you, David," he says. "You have no idea how much it means to us to have Lilly here at last."

Sniffling, wiping tears out of her eyes, grinning, Deb introduces the elderly woman to Ma and me as Renata Martin.

"And, Ma, guess where Renata lived the first seventeen years of her life?"

"I don't know. Paris?"

"Close," Deb says. "Staten Island."

"Oh, my goodness. No! Where?"

"Well," Renata says, laying her thin, silver-braceleted hand on Ma's wrist, "our first house was on Jersey Street in West Brighton. My father worked at the Moran tugboat yard there before the war."

"Goodness gracious, my best friend's father worked there. Julia Wiaczievski. It was right near the Empire Theater, remember? We used to go every Saturday for the double feature, and afterwards we'd go stand by the water and watch the tugs going in and out. Oh, I loved doing that."

"I adored the Empire Theater," Renata says. "You know, I have some marvelous pictures that I'm dying to show you. Not everybody appreciates them the way I expect you will."

"Oh, goodness gracious, I will," Ma says. "I definitely will."

We tour the place on foot, Deb's kids vying with Renata for Ma's attention. There's no doubt about one thing: the place is not only gorgeous, not only designed with impeccable taste, but it feels genuinely *warm*; it feels like, if not home exactly, then a pretty fair substitute. Everyone we meet is friendly, and several people offer Ma a place in their daily card game or their weekly shopping trip, or a movie date or bowling excursion. Ma looks both thrilled and maybe a tad dismayed, like a poverty-vowed nun who just found out she's won the lottery.

And Debbie—I can't quite put my finger on it. She's always been the cocky one, the one imbued with a sense of entitlement, the queen bee— but those traits come across now as transformed into confidence, self-assurance, maturity. I watch her closely, fascinated, attracted by the way her eyes shine and her voice lilts when she interacts with the residents, or Clint (with whom she's constantly holding hands), or her kids, who are, I have to say, growing into delightful and engaging children. Residents and staff alike seem to adore my sister. She strikes me as highly competent in her role, born to it, in fact. And she keeps turning to me, touching my arm whenever she wants to show or tell me something. *Learn from her*, I tell myself.

* * *

After the tour, Deb and Clint take us to the big Victorian house where they live. It sits shrouded in the piney forest, a quarter of a mile from the other buildings, like something out of a fairy tale.

As we walk up the front steps, I let everyone know I'm going to be heading home in a few minutes.

"*What*? No way," Debbie says. "You're absolutely not leaving here until at least tomorrow."

"I have to go. I've got some issues to deal with that can't wait."

"Surely they can wait one day."

I turn to Clint. "Debbie," I say with a smile, "was the only one of us who ever figured out how to get exactly what she wanted every time. A gift I envied but never possessed."

"A useful trait to have in this world," Clint laughs. "She certainly employs it to good purpose around here." He rubs his clean-shaven chin. "What exactly is it, do you think, that enables her to work her magic? I've never quite gotten to the bottom of it myself."

We enter the foyer. The inside is cozy and rustic, post-and-beam, big windows bringing in western light. I look at Deb, who waits, bemused. "Pure force of will."

Clint turns to Ma. "And was it you who passed along that trait, Lillian? Or did that one derive from your husband?"

"Oh, that was Bernie," Ma says. "I'm still trying to learn how to be a little more that way myself. What's the word for it? Assertive. Edna's always telling me to be more assertive."

"Stick around," Clint says. "You'll get plenty of good modeling."

"Well, now that you've all analyzed and dissected my personality," Debbie says, "I repeat: David, you are not going to leave tonight. No way."

I breathe and steady my voice. "Deb, I've got a serious problem I've got to try to fix back home. I don't want to elaborate right now, but trust me, it can't wait. And look, I promise—if everything works out—I'll come back up here with the whole gang real soon. Maybe over Christmas, if that's okay with you guys. This seems like a nice place to be at Christmastime."

Deb frowns, then smiles. "You promise? If you promise to come here with your family at Christmas, I'll concede."

"I don't think you've ever had occasion to concede to me before."

"There's a first time for everything," she says, and she leans up and kisses me, lightly, just beside my right eye.

* * *

The evening clouds are bright-edged drifting ships. Clint tells me that out here this time of year it stays light almost till ten, so I'll have at least three hours before it gets dark.

The van's engine's running and ready for the long push home. I've said my goodbyes to Debbie, Clint and the kids, each of whom has thanked me fifty times. Finally, Ma steps up beside me. Fighting her fear of touch, she puts her arms around me and I can feel her body trembling, feel the age in it and the wear and tear of all it's been through. I don't know what she feels in mine, but I hope it's close to pure love.

"I like it here, David," she says. "Everybody's so nice. It isn't Staten Island, but it's beautiful."

I chuckle at the understatement. "You're in good, loving hands, that's for sure. Really, you can't ask for more than that in life, can you?"

She turns her head away. "I've always been in good, loving hands." Sniffling, she says, "You be careful driving. Call us every day."

"Okay, Ma."

"Tell everybody I miss them already. Bring them here at Christmas, okay? Oh, goodness gracious, won't Marie and the kids love this place?"

"I think they will."

"Thank you, David. God really blessed your father and me when it comes to our children."

"Well," I speak into the green/gray pools of aging old eyes. "I'm glad you feel that way."

"And I'll be praying for whatever your problem at home is." Her head twitches but she looks me in the eye. "Marriage is hard sometimes. But it's worth it. You know it when you…" she looks into the tall, refulgent pines for words "…you know, get past some problem and then see the love again. Sometimes you see it even more clearly. Like it's more the real thing, you know?"

* * *

Daylight hangs above the forested hills, though in my rearview mirror the sun has fallen below them. I-40 *East*.

I've got a gun to get rid of. (God knows I better not have it when I get home.) Maybe I'll fling it into the Mississippi, the iconic American river.

Something appropriate about that.

Wherever I decide to stop for the night—I'm shooting for at least the New Mexico border, and I feel wired enough to get there—I'll call Marie. She's called twice since I began driving home, but I couldn't bring myself to answer. She left voicemails, but I haven't listened to them yet. When I do speak with her again, I want to be ready: I want to be loving, and I want to be wise, and I want to be strong.

But, my God, how to describe the pain when the thought of Marie making love to Brandon recurs, as it does, unbidden, mile after mile? And because, corny as it sounds, over time I've come to think of her and myself as *one being*, it's as if I've discovered now that I've been in possession of a false soul, a mock life, paper-thin. And yet....and yet if I'm honest, I have to acknowledge that simultaneously there's something else going on inside me. Something, counterintuitively, driven, charged with life, with drama, yes, but with opportunity, too. Along with the most excruciating pain I've ever felt, a force, a wellspring of energy has erupted in me. Driving home to the great challenge of trying to save my marriage and family, I feel in some ways more alive than I ever have. I swear I feel sparks in every atom in my body. What *is* that?

* * *

The phone trembles against my ear.

David, I want you to know that I stopped it before we... before we even came close to...I hope that matters. I hope you believe me. It does matter, David. He was unbuttoning my blouse, it's true, and we were kissing and touching, but, David, that's when I realized...that's when it hit me: No! No! No! And I told him that, I told him no, I can't do this, and, to his credit, he stopped right away. He tried to say it was okay, that we were just having a little well-deserved adult fun and it wouldn't mean anything in the long run, but I said it did mean something; I said it meant everything. He stopped. I told him I regretted the whole thing, starting to give in that way, being weak. I guess I was swept into the thrill of it. You know what I mean, honey. And, yeah, it was, for a while, a kind of thrill.

But, oh, God, David, the whole world seems so weak to me right now.

Shoddy and weak. I realize Brandon is a weak man. Ugly and needy and manipulative. He knows I'm married; he knows we have kids. But worse, much worse, is how I see myself. I'm a weaker woman than I ever thought I was and, God, how it hurts to have to see that. I don't know if I'll ever.... Beep.

A second message.

Please call me back. Let me hear just a trace of understanding in your voice. Oh, God, David, here I go crying again. I can't stop crying. The kids keep asking me what's wrong and I keep telling them it's just that I miss you so much. And I do. Then we all start crying. Even Teddy. And I want you to know Teddy only saw us kiss before he went upstairs. I hate that he saw anything at all. I hate that there was anything to see.

I feel so empty and cheap and weak. I won't stop crying until you tell me to my face that you forgive me. I need you. We all need you. Please, David, hurry home.

She's suffering. Good God, I've got to talk to her.

I forgive you, I realize I'm saying out loud. *But you have to forgive me, too.*

What I don't realize, until I happen to glance down at the speedometer, that is I'm going 101 miles an hour.

Epilogue

By the time I pulled into the driveway at a few minutes before two a.m. this morning, I'd spoken with Marie on the phone from the road at least four times over the two long, mostly quick-nap days it took to get home. Besides telling each other how sorry we are for letting things crawl toward some kind of marital brink, I asked her to find a good marriage counselor and to schedule a first session for as soon as possible, even if it had to be the day I got home. "Yes," she said. "We've got work to do. I know that. But, David, it will be a new beginning for us." I liked that she that, that life is forgiving, or at least it can be, if we cooperate with its grace when it's offered. So, we're seeing someone tomorrow morning. I will tell her about the hotel room, and I will tell her about what happened with Sheri. In fact, I can hardly wait to unburden myself of those moments. I also told her I thought we should consider moving out of the neighborhood, maybe find a more rural place, but not too far away, so that the kids might be able to stay in their current schools. She agreed to that, too. "I'll go anywhere with you," she said, which were possibly the most glorious, life-saving words I've ever heard.

She was there in the foyer when I walked into the house, my bones aching and my eyes throbbing. She was in her pajamas, and looked like a girl. Suddenly wide awake, I felt blood zinging through my body. We hugged and hugged and hugged, and at last we went into the kids' bedrooms and I drank in their wonderful dreaming bodies, and then Marie and I retreated to our bedroom, where, within minutes of lying down, we fell asleep holding hands.

* * *

It's morning, and I've got to do this sooner or later, so why not now, while I'm feeling strong and experiencing a strange but welcome sense of inner calm. The sun is pouring down like milk over the houses and rolling lawns and lushly green trees, and the sensation of the kids' welcome home hugs and kisses still reverberates in my bones in warm, pulsing waves. I feel them when I knock on Brandon's door, which, after a pretty long time, he opens. He looks bleary at first but quickly turns guarded.

"Hey," I say.

"Hey."

"So, I know what happened."

He seems unsurprised. "Yeah. What happened wasn't much."

"Says you."

"She'll tell you the same. And look, I didn't force anything. Takes two. But nothing happened, so…"

"I don't think it was nothing, Brandon."

"Okay, okay, spare me any lectures before you even start. We didn't do it, and I went home, and the case is closed. So, are you here for any particular reason? You here to shoot me for having a little mutual flirtation with your wife?"

I laugh. "No, no. Though I did fantasize about that from Flagstaff right to the banks of the Mississippi."

Remembering my flinging the gun into the river, late at night under a bridge, Sheri flashes through my mind. Good God, I hope she's made it home. I called her on the drive, twice, but she didn't answer either time. Maybe she's embarrassed about what happened in that motel room, which still feels to me like a nightmare and not an actual event I participated in. I hope she's made it home.

"Lucky me, huh?"

"Maybe. Anyway, I just came by to let you know I'm home."

"Thoughtful of you."

I never noticed much about Brandon's face before, except that it's a handsome, rugged one. Not hard to see why a woman might be attracted. But I see now, looking closely, that his shiny, well-groomed black hair has some gray streaks in it, and that his right eyeball is marred by a tiny bloodspot just below the gray/blue iris. I never realized that he's a good six inches shorter than I am. None of this means anything, I suppose, but…well, suddenly, and honestly only for an instant, I feel an intense loneliness, a lostness, emanating from him like a gust of artic air.

"Okay. See you around."

"See ya," he says and swings the door closed.

A little shaken, I cross the street, breathing in the rising scent of sun on grass and soil and asphalt. *Be calm*, I hear myself say. *Be calm*. And that allows me to come back to where I am, to notice, as if I'd arrived here for the first time just now, how lovely this little piece of earth is in full-bloom summer, everything alive, thriving, growing. Who knows? Maybe we won't move. Maybe we'll stay; stay and grow.

Maybe I can forgive Brandon. Hell, if I can do that, someday, maybe I can forgive myself, too.

Before I get back to the house, the front door opens and Teddy steps out onto our small front porch. He's wearing a baggy white tee-shirt and green shorts. I suspect he watched my encounter with Brandon from the window. He looks, somehow, both relieved and anxious; a young man with lots of hope for things to come but still a frightened boy.

"Dad, grandma called," he says.

"Did she?"

"She told me to tell you she's having so much fun and thank you for driving her and everything."

I nod. "Oh, that's good to hear."

"…and she said to make sure, you know, to tell you that she loves you and all."

"That's always good to hear," I say. "Never fails."

Teddy doesn't turn back to the house, just stands there, awkward but brave.

"You know how you always used to say to me when I got home from school, 'what did you learn today?'"

"Yeah."

"Did you learn anything on your trip?"

I stare at my hands; my fingernails are long.

"I think I'm learning that I still have a lot to learn."

"Even adults learn that, huh?"

"If they can. If they're lucky, I guess."

Before he can turn and go back inside, I say, "Hey, kiddo, you feel like going for a little ride? Drive around a while on the old highway and then maybe get some breakfast? We can talk about what both of us are learning, or we can just cruise around and then get a bite to eat. I don't want that van to get complacent just because I'm back home. What do you say, Ted?"

He looks at the van and so do I. A brilliant, plump Cardinal alights on the hood ornament but quickly takes off again. Trying to follow it, Teddy searches the sky. At last, he looks at me. "Okay, Daddy," he says, and that word almost buckles my knees. "Let's hit the road."

Lefora Publishing

Our mission is to publish new literature, including fiction, poetry, memoir, and criticism, with a focus on contributions that best serve to enhance and represent the intellectual life of the New England region.

Lefora seeks to support a vibrant community of writers...

•by stewarding writers through the editorial and marketing process,
•by working with emerging talent as well as seasoned writers,
•by sharing in the development of their careers,
•by hosting an online journal,
•by sponsoring writing contests,
•by offering speaking opportunities,

and we will do each of these as we create the Lefora Publishing legacy.